The problems were tremendous . . . . No such climb had ever been attempted . . . Hope alternated with despair. The men struggled with the mountain and their inner selves.

—Chris Jones, *Climbing in North America*

A mountaineering classic . . . .

— *Anchorage Daily News*

A timeless tale of courage on North America's highest, coldest mountain . . . an inspiration for anyone.

— John Waterman, author of *Surviving Denali*

Why?

WE EACH PACKED our own lodestone up the mountain in the winter, and we each would offer different answers to the questions: Why do you climb? What did you get from the winter expedition?

We solved none of life's problems, but I believe all of us returned with a new awareness of some of its realities. Each of us may have realized in his own way, if only for a moment, what Saint Exupery spoke of as ". . .that new vision of the world won through hardship."

MINUS 148°:
First Winter
Ascent of
Mt. McKinley

MINUS 148°:

First Winter Ascent of Mt. McKinley

by Art Davidson

THE
MOUNTAINEERS

Published by
The Mountaineers
1001 SW Klickitat Way, Suite 201
Seattle, WA 98134

First printing 1969. Second printing 1986 by Cloudcap
Third printing 1999 by The Mountaineers, fourth printing 2000, fifth
printing 2002, sixth printing 2003, seventh printing 2004, eighth
printing 2005, ninth printing 2007

Manufactured in the United States of America

Printed on recycled paper
ISBN 10: 0-89886-687-1
ISBN 13: 978- 0-89886-687-2

*For Mairiis and all others who at some point
in their lives turn to the wildness in nature.*

Contents

Acknowledgments and Photo Credits	1
Introduction	3
Prologue	9
Inception	19
My Daddy Can't Climb That Mountain	30
Crevasse	37
Blizzard	55
John's Fall	68
Psyched-out	77
The Climb to 17,200 Feet	95
Alone	115
Darkness	129
March 1: − 148°	142
March 2: "Light Breaks Where No Sun Shines."	154
March 3: "Pieces Are Coming off My Bad Ear."	161
March 4: Delusion	167
March 5: "Hope Gives Out for the Three Above."	175
March 6: "We Try to Avoid the Sentiments of Death."	183
March 7: Green Feet	194
March 8: Sunshine	201
Getting Back	213
Afterword	218
Appendix	229

ACKNOWLEDGMENTS

For encouraging me to tell this story I thank my companions on Mt. McKinley in winter, the Donners, Kay Hitchcock, and especially Dave Roberts. I am grateful to Mairiis Davidson for faithfully serving me endless cups of coffee during the months I spent writing. Special thanks to Susi Alexander for encouraging me to get out this new edition.

Introduction

by David Roberts

I WAS INVITED to be a member of the 1967 McKinley winter expedition. In Denver one evening the previous spring, Gregg Blomberg asked several climbers to come over to his apartment. We were, I recall, sworn to secrecy before Blomberg would reveal his plan. It didn't take me long to turn down the invitation. Blomberg's near-fanatic intensity unnerved me a bit. And as someone who had got quite cold enough in the upper regions of McKinley in **July** (on an ascent three years before), I did not relish the thought of trying to sleep on Denali in February. But mainly I said no because I didn't think Blomberg and his gang had more than a slim chance of succeeding.

Blomberg's dogged secrecy bespoke his own doubts. But at the same meeting I took note of Art Davidson's reaction. This Alaskan vagabond, whom I had first met the same week, seemed to be enwreathed in a blithe and naive enthusiasm. There was no question for him of participating. You would have thought from his response, however, that somebody had just offered him a two-week trip to the Riviera. Let Blomberg design the special sleeping bags; Davidson just wanted to get out on the Kahiltna Glacier and start walking.

Art had come down to Denver for the meeting, and while he was there he called me up and asked me out for a beer. The most casual occasions turn out to be pivot points of life. It would not be much of an exaggeration to say that it was a beer with Art at the Stadium Inn near Denver University that kept me from quitting climbing at age 22.

The summer before I had gone on my own third Alaskan expedition, on which four of us had succeeded in climbing a new route on Mt. Huntington. On the descent Ed Bernd was killed when his rappel failed. It was the third fatal accident I had witnessed in only five years of climbing, and it hit me hard. Although I was writing a book about Huntington at the time of Art's visit, I felt so depressed and freaked out about the accident that I had serious doubts about climbing again. Art took care of that.

He was a remarkable sight, sitting there in the Stadium Inn. I picture him in shapeless khaki trousers and an old plaid lumberjack shirt with holes in the elbows. "Scruffy" would have been too polite a word. He looked like an Icelandic warrior out of the Sagas, with his flaming red beard, his bizarre white eyebrows. He spoke like a poet, and the verses he intoned, in his deep yet dulcet voice, were ones of exhortation and enlistment. The text was a series of paeans to the gleaming untrod glaciers, the soaring salmon-colored granite walls, the green fire of the tundra and the dancing curtains of the northern lights in Art's adopted paradise, Alaska. Over the third beer he hit me with the clincher, "You want to go to the Spires?"

I signed on the imaginary dotted line. As it turned out, I had wangled a job that summer teaching on Elmendorf Air Force Base in Anchorage. No matter, said Art; we would do our expedition in September, even stay into October. My Huntington partner Don Jensen and I had been desperate to go to the Cathedral (Kichatna) Spires, and might have headed there immediately after Huntington, but for Ed's death. Art was equally enraptured with the place.

That summer I rented a squalid little shack in Spenard, a "suburb" of unzoned, booming Anchorage. Art came by daily when he wasn't in the mountains. He drove a dusty old truck, on the back of which he had erected a wooden shelter that looked vaguely like a dog house. The name of the truck was Bucephalus, after Alexander the Great's horse. Bucephalus also served as Art's domicile. It is hard to summon up a memory of what Art did to make a living at the time. He was paid a pittance to do physiological tests for some scientists at the University of

Alaska while he was off climbing. Money was not a central worry; his father, Art used to boast, had supported the family for several years by betting shrewdly on the horses.

We kicked around Anchorage that summer, becoming great friends. Art's diet consisted almost entirely of peanut butter, cottage cheese, raisins, and 20 or 30 cups of coffee a day. He loved music, having taught himself to play the flute and the piano. Late at night, when the impulse seized him, he would climb through a window in some empty building at Alaska Methodist University so that he could play a battered old upright piano. One day Art came into a little cash, so he went right out and bought 40 or 50 LP records. The only problem was, he didn't have a phonograph.

We climbed in the Cathedral Spires for all of September and the first week of October, making the first ascent of the range's highest peak, Kichatna Spire. The driving force among the five of us was Art, and it was his nerve and enthusiasm that got himself and Rick Millikan to the top of the mountain after weeks of buildup frustrated by terrible weather.

I doubt that he knew it at the time—do we ever stop to recognize those youthful spells of sheer excellence?—but Art was in the climbing prime of his life. He was almost entirely self-taught, so his maneuvers were eccentric at times, and his ice-chopping technique was as rough and brutal as it was effective. But he was at home in his beloved mountains as few climbers I have ever known learned how to be, and his appetite was boundless. In fact, during the 17 months from April 1966 through August 1967, Art went on **six** successful expeditions, one after another. I wonder if any other mountaineer has ever accomplished the like.

First came a smooth two-man ascent of Mt. Marcus Baker, the highest peak in the Chugach, unrepeated since Brad Washburn's first ascent in 1938. In May, Art summitted on the first ascent of Mt. Seattle in the St. Elias Range, on a typically impetuous Fred Beckey assault. In July Art was one of the prime movers in a very long ridge traverse of Mt. Logan led by Boyd Everett. Then in September he was the spearhead of our Spires expedition.

By next February, he was on McKinley. Despite almost dying on Denali, Art lived up to a promise and joined me and four others in the Revelation Range in August 1967. After his lengthy stay in the hospital, Art had been able only to limp around painfully for months. It was crazy to think of climbing again, but he talked his doctor into letting him visit the Revelation Range—"as long as you keep your feet dry."

Poor Art! In the Revelations, we hit the most fiendish weather I was ever to see in twelve Alaskan expeditions. The gales of rain, sleet, and snow threatened to wash our base camp off the surface of the glacier. We all had wish-fulfillment nightmares, dreams in which cozy log cabins vanished at the touch. Pots, gear, and hard hats blew more than a mile from base camp. We had to stay up all night sometimes with the stoves running in the tents to keep from succumbing to hypothermia. An igloo we built looked like a ruined beehive the next day. While we were in the Revelations, in fact, the Wilcox party was dying in a blizzard on Mt. McKinley—still Denali's worst disaster.

His own ordeal on McKinley the previous winter had left Art a shaken •
man—and perhaps the intensity of six expeditions in a year and a half was finally getting to him. I remember him hobbling around camp in his mukluks, looking up at the furious sky, and saying, "God, Dave, this is a foreboding place!" Yet he never gave in, and he treated the reduction of his footgear to soggy decrepitude as if it were some grand joke on his doctor. We invented a fierce game called Hole Ball; Art ran his patterns with complete disregard for his aching feet. A game, like a climb, was to be prosecuted with zest and passion, and to hell with prudence.

After 1967, understandably, Art tailed off in his climbing. His several years of achievement had had a meteoric brilliance about them, and I doubt that even the great campaigners of Alaskan mountaineering, like Washburn, Beckey, or Vin Hoeman, ever had a stretch so blithe as Art's in 1966–67, when they were quite so ready to meet every obstacle a mountain could offer. In Alaska, where more expeditions fail than succeed, and where many pack it in and go home before they even get started, Art's confidence and energy seemed to set an impossible standard. Of such panache the peculiar genius of mountaineering is made.

As I myself had, in response to a disturbing ordeal, Art immersed himself in writing a book. I remember well the false starts, the frustrations of the early drafts of *Minus 148°*. Art let me read his pages, and I could see two things happening. The first was that he had kaleidoscopic ambitions; in a way the book he wanted to write would have been a sprawling, picaresque celebration of Alaska itself, a kind of *Moby-Dick* of the 49th state. But in these wildly colorful early chapters, he was also avoiding McKinley. It was this, as much as anything, that revealed to me just how deep a horror those six days and nights of survival at Denali Pass had meant.

It took a while, but when Art finally settled in and faced his book, he pulled off a remarkable thing. Here was no simple tale of heroism and valor, like *Annapurna*, but rather a vexed, uneven story of doubt, failure, whim, courage, tragedy. The team was unbalanced, with the strong members far superior to the others. Perhaps the strongest of all was killed in an absurd accident within the first hours of the expedition. The leader himself seemed to lose heart in mid-stream. Yet everything was redeemed by the magnificent accomplishment of the summit in early March, and then by the even more magnificent survival of Art, Dave Johnston, and Ray Genet.

To my delight, the book Art wrote managed, as few expedition chronicles ever have, to deal directly with the conflicts that divided the party, to pay close attention to the personalities involved, to lay bare their weaknesses without disloyalty to the men (who indeed cooperated splendidly by lending diaries), and to narrate without flinching the details of the ordeal at Denali Pass. The potentially diffuse details of the plot came together in a compulsively readable story.

Minus 148° is one of the few true classics in the literature of mountaineering. It richly deserves a republication that will bring it a whole new generation of readers, hungry young climbers and armchair graybeards alike. It is an honor to salute the book's reappearance, and a pleasure to wish it well.

Prologue

ONE SUNNY MORNING in my twenty-first summer I was hiking along a mountain road in British Columbia wondering which mountain I'd climb next. The song of a thrush in the woods was interrupted by the roar of a car rushing by me.

If that car hadn't come to a screeching halt, I probably would never have become involved in the events which are recounted in this book. The driver offered me a ride. I asked him where to. He said he was going to Anchorage, Alaska, and did I want to come along. The mountains and wild country there were said to be unbelievable. I hopped into the car and was on my way to Alaska and to an improbable experience that would soon threaten to cut short my summer of wandering in the north.

At a roadside grocery I bought several loaves of raisin bread and a big jar of peanut butter. Whenever the man with whom I was riding stopped every few hundred miles for a meal at a cafe, I would order a glass of milk and make myself a couple of peanut butter sandwiches. All went well until we pulled into the customs station near the Alaska-Yukon border. A huge Royal Canadian Mounted Policeman, complete with moustache and braided golden cords swinging from his shoulders, yanked me from the car, frisked me, handcuffed me, and directed me to a backroom in the station house. As we passed the official at the front desk the Mountie called out, "We got our man, Frank!"

Sitting across an empty table from my interrogator, I figured

I was being mistaken for someone else, so I asked what crime I was supposed to have committed. The Mountie snarled; "Don't be funny! You know what you did!" He leafed through a folder of official-looking papers for several minutes, then crossed his arms and directed a well-rehearsed piercing stare into my eyes for a full forty seconds. Then his commanding voice broke the silence to say, "A hundred and eighty miles back, at Lake Kluane, did you eat a peanut butter sandwich?"

Stunned, I blurted out that, yes, I had eaten a peanut butter sandwich. A smile crept across the Mountie's face; he had his man. When I asked if there was a law against eating peanut butter sandwiches, he roared back: "You can't fool me, kid! We got solid proof! When our bulletin went out through the Yukon and B.C., it was only a matter of time before people along the highway would call in to identify you." With that he began rattling off the time and location of every peanut butter sandwich I had eaten along the highway. I confessed to each count; it looked as if they had me. Then he demanded to know where I had ditched the airplane I had stolen in Whitehorse. I declared I was not his airplane thief, and the man with whom I'd been riding stepped forward to assure the Mountie that even though I had eaten all the sandwiches recorded in the official reports, I had not snitched an airplane as we passed through Whitehorse. After additional checking the Mountie sadly concluded that I was innocent of the plane theft and let me go. Leaving this disappointed man with his folder of peanut butter sandwich documents, we drove into Alaska; mountains began to appear and I caught my first glimpse of a glacier flowing out of a rugged-looking range.

In Anchorage, the mountains seemed to fill the sky. There were the sharp ice and rock lines of the peaks in the Chugach Range to the east, the Chigmits in the west, and the Talkeetnas and the Alaska Range to the north. Thousands of unclimbed and even unnamed mountains rose straight from fjords of the Pacific, from spruce and birch forests of the interior, and from the treeless expanse of the Arctic tundra. Everywhere the land seemed to be bursting with incredible wildness. Volcanos erupted. Earth tremors and quakes set off avalanches and shattered rock ridges. Thirty-foot tides, among the highest and fastest in the world, flowed like massive, turbulent rivers. Whistling and trumpeter swans nested on outlying lakes. And one large lake, Illiamna, was even said to have a monster living in it.

I became especially intrigued by the few remaining blank areas on the maps. What glaciers were out there? What rock walls? What formations of ice? I decided to visit all the mountains, live on their ridges and walls, and drink from their streams. By myself or with others, I began setting out into the hills; sometimes I tried ascents that were at the very limit of my climbing ability and at other times I'd just poke around the woods and alpine meadows.

Occasionally, I'd return from these outings so dreadfully sun-burned or skinned up from scrambling over sharp rocks and edges of ice that friends would shake their heads and ask that question which has always made mountain climbers shudder: "Why do you climb mountains?" It's usually hard for a climber to reply because usually there are a number of very personal reasons why he loves to climb, and he's apt to be cautious about describing the simple joys of the mountains, like a sunrise seen from a lonely ledge of rock, because his words can never quite express what his experiences meant to him. When I'd be asked this "why" question, I'd often remember the climber who said, "I climb to escape tidal waves." Sometimes I'd offer my own version of this evasive answer by saying, "I climb because the mountains give me a tremendous opportunity to eat raisins and peanut butter sand-wiches without fear of being arrested."

As months passed, I began to feel the magnetism of Mt. McKinley, whose massive chaos of ice and rock is particularly inaccessible and therefore mysterious. Because this mountain can be seen from over two hundred miles away, Alaska's early explorers and pioneers often used it as a reference point before the country was mapped.

An old, blind Indian sage of Kantishna has told of the creation of this mountain. Hoonah, the sage, or shaman, as some have referred to him, recalled that before this great mountain was raised into the sky, Yako—the peaceful "Athabascan Adam" whose powers changed wicked men into animals, birds, and bees and who gave creatures of the forest immortality through vernal reproduction—journeyed to the sunset land in the distant west to find himself a wife. When he stroked his canoe to the shore of the village ruled by Totson, the raven war chief who delighted in killing animals and men, a mother with a happy face walked to the edge of the water and gave her beautiful young daughter to be Yako's wife. Totson, grown jealous and mean, sharpened his magic war spear, then pursued Yako across the sea. Totson's magic caused a great storm to blow in Yako's path, but the magic of the gentle giant Yako cleared a smooth passage through the wind and waves. Totson grabbed his spear, which had never missed its mark, and flung it at Yako's back. Yako, seeing the spearhead glint in the sun as it rose and arched toward him, called on his most powerful magic stones to send an enormous wave into the sky to deflect the spear. As the wave flew into the air it turned into a great rock mountain. The spearhead splintered into little pieces when it struck near the summit of the peak, and as Totson's canoe smashed into a sharp angular wall of the mountain, the war chief changed into a croaking raven. Yako traveled safely beyond the great mountain to his home in the east, where he fathered many children and allowed none of his people to possess a warlike spirit. Descendants of Yako, the Tena Indians, call the mountain *Denali,* the high one.

After many generations of Tena had lived in the shadow of Denali, white explorers discovered the mountain. They promptly measured the peak and to either repay or obtain a political favor replaced *Denali* with the name of an Ohio congressman who had never been to Alaska. Denali became Mt. McKinley, 20,320 feet high—the highest point in North America. The twentieth century was just beginning. In Alaska, shack towns boomed and were left deserted as the gold rush spread like brushfire. Riverboats chugged supplies to the outposts of civilization in summer, and dog teams ran on the snow and river ice in winter. Fairbanks and Anchorage became bustling communities on the edge of the wilderness. It was at this time that Mt. McKinley began to attract a public excited by its great height. In 1902 a race began to be the first to climb the mountain.

Two gentlemen of the frontier, Brooks and Wickersham, launched the first attempts, and failed. Belmore Brown's expedition was then frustrated less than a thousand vertical feet from the summit. The country's newspapers cried for a conqueror, and a Dr. Cook responded to the call of fame by publishing faked pictures with a fraudulent account of a summit climb he hadn't made. Then along came a batch of sourdoughs who boasted that miners toughened by Alaskan winters and work on their claims could climb McKinley before a phony eastern doctor (Cook) or any intellectual. With astonishing bravado and stamina, they lugged a fourteen-foot spruce pole to McKinley's north summit, but though it lay easily within their reach, they didn't try to climb the south summit, eight hundred feet higher. It remained for Hudson Stuck to plan and accomplish the first successful ascent to the very top of the mountain in 1913. An Alaskan missionary, Archdeacon Stuck's sensitive account of the climb reflects a man driven by spiritual aspiration rather than a quest for fame. He insisted on calling the mountain by its original Indian name, Denali.

As the years passed, mountaineers sought out the mountain's secrets; the great walls and ridges, each in its turn, were climbed. Naturalists, like Charles Sheldon and the Murie brothers, studied the wildlife around the base of McKinley, and their reports led

to the establishment of Mt. McKinley National Park. Sydney
Laurence and other artists filled their canvasses with the colors of
McKinley's mist and soft light. A young and energetic scientist,
Bradford Washburn, returned to McKinley several times to pioneer
the West Buttress Route (today the most popular climbing route
on the peak), to participate in studies of cosmic rays, frostbite, and
weather, and to produce a finely detailed map from the confusion
of McKinley's tumbling ice and rock ribs.

Although a mountain always remains enigmatic, by 1967
McKinley appeared to be hiding only one last mystery, an aspect
of the mountain not yet revealed to its visitors. Winter! What was
McKinley like during the winter?

I became intrigued with this season of the mountain when I
went on my first expedition to McKinley in the summer of 1965
with the Osaka Alpine Club and the superb Japanese climber
Shiro Nishimae, who taught me much of what I know about high-
altitude climbing. While Shiro and I watched huge cornices soften
and crumble in the July sun, we tried to picture the winter storms
that packed snow into these massive ice formations overhanging
the ridges. When we shed our shirts as we carried loads on the
glacier, we wondered what the temperature would drop to in
February. It might remain below $-30°$ F. for weeks. At these
temperatures, with hundred-mile-per-hour winds, could a person
survive, let alone climb? We shuddered to imagine McKinley's
most eerie winter aspect—the darkness. Perhaps the high ridges
would block out the low winter sun, allowing the basins to receive only a few hours of twilight between long nights.

During that summer expedition, Shiro and I caught only a few
glimpses of what the McKinley winter would be like, but they
were enough to infect us with what many explorers have described
as a fever to go back to a region or landscape that has a grip on
you. Not really understanding why they go, men have returned to

the sea or to deserts, to jungles or to frozen wastes in the Arctic, knowing they will be miserable and frequently in danger.

No sooner had Shiro and I come down from McKinley in the summer than we felt the need to go back in the winter; anticipation and the uncertainty of what we would find compelled us to go and live in the wind and cold, the thin air and darkness of Denali's winter.

MINUS 148°:
First Winter
Ascent of
Mt. McKinley

Inception

As a child I explored the unknown rivers and mountain ranges of wild continents while I forded puddles and irrigation ditches, searched my way through cornfields, and established trading posts in the wilderness of a neighborhood park. Despite my discouragement the day I learned all the continents had already been discovered, I grew up never quite losing hope of coming upon an unfound corner of the earth.

At twenty-two I came to regard the first expedition to Mt. McKinley in the winter as a journey into an unexplored land. No one had lived on North America's highest ridges in the winter twilight. No one knew how low the temperatures would drop, or how penetrating the cold would be when the wind blew. For thousands of years McKinley's winter storms had raged by themselves. No one had ever watched gentle light from the winter sun filter into McKinley's couloirs, basins, and cols. And, of course, no one had ever attempted to climb to McKinley's summit during the winter months.

When I asked a veteran Alaskan climber what he thought about a winter ascent of McKinley, he warned me that the combination of cold, wind, darkness, and altitude would likely be the severest conditions ever encountered by men. I couldn't believe it would be quite that extreme, but the information I was able to obtain from meteorologists and physiologists was not very encouraging. The temperatures could be expected to run into the minus sixties farenheit. The wind frequently blew 150 miles per hour. On December 21 the sun would rise at 9:45 A.M. and set at 2:30 P.M.; later in

February there would be as much as seven hours of direct sunlight. Bradford Washburn estimated that above eighteen thousand feet on Mt. McKinley a person is reduced to roughly 50 percent of his mental capacity, because of the lack of oxygen in the thin air. At high altitudes any physical activity is strenuous; a good number of McKinley climbers have been incapacitated short of the summit.

Perhaps I shouldn't have been surprised when it became difficult to find qualified climbers who wanted to try getting to the top of McKinley in the winter. When I asked one mountaineer who had already scaled McKinley in the summer whether he'd like to join a winter expedition he said, "Why try something so unpleasant?" Another McKinley climber declined to join a winter attempt because he figured there was less than a fifty-fifty chance of success. On the other hand, Shiro Nishimae, who had first put the notion of a winter ascent in my head, never faltered in his enthusiasm for a winter climb. The very uncertainty of success appealed to Shiro who took delight in doing things he had been told were impossible. Unfortunately, he was having financial difficulties getting through graduate school and there appeared to be no way he could afford a winter expedition which might cost over a thousand dollars a person by the time all the food, equipment, and transportation expenses were divided among the expedition members.

Shiro and I had a mutual friend, Dr. George Wichman, an orthopedic surgeon in Anchorage who told chilling stories about his struggles on McKinley in early spring. George and several companions had been caught away from their camp by a sudden storm and forced to bivouac without sleeping bags in subzero temperatures. Late one evening, after George had related the details of this fight against cold and driving snow, he gathered up the solid hulk of his body, lumbered once around the room without saying a word, then stopped and said he would like to try a winter ascent of McKinley. I was delighted and encouraged because, besides George's endurance and twenty-odd years of experience in mountains, his medical abilities would make him invaluable to an expedition.

Most of all, our expedition needed a leader, someone with a strong personality who could gather the right people around him and fuse them into a close-knit unit that could work smoothly under the most miserable circumstances. I thought Gregg Blomberg was the man, but the first time I mentioned climbing McKinley in the winter to him he thought I was joking. When he realized I was serious, he told me it couldn't be done. Then, after a pitcher of beer, his enthusiasm for the absurd and incredible caught fire and he decided it might be possible. By two in the morning he had accepted the leadership of the expedition and had already begun designing special clothing for the extreme temperatures we were anticipating. Gregg not only appreciated excellent equipment, he demanded it. Several years as the head of Colorado Mountain Industries had earned him the reputation of being a perfectionist in the manufacturing of climbing gear. One after another, Gregg solved our equipment problems with his inventive and thorough mind, but there remained another, more important, task with which he had difficulty coping—a team of climbers had to be brought together.

Since Gregg had taught at winter mountaineering schools for several years and had led a successful climb of a new route on Mt. Logan (19,850 feet high, the second highest peak in North America), he knew the type of men he wanted for McKinley in the winter, but he couldn't find them. Of the more than thirty top American climbers he contacted, only a few were interested, and none could arrange free time for a winter expedition that might take thirty to forty days or even longer. Gregg grew frustrated. When Shiro reported that he still could not finance the trip and it appeared that George might not be able to leave his busy orthopedic practice for the expedition, Gregg's enthusiasm disappeared. In Alaska I began receiving despondent letters from Gregg. The first week in July, 1966, five months before we had planned to depart for the mountain, Gregg wrote me that he was through with the expedition.

I answered him immediately:

I am convinced you and I are going to climb those last steps to the summit of McKinley together next winter. Have you grown old since I saw you last? Think of the magnitude of what we can do. Here we can extend ourselves and the limits of what has been done. It is perfectly understandable that others are not excited about this project. Who can imagine it? It is an act of imagination and inspiration. Gregg, you are a person of imagination and inspiration. This is your climb. You have worked on it more than anyone. We will make it. We need your leadership.

Gregg responded on July 7:

Art, your enthusiasm is the same as it always was, and would again convince me to go, if I hadn't already spent so much time with so little result. I am going to have to hang it up, as I don't believe there is enough time to do the climb in '67 the way it should be done. We haven't even a crew yet.

Without Gregg's leadership it appeared hopeless. Our expedition had collapsed. I was the only definite member. Perhaps Gregg was correct in thinking it would be four or five years before mountaineers were ready to accept the idea of a winter ascent.

Through the summer our expedition hung in limbo. Gregg registered in school for the winter quarter, and even I had all but given up the expedition as a nice dream. Then Shiro and George suddenly confirmed that they could definitely go. This encouraged Gregg to the point where he offered to lead the expedition if at least one more good climber joined us. By September two more climbers, both excellent men, were committed to the expedition.

One was Dave Johnston—a rare, almost mythical creature. He stands six feet seven inches, and has flowing, sandy-red hair and beard. His low, vibrant voice is nearly always singing. He has ridden freights and hitchhiked throughout the United States and South America to find enough mountains to climb. Although Dave holds a college degree in forestry, he doesn't pursue a career, but prefers to be a "climbing bum." I'd often seen climbers, myself included, seized by uncontrollable excitement before a big climb, but Dave's reaction to being included in the winter expedition startled me. Leaping several feet into the air and flapping and waving his endless arms, he started shouting, "Wow, honcho boncho!"

Dave's experience on numerous peaks above eighteen thousand feet, and on one ascent in particular, strengthened our team. He had already climbed McKinley. With him and Shiro in the party we had two climbers who had already been up the mountain. Two others, George and myself, had been on McKinley but had been stopped short of the summit.

The other climber who joined us was a New Zealander, Dr. John Edwards. After clambering about the mountains of his homeland, John had climbed in England and in the Alps during his student days at Cambridge. Biological research had taken him on an expedition to northeast Greenland, but for several years a physiological study of insects had tethered him close to a lab; understandably, he was just itching to climb McKinley.

Though none of us had met John, people at the Institute of Arctic Biology, where I worked and where he had once held a position, spoke of him as an extremely delightful overgrown elf. He was fabled to be amiable, boisterous, occasionally mischievous, and at the same time a thoroughly levelheaded and thoughtful fellow. My first meeting with John reaffirmed the legend. I had traced the sounds of a concert through several corridors at the Institute to a short figure hopping about from leg to leg while vocalizing the entire woodwind section of an orchestra. This apparition's large, elfin ears stuck out from generous locks of golden hair, his hands rapidly punctuated the air in time to the symphony, and his light-blue eyes flashed me a quizzical glance. It was John.

It would be good to have a comedian with us through the long, cold nights that lay ahead. All too often expeditions have floundered in depression because they couldn't laugh at their misery. We were well aware that the tensions of confinement during storms and the strain of altitude and darkness could easily break a climber's personality. Character strength would be as important as physical strength on this climb.

With the addition of Dave and John our expedition was complete with competent men. We had to discourage a number of people who wanted to go with us because their climbing qualifications weren't sufficient or their mental attitudes didn't seem appropriate for this venture. The six of us proceeded to select our food and collect our equipment. Then, in about the middle of December, only five weeks before we were scheduled to start up the mountain, Gregg in Colorado and I in Fairbanks, Alaska, began receiving long-distance phone calls from a man with a thick Swiss accent. His name was Ray Genet. Genet asked if he and his French friend Jacques "Farine" Batkin could become expedition members. Batkin we had heard about. He was said to be an incredibly powerful climber, noted for having pioneered long, difficult winter ascents of steep ice and rock walls in the Alps. Three years earlier he had climbed what many judged to be the most difficult route ever put up in Alaska; on this expedition with Lionel Terray to Mt. Huntington he was considered the best-liked party member and was chosen by the leader, Terray, for the first summit attempt. Farine appeared perfect for McKinley in the winter. It was true that we might have some problems communicating with him, since he had mastered only a few dozen words of English, but we were anxious to have him with us nevertheless. Genet, however, was a different matter. His mountaineering background wasn't particularly impressive. He cited his youth in Switzerland's Alps, cross-country skiing, and winter hunting trips as his experience. His most notable ascent was of a squat, roundish peak only forty-five hundred feet high. I considered his main qualifications for this climb to be his limitless enthusiasm and a determination to be included. Certainly enthusiasm and determination were important qualities for a winter

McKinley climber, but would they compensate for a lack of experience? It wasn't until much later that we learned how Genet had helped Gregg and me decide to let him join us. On the phone he had told Gregg I wasn't opposed to his coming. Then he called me to say Gregg approved his coming if I agreed. Before we realized it, Genet was a member of the expedition.

When I first met Farine and Genet they inspired opposite reactions: confidence and doubt. Farine, dressed in plain working clothes, was the most powerful man I had ever encountered. His large neck made his head appear small in comparison. He was short, with enormous shoulders and a barrel chest. His stocky legs reminded one of giant pistons designed for hard work. In fact, much of his life had been spent in strenuous labor. His career as a flour sack carrier was the origin of his nickname, "Farine," and also, no doubt, of some of his stamina. He had the humble appearance and quietness of a man who has confidence in himself.

Genet, on the other hand, seemed to be trying to prove something to us and, perhaps, to himself. He wore a shirt tied with rawhide thongs which opened on his hairy chest. He had on his climbing trousers and boots as if to convince us he had just come down from a mountain and really was a climber. A smile stretched behind his bushy black beard. His dark, deep-set eyes gleamed, and his voice boomed out a greeting—"I'm Ray Genet." At first sight I thought I'd never be able to take Genet seriously, but his infectious personality quickly charmed me into accepting his style and friendliness. Much as I grew to like him, I couldn't shake off the suspicion that we were being careless by bringing him with us. Both Farine and Genet earned our respect when we gathered in Fairbanks the last week in January for a series of physiological tests at the Institute of Arctic Biology. On the treadmill runs which indicate physical fitness Farine topped us all with an astonishing score which amazed even the scientific examiner. Not far below Farine in fitness was Genet. Dave and I were a little further down the scale, and the others followed us.

The three days of testing were the first occasion we (except for George, who was still busy with his practice in Anchorage) had all been one place at the same time. A group spirit began to develop.

Assuming the roles of guinea pigs in experiments designed to measure our responses to cold and altitude, we found it unsettling to watch our mental function, balance, and coordination deteriorate while heart rate increased as we tested at simulated altitudes up to twenty thousand feet in a decompression chamber. We contributed generously to blood and urine studies and allowed the imposing dials, switches, wires, and electrodes of an electrocardiograph and an electroencephalograph to chart the activity of our hearts and brains. To determine the effect the expedition had on our physiology we were scheduled to repeat the same battery of tests when we returned from the mountain, but one of the chief scientists looked me in the eye and said in a voice which might have been serious, "Do you really think you are going to return?"

During the expedition I would conduct tests with miniaturized equipment to observe how our physiology changed throughout the course of our climb. I had learned by testing for the Institute on previous expeditions that climbers usually return from Mt. McKinley physically weaker than when they started. While trips to lower mountains may help improve a climber's fitness, a McKinley expedition is likely to drain his strength and lead to deterioration of body functions.

On the mountain our ability to work and think clearly would be limited by our bodies' capabilities of extracting oxygen from the thin air and delivering it to the brain, the muscles, and other tissues. Above even moderate altitudes of thirteen and fourteen thousand feet a person's motivation diminishes, and lassitude undermines the desire to go on or to survive. The higher one climbs the more one's cold resistance is lowered—the chances of frostbite increase. Above fourteen thousand feet it is virtually impossible for the human body to recover from many illnesses and injuries—a head cold or diarrhea can become fatal. Altitude has often strained the nerves of climbers to the point where the best of friends come to hate each other. These effects of altitude would be more subtle than the cold and wind but every bit as demanding. Unlike these other elements, there is no escaping altitude by putting on more clothes or slipping into a tent or igloo. Since, like previous McKinley climbers, we were not going to use oxygen masks, relief from the rarified air could come only by descending the mountain.

When the tests were completed, we rushed willy-nilly into the final hectic week. Shiro supervised the packing of our fifty-five-day supply of food into cardboard boxes, each of which contained breakfast for four men, four individually wrapped lunches, and enough dinner for four. These units, which allotted each of us approximately fifty-two hundred calories a day, were expected to be easy to carry on the mountain.

With sweat beading from his forehead and his bloodshot eyes darting swiftly over endless lists and piles of gear, Gregg directed the organizing of our equipment. He regularly dispatched Genet to buy more matches, more candles, more gas for the stoves (besides cooking our meals they would melt all our water from snow and ice), more spare gloves and socks, more string, twine and light ropes, extra lantern mantels, needles and thread, more of everything we might need; once we were flown onto the glacier there could be no returning for forgotten items.

Gregg let us select our personal clothing from the heaps of down parkas, down pants, wind pants, wind parkas, sleeping bags, and packs which Alp Sport had prepared especially for our expedition. Knowing that a variety of colors would help each of us keep track of his own equipment, Gregg had requested quiet shades of green and blue and tan and a blazing orange. Seconds after he had laid the clothes before us, every orange garment vanished. Genet, heedless of the variety of sizes he was collecting, had scooped them up for himself. Although most of his orange regalia turned out to be either too small or too large for him, we let Genet keep these clothes because they seemed to fit his personality.

For further identification of our equipment we each wrote our names on our personal gear, and here again this strange man with a bushy beard surprised us. Instead of writing his name on each item, Genet painted a skull and crossbones on everything that was his. I wondered what it was going to be like living with this sort of being for more than a month. In any event, this insignia, along with Genet's loud voice and crackling laughter, earned him the nickname "Pirate."

With the packing completed, press conferences over, and farewell parties ended, we left for Talkeetna on the Alaska Railroad. From this tiny town, sixty miles from the Alaska Range, we would be flown onto McKinley by the rough-cut glacier pilot Don Sheldon. "Howdy," Sheldon hollered when we arrived. "Big wind blow'n up there now," he said, "tear a wing right off a plane, you bet. Tell you what, you guys can sleep in the hangar tonight. I'll get up at the crack o' dawn and take a look. If the wind is down we'll just huckldebuck on up there."

Twelve months earlier I had asked Don if he could land on McKinley in the winter. He answered: "Yowza, no problem. What you want to do, Art, is get yourself a hundred-pound sack a beans, fire yourself up, and climb that old mountain." Now he told me he never expected I'd get a party together to go on McKinley in the winter.

It was minus 30° F. when we laid out our sleeping bags. In just a few hours our umbilical cord would be cut. Set on the Kahiltna with a few boxes of supplies, the expedition would be on its own in fifteen hundred square miles of ice and rock. If we had an emergency below fourteen thousand feet, Sheldon would be able to land near us. If the radio didn't work or the weather was bad, as is often the case, he wouldn't be able to reach us at all. If an emergency occurred above fourteen thousand feet we would have to rely entirely on our own resources to evacuate an injured man or to retreat. We would be independent of the world we had left, and consequently dependent on each other.

As I went to sleep the questions that had been with me for over a year again ran through my mind. Would everyone make the summit? Would I stand on top of McKinley? What would I discover about myself in the critical situations we were bound to encounter? Would everyone return safely? Curled in the warmth of my sleeping bag, I thought again of the storms and long hours of darkness, the high glaciers of wind-swept ice that lay ahead; of the hardships I'd share with seven men. Out there in the night, under the full moon, somewhere beyond the streets of Talkeetna, beyond the frozen marshes and woods, was Mt. McKinley.

My Daddy Can't Climb That Mountain

"MY DADDY CAN'T CLIMB that mountain, it's too big," whispered George Wichman's five-year-old son, leaning against his mother at the end of Sheldon's airstrip. Through a partly iced-up window of the small silver plane he caught sight of his father wedged in behind Pirate as the Cessna raced off to the far end of the runway, whining and throwing snow in its wake. His eyes grew large and puzzled as the plane lifted lightly into the air, banked sharply, and flew off toward the big mountain.

Early that morning Sheldon had packed Gregg and Dave off in the first flight to the peak. In the still air, as they passed close to Mt. Hunter, the buzzing of the plane's engine had shaken loose an enormous avalanche. They laughed about its being a warning. Even though the West Buttress route we would attempt was relatively protected from avalanches, Dave and Gregg realized we would have to judge snow conditions carefully. On the ground an avalanche can't be outrun; once you are caught in a river of snow and ice blocks, there is little chance to escape being crushed or smothered.

Sheldon cruised low over the Kahiltna, turned east to a tributary glacier, and landed just outside the McKinley Park boundary at an altitude of seven thousand feet. Dave and Gregg immediately roped themselves together. Then, while Sheldon hurried back to ferry the rest of us onto the mountain, they set about to scout the first mile of the route for crevasses. The rope, tied tightly around each of their waists and stretching 140 feet between them, protected them from the crevasses. If one of them should step into a crevasse hidden under a crust of snow, the rope, linking him to his partner, would keep him from falling to the bottom of the crevasse.

Fortunately, most of the crevasses that spread like intricate lacework before Dave and Gregg appeared to be filled with snow. Cautiously, the two searched out a safe path through the crevasse field. Already they had started toward the summit which lay at least three weeks and five or six camps away.

Several hundred yards beyond the landing site Gregg and Dave peered around the end of a small ridge to see the route stretch seven miles north on the gently rising Kahiltna Glacier to a point immediately below Kahiltna Pass. Hidden from their sight, the route turned east and upward toward Windy Corner—13,000 feet. A mile beyond this natural wind tunnel a steep ice slope rises to the crest of the West Buttress. A mile-long rock and snow ridge leads to a basin below the ice wall rising sharply to Denali Pass—18,200 feet. A final two miles of ice separates Denali Pass from the 20,320-foot summit.

By the time Gregg and Dave had returned from their route-finding hike several hours later, Sheldon had flown everyone to the glacier but Shiro and me. Winding their way back through the crevasses, Gregg and Dave were somewhat alarmed to be greeted by a playful Farine. The bareheaded Frenchman came bouncing toward them alone and unroped with a big grin on his face. Farine was obviously delighted to be in the mountains again. He waved both arms, then jogged toward Gregg and Dave, his eyes shining.

The two who stood roped together were happy to see Farine so ebullient, but, at that moment they couldn't share his excitement, because they were shocked that he had nonchalantly charged off by himself before he knew whether there was a safe route through the crevasses.

Even though Gregg and Dave were disturbed by Farine's apparent carelessness, they chose to say nothing about the incident since Farine spoke no English and they spoke no French, they figured it would be nearly impossible to caution him without insulting him. After all, Farine had more experience on glaciers than either of them had. Gregg had told me that his sense of leadership compelled him to feel responsible for everyone's safety, but he let this incident pass. Farine was safe. The route was now clearly marked with willow wands. What did it matter?

Evening was already in the air when Sheldon took off with Shiro and me on the last flight to McKinley. The sun had begun setting by the time we left the forests behind and began flying over the moraine of the Kahiltna Glacier. Noticing the long shadows cast by the peaks and the dim light in the basins, Shiro and I decided Sheldon would be unable to land in the poor light. Touching down on a glacier requires excellent vision to judge the slope and to calculate the position of crevasses and bumps. We had resigned ourselves to returning to Talkeetna for the night and coming back the next morning, but suddenly we felt that weightless sensation which meant the plane was losing altitude fast. Since it seemed impossible that Sheldon might be heading down for a landing, I shouted over the roar of the prop to ask him what was wrong. He clicked on a headlight and yelled, "Let's give her hell, boys!" Shiro and I exchanged worried glances and braced ourselves for the crash. Sheldon hollered, "Geronimo!" The glacier rushed up toward us. Sheldon stared straight ahead, and I watched him so closely that I almost failed to notice when the plane's skis touched the snow and skimmed smoothly along the surface.

Anxious to get in the air again before it was completely dark, Sheldon heaved our gear onto the snow, checked his instruments, then barreled down the slope. Shiro and I watched the plane's red light rise over the Kahiltna and disappear beyond a ridge of Mt. Hunter. Long after the plane was out of sight we listened to its buzzing. At first the noise bounced off the ridges and sounded like several planes. Then a single faint sound remained, till eventually our straining ears heard nothing. We had listened intently because the disappearing plane was the link to families, friends, and comfort, to our regular lives.

As my eyes traveled over the dark outlines of ice and rock rising from the Kahiltna and my ears listened for some sound in the still air, I began to feel uneasy. The weather was calm and the three inches of soft snow beneath our feet had a gentleness to it, but the impact of the emptiness of this barren landscape made me feel very small and somewhat vulnerable. Snow and ice and rock—that's all there was.

Shiro winked at me; we smiled and slapped each other on the back. I remembered belaying Shiro by moonlight as he had climbed onto the tiny summit of a previously unexplored mountain in the Chugach Range; on the summit snow we'd seen the tracks of a dall sheep that must have been watching us climb up the snow and rocks. And I thought of the time on McKinley in the summer when Shiro and I had traveled roped together along the Kahiltna while the sun's light filtered through a continually shifting mist.

A sharp call from down the glacier turned our heads. Shiro recognized Pirate as the lone figure tramping toward us. Pirate was evidently returning to the landing site to fetch an extra load of supplies while the others were resting or cooking dinner. I knew what prompted him to work so hard; once I had also been the least experienced member of an expedition and had tried to compensate by carrying more loads than the others.

The moment Pirate reached us Shiro asked him why he wasn't roped with someone else. Pirate shrugged his shoulders. "There's a path. No danger."

The surface of the glacier was completely dark by the time the three of us began following the trail marked every 150 feet with the three-foot willow wands Gregg and Dave had stuck in the snow. Shiro's headlight lit a small area in front of our feet. Beyond this patch of light, perhaps as large as ten square feet, all was darkness; some of the wands were difficult to find. The route twisted and turned to avoid the crevasses which loomed as dark pits at the edge of Shiro's light. We were not roped together because Pirate assured Shiro and me that the others had found the path safe enough for unroped travel. I stayed a step or two behind Shiro, who moved slowly, cautiously. Pirate, overly excited or impatient, kept ahead of us; sometimes he'd even venture a few feet beyond the light. We warned him to stay within the range of the light to be certain of his footing. For a few minutes he would manage to go slowly; then his enthusiasm would get the better of him and he would move ahead of us.

Third in line, I kept my eyes on Shiro's feet to know exactly where to step. Suddenly Shiro stopped and turned around. In his soft-spoken voice, with no trace of panic he said, "Pirate's gone; he's fallen in a crevasse."

Pirate had vanished. We followed his footsteps to where they suddenly stopped at the edge of a crevasse. Beyond his last boot-mark in the snow there was only darkness; we couldn't see the bottom of the crevasse or the other side. When we first called there was no answer. The second time we yelled for him Pirate answered faintly: "I'm down here. I'm O.K."

Pirate had rolled twenty feet down the side of the crevasse. He hadn't fallen further because this crevasse was partly filled with snow. Even this fall could have broken an arm or leg. The bottom of the crevasse opened onto the slope below, allowing Pirate to walk out by himself. He tried to laugh it off, but the silence of Shiro and myself embarrassed him; he grew quiet. Taking his fall seriously would not have been in keeping with his "pirate's" personality. It also would have been admitting he had been careless.

The three of us roped together and, with Shiro in the lead, slowly found our way toward camp. Walking in the dark, Shiro told me that he thought it would have been more sensible for the others to camp at the landing site. "Rushing off is no good." he said. "Each person needs a little time to make adjustments in his mind to being in the mountains. The expedition should feel like a team before climbing." I agreed with Shiro. And Bradford Washburn, I remembered, had predicted that our success would depend on patience as much as guts and experience.

When we reached camp I pulled Gregg aside to talk with him

alone. I told him about Pirate's fall and how I thought going unroped and having to reach camp by traveling through a crevasse
field in the dark before we had seen it in daylight were examples of
the impatience Washburn had warned us about. "Gregg, I think
we're off to a horrible start." I said. Gregg disagreed. He thought
we were off to an excellent start. He was glad we had been able to
to move up the glacier on the first day. Gregg supposed that Sheldon
knew camp wasn't at the landing site. He should have had better
sense than to bring two climbers in after dark. No one was harmed,
Gregg argued. He finished by telling me that when he and Dave
had seen the first star that evening, they had wished first for safety
and then for success.

I didn't question Gregg's concern for safety. And he was right;
we were all safe. Nevertheless, I was still troubled by the near-
accident and by what I thought was impatience. Perhaps I was
being fussy because of the strain of the last week of preparation for
the expedition. A hot meal of dried beef and mashed potatoes, along
with everyone's delight at finally being on McKinley, helped ease
my anxiety.

Because it was only $-12°$ F., Pirate and I chose to sleep in the
open rather than in the stuffy tents. The extremely low humidity
made the stars brighter than I had ever seen them. Watching them
flash and sparkle, I had an overwhelming feeling that the sky was
alive.

The following day passed so smoothly that my uneasiness gradually dissipated. Everyone was eager to work and optimistic that
we would be moving up to higher altitudes without delay. Carrying
moderate loads of fifty to sixty pounds, we transported most of our
provisions from the landing site to a temporary cache two and a
half miles up glacier. By evening there hadn't been a single incident
to make me suspect we were climbing carelessly.

I think we all shared the warmth and confidence reflected in
Gregg's journal entry that night, January 30:

The darkness of the night is no match for the intense happiness and comradship inside the tents. Our laughter spills out onto the snow with the light of the Coleman lanterns. The jabber of our group in its many accents is music to my ears. Boy, I can't believe it; on our third day we may be as far as four miles from our landing site. This is due to good snow conditions and weather, and partly due to a hell of a fine crew. I'll be happy when the first week has passed; I'll be in shape, and everything will be easier and more routine.

I snuggled down into my sleeping bag, drifting off to sleep, warm and excited about the climbing ahead of us. Then in the night I had a vivid dream: *I was walking on the glacier and suddenly fell, almost floating, down into a very dark place. Far off, I saw a pinpoint of brilliant light that began growing larger. I heard beautiful music, a symphony and singing. All the darkness disappeared and I was sitting in a lovely forest. Birds were singing and there were flowers. I was ok.*

Crevasse

As WE BEGAN dressing, a pale light slipped into our tents. It was —20 F. The tent walls sagged with the weight of ice which had crystalized out of moisture from our breath while we slept. Every time anyone moved a sprinkle of crystals was set off. Invariably, the tiny flecks found their way onto our faces or down our necks. To defend ourselves we either dressed quickly or ducked back into our sleeping bags to hide until breakfast was ready.

Farine, however, calmly let this morning ice shower fall on him as if he didn't feel it at all. I thought he might even be enjoying the cold tingle when the ice touched his skin. Later, when Dave had fired up the little cooking stove, Farine handled cold metal pots with his bare hands as if this were the natural thing to do. I tried it, but my skin stuck to the metal.

Chattering busily over the muffled roar of the stove, we prepared for the day. Dave hunched his lanky body into one end of the tent in order to cook oatmeal and hot jello. I sorted my film, imagining the movies I'd shoot when the sun came up. Pirate teased George for crawling out of his sleeping bag, bleary-eyed and mumbling, like an old grizzly emerging from its hibernation den. John, Shiro, and Gregg discussed how we could best take advantage of this day of clear weather. It appeared unlikely that a storm would disturb the calm and cloudless sky before nightfall. Gregg figured it was a perfect day to move camp. With an early start, he thought we could cover four miles and camp that night where the glacier rises suddenly toward Kahiltna Pass.

While we gobbled down the oatmeal Dave had cooked up, and

crunched on dry bread, two or three separate conversations rattled on. Only Farine was quiet. As his eyes followed our expressions, I wondered whether his poor English alone kept him from talking, or whether he preferred to be silent. His eyes were direct; there was an intense feeling in them. Before we had flown onto the glacier I had thought this feeling was loneliness; now it seemed to be a deep peace of mind. Once, before we had left Anchorage, I had asked in my broken French; "Farine, when are you going to get married? Here in Alaska there are many beautiful Eskimo women. I hear that some of them make very good wives."

He had answered with a slight smile: "No, I am a simple man. I live in the mountains."

I noticed Farine was waiting quietly while the rest of us packed our personal gear. He, of course, was ready to climb. Feeling an orange in my pocket, I offered it to him. He said I should eat it because he had eaten one the day before. He really deserved this orange, so I insisted: "Thank you, Farine, but I have eaten fifteen oranges this morning and cannot eat one more."

He nodded without cracking a smile and answered: *"Vraiment? Mais, J'ai mangé quatre kilos des oranges ce matin, Arthur. Mangez cette orange."* (Really? But I have eaten four kilos of oranges this morning, Arthur. You eat this orange.)

He had deftly turned my joke back at me, and though I insisted that I had just stuffed away thirty pounds of raisins, he wouldn't take the orange.

When the sun suddenly lifted above a ridge and flooded our tents with its strong light, everyone became eager to set off. In the sunlight it felt thirty degrees warmer, though the air temperature rose to only —14° F. Gregg, Dave, Farine, and Pirate shouldered sixty- to seventy-pound packs of food to be deposited at the cache two and a half miles up the glacier. They would have to return for some of their personal gear, then head up the glacier again to arrive late at the new camp, perhaps after dark. They sauntered off unroped because the route had already been established. There were no exposed crevasses; it appeared to be safe. As they left I filmed them moving slowly out onto the white expanse of the Kahiltna. Through the lens I followed them as they grew smaller before a backdrop of ice ridges and blue sky.

The rest of us packed up the tents and picked up the odd pieces of equipment. We would go directly to the new campsite to pitch the tents before the others arrived. When we started off, each finding his own pace, the Kahiltna lay before us in the sun. We wondered if this was really an Alaskan winter—on Mt. McKinley. There was no wind. The sun shone so brightly that we shed our parkas to stay cool while we lugged the heavy packs. The entire glacier was wind-packed; the hard snow made perfect walking. Summer load-carrying on the Kahiltna would never be this easy. One would have to plow through soft snow in June and July. Now, on the last day of January, our boots barely sank in. Our feet were light.

When we met someone coming back for another load or stopped to rest, our excitement bubbled over. We sang, John symphonized, and Pirate bellowed out the greetings of a true buccaneer.— "Ahoy!" and "All right, you guys!"

When I met Dave on the trail he was all buzzed up. He told me how he and Farine, walking together, had figured we'd get up McKinley in about two weeks. Then they would climb Foraker together. Both powerful climbers, they had an affinity for each other. Dave said he and Farine were eyeing an unbelievably steep ice and rock route on Mt. Hunter. Maybe they would attempt it in the spring. I could tell the sunshine was expanding Dave's confidence. It was also affecting me; I began wondering what I'd do if we got up McKinley in a couple of weeks. It would be a shame to leave the park without even trying Foraker.

Later, Gregg and I shared some lunch. We felt like brothers who had quarrelled and made up. In the year of preparation we had sometimes vented our frustrations on each other. Now, all that forgotten, we felt closer than ever before. Forgotten also were the impatience and recklessness I had charged Gregg with that first night on the glacier. With perfect weather and snow conditions it was understandable that we were climbing faster than we had ever thought possible.

As Gregg and I warmed each other with our joy and confidence in the expedition, Farine chugged by. He had a big smile on his face. *"Il fait beau!"* He greeted us with French words simple enough for us to understand. *"C'est tres bon, n'est-ce pas?"*

"Oui, c'est tres bon, Monsieur Farine," I answered.

I told Farine that all I was carrying were thirty kilos of oranges so he wouldn't get hungry. He laughed, and when he turned to go his hand thumped my back. There he went, a happy child, bouncing away, his parka off, gloves off, hat off—on Mt. McKinley in the middle of winter. Without a hat covering his head, I noticed again the jagged scar showing through the hair on the back of his head. The scar seemed to command respect. How had he gotten it? While climbing, no doubt. It was easy to picture Farine, his head torn up (perhaps from a falling rock), trying to escape from an iced-up north face in the Alps. The scar was almost an heroic mark, a sort of medal one wears only after many battles on steep rock and ice.

Much later, Pirate happened to mention the scar to me. It had come from a climbing accident. In Europe, Pirate told me, Farine was not considered a very cautious climber; some had even said he was slightly accident-prone. Farine had taken some rough falls.

Gregg took off down the glacier after Farine to get his personal gear; I wandered slowly up the glacier toward the new campsite. The sun, moving lower in the west, cast intricate and rhythmic shadow patterns on the snowdrifts. Like desert sand, the snow had been woven into intertwining drifts by the wind. I spent much time photographing them from different angles, framing them with different lenses. I experimented with several exposures, hoping the film would capture the blue in the shadows. I would finish filming, pack away my camera, and hike only a dozen or so yards before stumbling onto another network of delicate carved drifts more beautiful than any I had ever seen. Again I would lie flat on my stomach, camera before us, trying to catch the spirit of the wind in the drifts.

Around two o'clock I gained the crest of a slight rise and could see several people about a half mile ahead. Evidently, they had located the new campsite. I looked back down glacier; no one was in sight, though Dave, Gregg, and Farine were behind me on the trail.

I decided to fasten the waistband on my pack. I rarely used it, but now, at the end of the day, my shoulders were sore from carrying the load. Once fastened, the waistband supported much of the weight on my hips. As I moved on I noticed that the afternoon sun had already begun to fill the air with the first hint of reddish light. Step after step my feet glided over the hard snow. Then I fell.

My arms went out; I was stuck waist-deep in a crevasse. Below, sixty or eighty feet through the shadowy half-light I glimpsed ice and rock. If the snow bridge collapsed I'd be smashed onto those rocks. Some of the snow gave way; I fell up to my shoulders.

I kicked into the side of the crevasse. My feet couldn't find a grip; I began slipping. My arms were weakening from holding my weight. Again I caught sight of the dark rocks below. I arched my back, trying to force some of my weight against the snow behind me. I stopped slipping.

Gently, so as not to disturb the delicate balance that held me from falling, I nudged out a small niche in the snow with the toe of my boot. I set one foot. Bracing my body as still as I could, I kicked a hole for my other foot. Trying not to jar the snow, I pushed upward, but I couldn't move. I was stuck! My pack had caught the lip of the crevasse. It had helped keep me from falling; now it kept me from getting out.

Slowly I turned my body to loosen the pack; I could feel it working free. When I pivoted more forcefully it jerked loose, but the sudden movement knocked my feet from their holds. I sank down, supported only by my arms across the thin snow covering which groaned from the shift of weight. As snow fell away from the hole, more light filtered down to the bottom of the crevasse; it only made the shadows appear darker and the rocks colder.

I could clearly see the walls of the crevasse fall away below me to form a cavern fifteen or twenty feet wide; toward the bottom, near the rocks, the walls came together again. I was pawing frantically with both feet. They suddenly caught, but as I lunged upward the snow crumbled from under one boot.

While I told myself, "Don't panic, don't panic Art, don't panic . . ." I tried patiently to enlarge the small footholds I had managed to make before. I kicked and kicked with the free foot; gradually the ledge in the hard snow grew larger. I started on another one. When it was done I began one more. Each foothold seemed to take an eternity to kick out, but if they weren't solid I'd end up pawing and scraping at the hard wall in front of me.

Straining to shift my weight smoothly, I lifted a boot into the top hold I had kicked out; it held. Then I pushed, my back arched backwards. I came up! All at once I was out, stretched flat on the snow. I rolled away from the crevasse and stood up on shaking legs. My lungs heaved wildly to catch their breath. I was shivering. My head was roaring. I wasn't going to fall onto those rocks. My body trembled. I was content to simply breathe.

It was all over. "Safe," I whispered, "I'm safe." Hurriedly, I strapped on my snowshoes; I hoped their webbing would distribute my weight enough to prevent me from breaking through again before I reached camp. As I tightened my pack's waistband, I realized how fortunate I had been to have had it fastened. Without this band helping to secure my pack to my back, my weight could have easily broken the shoulder straps, or I could have slipped out of them; either way I would have gone all the way to the bottom of the crevasse.

The small hole my body had punched in the surface of the glacier was the only indication that a crevasse, probably a whole system of crevasses, sprawled before me. Everywhere the wind-drifted snow appeared the same; in some places it covered solid ice; in others it concealed crevasses. It was unnerving to see the course my footprints marked in the snow; the zigzagging tracks showed where I had strayed off the trail while filming; they wound over the crest of the rise and ended abruptly at the edge of the hole. I thought of Dave, Farine, and Gregg plodding along somewhere behind me. They would have sense enough to stay on the marked path; they'd miss this crevasse. Nevertheless, as I turned to go, I wished I had some willow wands to mark the area. My hands still trembled occasionally; I was anxious to reach camp. Circling far to the right of the crevasse, I rejoined the trail and headed toward the new campsite.

The drifts in the snow were no longer things of beauty I wanted to film. Rather, every shadow suggested the outline of a crevasse. I knew I was treading over a thin roof covering a maze of caverns. The crevasses were there under a crust of snow, in the darkness just below my feet.

The sun and snow conditions had made us overconfident. The glacier was not safe. I felt we were fortunate to have discovered the hidden crevasses without anyone being injured. I would make certain we were all roped from now on.

Though I'd be able to warn the others and insist we all climb more cautiously, I realized I had learned something I'd be unable to share with anyone. The horrible darkness I had seen at the bottom of the crevasse, those dark cold rocks, they had been very close.

I found George, John, and Pirate setting up camp. Quietly I related my struggles with the crevasse. John and George were immediately concerned, but Pirate took it lightly. Despite his reluctance to take anything seriously, though, Pirate agreed that none of us would climb unroped on this glacier again.

Yet at that moment Shiro was by himself, looking for the airdrop Sheldon had made. We were more worried about Shiro being alone than about the three others—Dave, Gregg, and Farine—even though on their way to camp they were certain to pass near the crevasse I had fallen into.

It was encouraging to see two figures appear on the rise a half mile away. They were close to each other and might be roped together. We busied ourselves building a tent platform. To pack a solid base from the soft snow three of us stomped back and forth in a rectangle large enough for three tents. One person smoothed the surface with the aluminum shovel. We stomped and shoveled until George paused to stretch for a moment. He stared down glacier; where there had been two people he saw only one.

We watched, waiting for the second figure to appear. We tried to remember whether there wasn't a slight hollow, a shallow ravine on that part of the trail. Perhaps the second person was walking through it, hidden from our sight.

A minute passed—then two or three. Still we could see only one climber. He kept coming toward us at a steady pace. If one of them had fallen in a crevasse, surely the other would have heard and stopped to help. Maybe one was resting where we couldn't see him. Or perhaps he had dropped something on the trail and had gone back to find it.

We were alarmed, but we waited. We didn't want to believe someone had fallen; it was as if believing would make it happen. We called to the person climbing toward us. He was near enough to be recognized as Dave. He yelled back. We asked him where the other person was. Dave answered with a happy yodel; evidently, he hadn't understood our question and thought we were welcoming him to camp.

We waited.

As Dave approached camp we called again. Still he couldn't understand us. When he finally reached us we could hear him humming to himself. He hollered out about how great a day it had been. We asked him about the other person; he looked puzzled.

For the first time Dave turned to look behind himself. His face went blank with shock, then tightened with anger. Where he had expected to see Farine there was only an empty glacier. Pirate quickly lashed on his snowshoes. I whipped on George's skis. Together with Dave, Pirate and I raced down glacier.

In the distance a figure was coming toward us. For a moment we thought it might be Farine, but it was Gregg. When he suddenly stopped and bent down to the snow there could be no more doubt that something was wrong.

We ran up to Gregg out of breath. His eyes were glazed and frantic. He was yelling into a hole in the glacier. "Thank God you guys are here!" he cried.

Bending over the hole again, he screamed "Dave, Dave, Dave, can you hear me? . . . Dave!" Though Dave was standing beside him, getting a rope ready, Gregg didn't yet realize that it was Farine and not Dave who had fallen into the crevasse.

Both Dave and Pirate declared that they were going down into the crevasse to rescue Farine. Gregg insisted that only one should descend; he knew that two people down the hole would create confusion. Without hesitation, Gregg decided Dave was the one we'd lower down; he had more rescue experience than any of us. Pirate accepted the decision without saying a word; I noticed that his hands were knotted into tight fists.

Edging his way carefully to the lip of the crevasse, Gregg shouted again into the dark hole. "Farine! Farine!" His voice was cracking. "Farine! . . ." There was no answer.

Gregg turned to us with a frantic sigh. "Oh God, I don't know if I can face a body."

Gregg and Pirate anchored themselves thirty feet from the crevasse. Two ropes ran from them into the hole. Dave fastened Jumar ascendars, small clamps that grip a fixed line, to the rope he would descend on. He tied into the other rope for protection. Flicking on his headlamp, he disappeared down the hole.

Because the snow absorbed Dave's voice as he descended, Pirate and Gregg couldn't hear him. I lay down at the lip of the crevasse to pass messages between the two ends of the rope.

Farine's pack, the shoulder straps broken, lay a dozen feet from the crevasse. In his frenzy Gregg had yanked it from the hole and thrown the fifty-pound pack this incredible distance. I swore silently at Farine for not having fastened his pack's waistband; it might have held him above the crevasse as mine had.

I suddenly realized that this was the same crevasse I had fallen into. Only thirty feet away gaped the hole I had made forty minutes earlier. I damned myself for not having waited at the crevasse to warn the others. Here, where Farine had plunged through the snow covering, the side of the crevasse was bloodstained; it could so easily have been my blood on the snow. Maybe he had fought the way I had, before he fell.

Dave descended through a wide cavern a few feet below the surface. Twenty-five feet down he slipped past a sharp projection of ice. Had Farine hit it while falling? Fifty feet down lay a shelf, the floor of the cavern. Below that the crevasse narrowed again and disappeared into the darkness of the subglacial rocks.

Dave found Farine lying unconscious on the ice shelf. Only six feet above the body Dave's ropes jammed. He yelled and swore at me to lower him. I shouted at Gregg and Pirate to give him slack.

They worked furiously on the ropes while Dave cursed. Pirate's hands darted swiftly among a tangle of ropes. Though he had no experience with rescue techniques he quickly had the lines straightened out; he worked fast under pressure.

With the rope freed, Dave reached Farine. With startling speed he tied the hauling line around the limp body. While he worked I could hear Dave talking to his friend; "Come on, Farine baby . . . you'll make it. . . . Won't be long, Daddy. . . . We'll get you out of here."

Dave carefully tied the rope around Farine's chest; he didn't want his breathing restricted—if Farine was breathing.

Dave signaled; we began pulling. Slowly the slumped body rose from the ice. I heard Dave calling after it; "Go man. . . . Don't hang up. . . . You can do 'er."

At the other end of the rope Gregg began gasping. The rope stopped moving. In the excitement Gregg had tied the hauling line around his waist with a slipknot. When he had pulled, the knot had tightened, squeezing the breath out of him. He had fallen onto the snow and nearly fainted, but was trying desperately to undo the knot and regain his breath.

The rope began moving again. We hoisted Farine up ten or fifteen feet before we had to stop to rest; then came another haul, and another rest. Looking down into the darkness of the crevasse, I could see Farine's body coming out of the shadows. Further down the yellow glow of Dave's headlamp reflected against the black ice. I could hear his jumars clicking and sliding on the rope as he ascended the fixed line.

Farine reached the top of the hole, but there he became snagged on the sharp lip of the crevasse. While Pirate and Gregg pulled on the rope, I grabbed Farine under his shoulders to try to draw him up over the edge. Within seconds he slid out onto the flat snow. Quickly I loosened the hauling rope around his huge chest. His face was bloody; the lower lip was torn.

George had arrived, and, running his hands firmly over Farine's limbs, thought he felt some broken arm and wrist bones. I couldn't detect any breathing, but he might be alive. We slipped Farine into a sleeping bag to save all the warmth left in his body. His eyes were open, staring blankly. George couldn't find a pulse.

Kneeling over Farine, I wiped some of the blood and mucus away from his mouth with my finger. I began mouth-to-mouth resuscitation. While Gregg held Farine's nostrils shut I breathed deeply into him. There was a rasping noise. The air passage sounded blocked. I pressed my mouth harder to Farine's so no air would escape; I breathed and breathed and breathed. While I tried to force breath back into his body, George massaged his heart and applied rhythmic pressure to his chest. Dave had clambered over the edge of the crevasse and moved in to relieve George. There was still no sign of life.

George knew how to make a decisive check. He shined a flashlight into Farine's eyes. There was no contraction of the pupil. When he took the flashlight away the pupil remained the same size. "He is dead," George sighed.

Dave and I wouldn't stop giving resuscitation. Perhaps the heart would start again if we kept trying. I breathed into Farine, then Dave applied pressure with his strong fingers. I breathed and he pressed. I smelled and tasted something from Farine's stomach. It made me nauseous for a moment.

The others silently watched Dave and me work. We listened for the faintest gasp. Dave was mumbling to himself. Every few moments he'd talk to Farine: "Come on, ole heart . . . start up. . . . Come on, you old bastard, start up. . . . You can do 'er."

I breathed with all the strength in my lungs. Dave pressed harder. Several minutes passed before George shone the flashlight on Farine's face again. There was no movement of the pupils; no reaction. There was no pulse. The face was purplish. George pronounced him dead.

The glacier was dark in shadow, but McKinley's summit, blazing with alpenglow, was almost frighteningly red. We didn't cover Farine but left him in his sleeping bag on the ice.

My fingers fumbled for the cottonwood bud in my shirt pocket. My wife had given it to me to carry during the expedition to remind me of her. She had wanted me to carry a little piece of spring with me. It was green and smelled green. In all these hundreds of square miles of ice and rock it alone held the scent of warm earth and new leaves. No one saw me drop it into the crevasse that had taken Farine.

The cottonwood bud had been wrapped in a prayer of St. Francis of Assisi. When Gregg noticed me saying the prayer to myself, he asked me to read it aloud.

I began uneasily, almost afraid to hear myself speak, and I finished with only a slightly steadier voice: "And it is in dying that we are born to eternal life."

The five of us tied into one rope. Then, guided by our headlamps, which seemed incredibly faint in the darkness, we began walking toward camp. No one spoke. The silence seemed to be amplified by the broad span of the Kahiltna stretching away in the darkness. I heard only my heavy breathing and my boots squeaking on the dry snow. Leading, I couldn't see the others. Occasional gentle tugs on the rope from behind were comforting reminders that I was not alone. That rope, linking us together, was a single reassurance against the loneliness that echoed in the crunching of snow beneath our feet.

I was too numb to feel the horror. Rather, I felt guilty. Though I didn't want to admit it to myself, I knew I should have stayed by the crevasse when I fell—to warn the others. At least I should have marked the hole with something. If I hadn't been in shock, if I hadn't been so anxious to leave the place where I had fallen, Farine would still be alive.

I sensed that the others were also accusing themselves. Genet probably felt responsible for bringing Farine onto McKinley in the first place. Dave realized that if he had simply looked behind himself earlier he might have noticed in time to rescue Farine. Gregg knew that, as leader, he should have insisted that everyone rope together; this is the first lesson of glacier travel. If Gregg had only reprimanded Farine that first afternoon when he had come bouncing, alone and unroped, through the crevasse field. I imagined Gregg felt that the wish for safety he had made on a star was mocking him.

Our procession stopped once because someone was dizzy. I took off my mittens to feel something caked around my mouth. I was startled when I realized it was blood, but I was careful not to wipe it away. The blood made me strangely exuberant. It was as if Farine were right there. He hadn't disappeared. The blood eased my loneliness. It also seemed to ease my guilt; maybe it helped convince me that I had done everything possible for Farine.

The moon hadn't risen yet. Ahead of us, high above Kahiltna Pass, a pale-green band of northern lights glowed and shifted across the black sky. Already the inevitable question was forming. Would we leave the mountain or continue?

A headlamp bobbed a few hundred feet in front of me. John, or maybe Shiro, was coming to meet us. I liked watching the little light. It was so friendly.

Seven of us crowded into a four-man tent. The air was thick with moisture from our breathing. When someone lifted the lid off the boiling soup I couldn't see the other end of the tent through the steam. Gregg dipped his handkerchief in hot water and scrubbed at the blood around my motuh; some of it was crusted into my beard. I wanted it left alone, but the expression on Gregg's face made me realize how it must have looked to the others. I suddenly became self-conscious and let him wipe it away. No one had spoken except to ask for more soup or rice.

When Gregg finally spoke he tried to be matter-of-fact. He said we had to decide whether or not to abandon the expedition. His feelings were clear: "This isn't Everest, guys. It's not a once-in-a-lifetime deal. We could take all our gear and save it for the next expedition in winter. We could return again ourselves." Gregg went on to say that the expedition was a failure. He said that for him reaching the summit would be meaningless. He asked how I felt.

"I want to go on more than ever." I tried to answer calmly, but I must have sounded fanatical. "We've got to reach the summit. I'm certain Farine wouldn't have wanted us to quit. If we give up, his death was for nothing. We've got to go on because of him, not in spite of him."

"No. I don't understand," Gregg shot back. "I guess I climb for different reasons. I climb for the joy of the beauty . . . joy of wind, sun, and cold. All the joy of this climb has left me with Farine's death. I don't climb for something like this."

"None of us climb for this." I answered. "We don't climb because of the danger, but with it. You have to accept the risk that someone, maybe yourself, might be injured or killed."

"You don't understand, Art. I'm the leader. I'm responsible. I can't risk taking you guys up higher after this has happened. God, what if someone else died!"

"Gregg, we simply won't have another accident." I said. "And this one is as much my fault as it is yours or anyone's."

Pirate tried to comfort Gregg by saying that Farine would have been the last one to put on a rope. "You saw him that first day . . . sure of himself . . . by himself. . . . He was happy that way. It wasn't your fault, Gregg."

Pirate's tenderly spoken words were a slight relief for all of us because they suggested that it had been Farine's choice to climb the way he had; we weren't to blame. Farine had known it was safer to be roped. He must have realized it could be dangerous to wander off the established trail. We wanted to believe that Farine's carelessness, not our own, had killed him.

Gregg said that mountaineers would condemn us for the avoidable accident, and that the public would condemn us if we continued. He asked whether we had a precedent in American mountaineering, whether another expedition had continued after one of its members had died.

Dave and I reacted simultaneously. "It's not a matter of precedent," we blurted out. Dave added that it is not what people think that matters but what we feel.

Gregg then asked each of us in turn how we felt, what we wanted to do.

Dave said he wanted to go on, but added that he thought his reasons were selfish. He didn't think he would be able to afford trying again. He also told us he wanted to continue for Farine's sake, to complete the climb for his friend.

Pirate made no attempt to conceal or apologize for his desire to reach the summit. "On construction jobs I've had friends killed only a few feet from me. . . . The work goes on. We should keep climbing."

Pirate had been closer to Farine than any of the rest of us, yet he appeared to be the least shocked. I couldn't tell whether he was capable of casually accepting the death as something natural, or whether he was protecting his real feelings.

George reminded us of the legal considerations, of a death certificate, of funeral arrangements. He made us realize that there would be repercussions when the story was picked up by the press. George's unusual quietness since the accident and his tired face revealed his deep hurt. He appeared reluctant to complete the climb, and admitted in a roundabout way that he was more inclined to return to Anchorage. He even suggested we might continue without him.

John, who hadn't been at the scene of the accident, but had been preparing a tent in case we brought Farine back injured, spoke from a different perspective. "Look," he said. "We're all in shock. Let's wait a day or two before making a decision."

Shiro agreed with John that it was pointless to talk that night, but, in no more than a whisper, he added that he wanted to go on. This would be Shiro's only chance for McKinley in the winter; he had made tremendous personal sacrifices to be on the expedition. Since his visa would expire in March, this would probably be his last climb in Alaska's mountains.

The conversation shifted for several minutes to what we would do with the body. Send it to France, or bury it in Alaska? Pirate told us that Farine had only one close relative, his mother. She had called her son "mon petit Farine." They had lived together in Paris. She was destitute, Pirate said, and, if we wanted to send Farine to France, we should pay the shipping bill and funeral expenses.

We avoided talking about Farine himself. To remove ourselves from the immediacy of our horror we abstracted it, spoke of it in general terms. Gregg said you couldn't equate a life with a climb; no climb was worth it. Dave said he hoped he would die climbing and be left in the mountains he loved. George declared that "there is no joy or satisfaction in climbing to compensate for death." Pirate mumbled "We all go sometime. Dying is a part of climbing."

Reluctantly, we each came to realize that John and Shiro were right; we were too deeply in shock to think clearly. Distraught because we couldn't moralize away the death nor shift the responsibility for it from ourselves, we blew out the candles before it was decided whether to give up the expedition.

Sleep did not come easily. With my head deep inside my sleeping bag I stared into the dark for what seemed like hours. As I began to relax, I caught myself wondering whether I really wanted to complete the climb. My snug cabin near Fairbanks, the woman I loved, and a pile of books were suddenly more desirable things to spend the winter with than the crevasses and long miles of snow and ice that stretched toward a summit which seemed impossibly far away.

I had spoken bravely to Gregg, but I knew I was afraid. Perhaps the fear itself had made me wildly want to go on climbing the mountain. I had an irrational desire to reach the summit, greater than I had ever felt on any other mountain. But maybe my feelings of guilt had made me think pushing on would be an escape from the body, or from the outside world, or from the expedition's or my own failure. Another moment I was just as convinced that a faithfulness to Farine, to his love for cold sunrises, for wind and snow whipping his face, was compelling me to go higher. The ghastliness of what had happened that afternoon made me distrust my thoughts and emotions.

The body haunted me. The gentle strength had left it. The tissues would all be frozen by morning. I was horrified because all that had been Farine was gone, because I knew how easily it could be my body lying out there on the glacier.

I remembered a dead magpie I had once seen lying in the snow.

Four or five cawing and screaming magpies had flown above it and jumped around it on the ground. They had been terrified. Without words and thoughts to help them grasp their horror, their panic had been undefined. They probably missed their old companion, but I had sensed that they felt threatened themselves, not by any specific danger, but by the horror they couldn't understand.

When I pushed my head out of the sleeping bag for some fresh air, I heard the deep, regular breathing that meant someone had been able to sleep.

Dave, however, had lit a candle, and was writing in his journal:

It's real. It's like an underwater nightmare that never really happened. In retrospect, only this exists: my love for Farine.

He seemed to have a special, glowing smile for me; the kind you get from your partner after a hard lead. It was a smile you felt; one I could feel and return, and know he felt the return. His love for climbing was written all over his face.

I remember his freedom, like an untethered bird, as he wandered uncapped, and unmitted, and unroped about the glacier. His deep pleasure and peace of mind were written in his eyes when he wandered this way. He was happy and content with so little.

Blizzard

WE WOKE TO SEE A storm front sweeping in from the south. A high overcast already stretched to the north; dark purple and gray clouds, packed up against the mountains to the southwest, were rapidly forcing their way up the Kahiltna. The summits of McKinley and Foraker were obscured by lenticular caps. We spotted whirling clouds of snow being torn from the high ridges by a wind. Standing outside our tents, the air around us still, we knew the sky was about to crash down upon us.

Camp had to be moved because the tents were pitched under a slope that would avalanche if there were a heavy snowfall. There was little time to think of the previous day.

We should have secured ourselves in igloos before the storm struck, but even as we retreated down glacier, snow carried on a fifteen- to twenty-mile-per-hour wind flew into our faces. We reached Farine's body. Swallowing hard, I tasted again, this time in my memory rather than my mouth, that stale sweetness from Farine's crushed insides that had been smeared on my face. There was time only to mark the body with a bamboo pole which would help us locate him again if twenty to thirty inches of snow accumulated before we could return. Moving on, our emotions were caught between anguish for the corpse and apprehension for the storm and the campsite we hadn't found yet.

Although we had set out to find good igloo-building snow about a quarter of a mile below Farine, I felt we were wandering aimlessly. Snow obscured the peaks. We were walking in a near white-out. As it snowed harder everything became white; the ground and the sky appeared the same. Contrast disappeared. We could see only about fifteen feet ahead.

In ropes of two we groped and wandered in a desultory manner, looking for snow packed into the hard consistency needed for igloo blocks. Often we lost sight of the others; only by calling out could we rejoin them. For several horrible minutes we all just clustered together in the driving snow, no one speaking, no one knowing what to do.

Several voices, muffled by the storm, said we ought to pitch the tents. Someone growled that the tents might rip apart if the wind continued to grow stronger. Again, we set off in pairs to search out a patch of glacier where the snow was soft enough for our saws to cut and hard enough to hold when erected into an igloo wall.

We stumbled about. We poked the points of our axes hopefully at the frozen surface. We cursed the blizzard. Frantic visions of Farine's bloody face and the mushy sound inside his chest darted through my mind. At length we found snow that would make adequate blocks. Gregg and two others headed back to yesterday's camp for supplies; four of us started an igloo.

Not only did we not work efficiently as a team, but we each had a different idea of how the igloo should be constructed. George suggested we cut large thin slabs, as the Eskimos do. I insisted we ought to make the blocks thick and solid. Dave quite understandably wanted a high ceiling. Someone else wanted to simply dig a pit and block in a roof, never mind how high the ceiling.

Shiro took the key position in the center of the area we had scribed off for our igloo. We cut blocks and passed them to him. After the bottom row had been carefully set in a circle, George stepped up to help Shiro; he propped rough blocks in place while Shiro shaped them for a tight fit. I quarried the blocks several yards away. No sooner would I cut one from the packed snow than Dave's long arms would reach for it and pass it to George.

It had taken us more than a half hour to put up the first row, partly because the circumference of this foundation would be larger than that of suceeding layers, but mostly because we took special care to construct a solid base—one weak or misplaced block in the bottom row could bring the entire structure crumbling down unexpectedly. As our building system improved and each higher row shrank in size, the structure gradually took the shape of a three-cornered hemisphere. The faster we worked, the less we thought of Farine, and the more we felt like a team.

Hours passed. It began to grow darker. The whiteout became thicker. Every few minutes we yelled, then listened for a reply from the three who had not returned from the previous campsite. At length, one of our cries was answered by a faint, high-pitched yodel. Shortly, three figures, their heads bent to shield faces from the wind, trudged out of the wall of grayness that surrounded us.

With all our efforts concentrated on the igloo, its main chamber was quickly completed. While Dave and I cut and laid blocks for the arched entrance, a tent was set up; stoves were started; food was unpacked; sleeping bags were thrown out. In a great shuffle of elbows, shoulders, and legs we sprawled about the floor of our new home to finally eat our first real meal of the day.

"Gentlemen," George stated with mock gravity, "it gives me great pleasure to announce the opening of the Kahiltna Hilton, built by the famous Eskimo architect Shiro. This premier banquet, prepared by chef Gregg, appears to be a smorgasbord of dehydrated pork chops, diced ham, rice, cheese, dried potatoes, applesauce, powdered milk, instant chicken noodle soup, turkey boullion cubes, *au jus* gravy mix, and dried green peppers all cooked and served in one pot."

"It's a super glop!" Dave chimed in. "And well seasoned with bits of yesterday's Tang and oatmeal."

Leaning against Pirate's back and half buried under Dave's seven-foot sleeping bag, I stuffed myself with glop till I grew drowsy. As I drifted off, half daydreaming, only snatches of the conversation registered in my sleepy head.

"This storm has helped us," I heard Shiro say to Gregg. "It's driven us together, by forcing us to act."

"Yaaa." Pirate's voice lifted above the others. "I like this weather!"

Eventually someone nudged me awake to get me to spread my foam sleeping pad and bag alongside Pirate's. Dave and Shiro had gone out to sleep in the tent. John and George appeared to be asleep already. The lantern was turned off; for a while, Gregg scribbled away at his journal by the light of a single candle; then it too was blown out. I was thankful that some humor had returned to us; it made me more confident that we could still take care of ourselves. Our igloo was cozy. The snow blocks muffled the sounds of the blizzard; I had difficulty picturing the wind and snow that were swirling across the glacier. Farine's image came to mind. It seemed to always be right at the edge of my thoughts. Often I'd see him standing in the doorway of Sheldon's hangar with those huge moose antlers balanced on his head. Whenever this image returned I felt a tenseness begin to mount somewhere inside me, as though I wanted to shout or begin running. Even during our most relaxed moments this evening I knew the others had felt this underlying tension in their own way. It was probably best that we hadn't tried to voice our emotions.

"Art," I heard Gregg whisper from the other side of the igloo, "are you talking in your sleep."

"No, I'm awake."

Gregg felt like talking a little. He told me that Shiro and Pirate had volunteered to hike four miles down the glacier, as soon as the storm eased off a bit, to call Sheldon with the radio we had left at the landing site. The rest of us would have to haul the body to an area where Sheldon could land.

"Until Farine is taken care of," Gregg said, "we can't very well continue the climb, or even know whether we will go on."

Gregg went on to tell me how alone and morbid he had felt the previous night. I told him we had all been confined in our thoughts. He said he thought that sense of separateness was giving way to the feeling of being part of a group. The expedition seemed to be reasserting its identity.

The sky wasn't clear the next day, but for brief moments the sun did manage to hit us directly. The wind was down, and snow fell in only light and occasional flurries. Shiro and Pirate set off down the glacier to the radio. It was possible that Sheldon might make it in for Farine before nightfall. Five of us went to haul the body.

We found it half buried in snow. Dave and Gregg hurried about the unpleasant task of binding ropes around arms and chest and legs. We attached three hauling lines.

Before we stepped into our traces, George took several pictures of the hole and the body; I filmed the scene with the movie camera. Our first steps were unsteady, but we found a rhythm and began to pull together. Head first, the body slid over the wind-swept ice, gouging into the surface only when we crossed areas of drifted snow. Always we leaned far forward. The ropes cut into our waists, forcing us to fashion a harness around our shoulders and chests. It was not a light load.

We aimed ourselves at the cache site Sheldon had choosen for a landing strip several days earlier. We quickened our pace when the glacier tilted downward, and strained to keep the body moving when we had to gain a slight rise.

The first time I asked whether I could leave my traces to film our procession, Dave shouted at me to hurry up. The second time I left the others to film from a dozen yards away, Dave, anger rising in his eyes and voice, asked me why I was filming this macabre scene. "You're sure irritable today," I told him. "We have to document this situation."

Dave grumbled and looked away from me. I didn't think he had accepted my answer. At the time, I didn't stop to really question why I had an obsession to photograph our efforts to drag the body across the glacier to the landing site. I simply obeyed a compulsion to film, to record our trek, to get it all down on celluloid.

Later I realized that my desire to photograph had been an attempt to escape and defend myself. Filming, I could occupy my mind with exposure readings and shooting angles. When I framed the scene through the lens, our horrifying task became an event; all I had to do was hide behind the camera. I escaped, if only momentarily, from being a participant by becoming an observer. Besides seeking refuge from my confused emotions by considering our death march an event, I defended myself by treating it as a subject that I could grasp and define with the means of cinematography; this allowed me an illusive sense of control over the situation.

When we had reached the landing site there was nothing we could do but slide the body snugly up against the food boxes and plod on back to camp. It was dusk when we threw off our packs in front of the igloo. Shiro and Pirate hadn't returned. We tried to force out of our minds thoughts of their being caught in an another crevasse. We ate. We waited. I often crawled out of the igloo to try spotting their headlamps. We discussed what we'd do after Sheldon took Farine out. We began to wonder what to do if Shiro and Pirate didn't return. It would be reckless to begin looking for them before morning.

We had all but resigned ourselves to setting out early the next morning to search for the missing two when we spotted the distant twinkles of their headlamps far down the glacier. In another hour they sat with us, drinking soup and digging into a rice glop thick with cheese and tuna fish. They said they had tinkered with the radio for four hours, stretching the wire antennae in several directions, warming the battery, but whatever they tried the obstinate box of tubes and wires hadn't encouraged them with even the slightest sputtering of static.

The radio failure meant we had no way of knowing when we would be able to establish contact with anyone. Our best bet seemed to be stamping a message in the snow in the hope that Sheldon would spot it if he happened to fly some tourists around the mountain in a few days or a week. It was unsettling to realize that if one of us were seriously injured in a crevasse fall or an avalanche there would be no way of calling for help. Had we hauled Farine out of the crevasse alive he probably would have become delirious because of his head injury, and since we would have been unable to get him to a hospital, he would have died in our hands.

Before we could continue toward the summit of McKinley we had to offer an explanation of the death to that remote place we had begun to call the outside world. Pirate volunteered to escort the body to Anchorage whenever Sheldon reached us. Gregg tried to write a press release to relate the manner of death and communicate our reasons for wanting to complete the climb. It was a difficult explanation made all the more difficult by Gregg's mixed emotions and attitudes. None of us, for that matter, had fully resolved our conflicting reactions to the accident. Nevertheless, we tried to help Gregg write a statement that was straightforward.

Although we didn't feel free to climb upward until Sheldon took out Farine and Pirate, we expected that if we simply waited in the igloo with nothing but morose thoughts to occupy our minds, depression would make us jump at the opportunity to leave the mountain when Sheldon eventually arrived. We believed that we had decided to continue, but it was hardly a decision, for at that moment there was no way for us to return.

The following day we ferried loads in a perfunctory manner. We could muster little enthusiasm for our labor because we knew an adverse reaction to the accident by the outside world might neccessitate our departure from McKinley. And it was difficult to work so close to the frozen lump that had been our friend.

By evening the low, dark clouds that had bullied their way among the peaks all day had settled down to the surface of the glacier. Under the cloud we lit all our lamps and a good many candles to brighten the igloo and the tent. This night may not have been much darker than previous ones, but the oppressive fog of minute ice crystals made us want light. I even suspected Gregg and John of hoarding more than their share of the candles in their corner of the igloo, and when Dave and Shiro left the igloo for their tent I regretted they had to take one of the lanterns with them.

I went to sleep expecting that a blizzard would have us shut into the igloo by morning. Hours later I woke blinking and rubbing the sleep from my eyes; the sound of John rustling through his pack for his camera had roused me. "Art," he whispered loudly, "it's the most beautiful sight man's ever witnessed! I think it's the dawn of creation!" With that he wheeled around, scurried out the igloo entrance, and was gone in a flash. I sat up in my sleeping bag, still blinking my eyes.

Several minutes later I stood next to John, fumbling to mount my movie camera on a tripod. "By God," he said, looking to the south, "we certainly live on a beautiful planet."

A hugh, soft, pink cloud was lifting over Foraker; the rock was lit with a yellowish glow where the sun struck it. Mist clung to the ridges of McKinley and Hunter and everywhere the clouds were pastel shades of pink, yellow, and silver. It seemed as if the sky were splitting apart where the sun broke through the mist and clouds.

I filmed until someone had cooked breakfast and only wished I'd been waked sooner so I could have begun filming the first stages of dawn. Since Dave had been awake at first light, I asked him why he hadn't waked me up to film. He looked up from his journal to glare at me with a stony, faraway expression. "It's your own damn fault that you slept too late," he said, then turned back to his journal.

This didn't seem like the old Dave I had climbed with before. Maybe there had been too much irritation in my voice when I had spoken to him. I wondered what he was taking so much time to write about in his journal.

Dave's journal, February 4:

Dawn is beautiful. A cloud half-covering Foraker radiates warm
pinkness from its bottom, causing the east-southeast rock buttress to
glow warmly in the mist. When Art finally gets up he blasts me for
not waking him. In a frenzy he photographs everything in sight. I'm
envious of his camera gear, and p.o.ed at him too. I carry his 35 mm.
camera, which he said I could use on the climb, but he reclaims it
when he wants to take a picture.

Today I am a proponent for the fast group, so the slow ones bug
me . . . especially Art, who doesn't seem to care how much he holds
everyone else up while he photographs, but who nearly has a fit should
anyone hold him up.

After breakfast we split into groups of three and four; Gregg,
George, and Pirate started across the glacier to shuttle loads from
the air drop; Shiro, Dave, John, and I began setting the route to
Kahiltna Pass and packing up the first supplies to stock the next
campsite.

The irridescent colors of dawn had been replaced by bright sunlight and a mostly clear sky. Much of our gloom of the previous
days was lifting with the weather; a few minutes of sunshine were
doing more to inspire us to continue the ascent than had all our
discussions and self-analysis. Several hundred yards out of camp
Dave stopped to talk to me.

"I'm sorry about this morning, Art," he said. "Guess I just need
to get out on the trail to pull my spirits up."

"Forget it," I answered. "I was a little grumpy myself."

The few clouds in the vicinity shifted about; usually we climbed
in direct sunlight, but occasionally a shadow would cross our route.
John and I poked along nearly a half mile behind Dave and Shiro,
who were breaking trail with lighter loads in their packs. The
higher we climbed the more dramatically the Kahiltna flowed away
behind us. Down below, our camp had become a cluster of dots;
miles beyond the specks that were the tent and igloo the glacier
turned behind Mt. Hunter to disappear from our sight. I felt frustrated trying to film the drama of the landscape. Perhaps with care-

ful editing my film could convey an impression of our gradual ascent by showing the ridges and the Kahiltna growing smaller behind us, but I knew I could never express on film the imperceptible but overpowering descent of the glacier itself. Among the filming speeds on my camera there wasn't a setting for geological time. It might be a thousand years before the ice we were climbing over would reach the great bend the Kahiltna makes near Mt. Hunter. Another thousand years might pass before this snow and ice would reach the end of its journey on a gravel bar among willows and alders.

We were still two miles below Kahiltna Pass when I thought I heard the sound we had been listening for through the last three days.

"Hold up a sec, John. Hear anything?"

"No. . . . Yes, I hear it now!"

A small plane was soon circling above us; it was red; it couldn't be Sheldon's. The plane banked gracefully several times before it sent down a little parcel. John and I threw off our packs to scramble after it. In a wadded-up paper bag was a note: "Do you guys need anything besides wine, women, and a sauna bath?"

Though we couldn't help laughing, the note was a reminder that the secret we had been quietly trying to forget was about to become public knowledge.

The plane swung down the glacier, over our camp, and evidently the pilot noticed the signal—LAND—which we had stamped in the snow, for he began circling as if looking for a place to touch down. A mile and a half below camp Pirate, Gregg, and George began hurrying back to the igloo.

John and I decided to return to camp also. By the time we had cached our loads and started down the slope, the pilot had landed. We watched him disappear into our igloo, then reappear again after he found no one at home. We were still a mile above camp when, to our horror, the pilot began walking in our direction. Between him and us lay the crevasse field. He was heading straight toward the crevasse that had claimed Farine. John and I tried calling to him, but we were still too far away. We began running.

When we finally came within shouting distance he was only a few yards from where the hidden crevasse intersected our marked trail.

"Stay where you are!" I yelled.

He stopped. I recognized him as an old friend, Jim Cassidy. Immediately, we tied him into the rope. Stammering for the best way to say it, I told him why we were so worried about his having walked unroped. Quietly, Cassidy offered to call Sheldon for us.

When Cassidy had landed, one of the supporting rods for his plane's skis had snapped. From odd corners of his plane he dug out bits of rope and wire. Calmly, he began lashing the ski back in place. I started to offer him some adhesive tape I had in the igloo, but I judged he was taking the damage too seriously to appreciate this suggestion.

When Cassidy ran out of wire and twine he did ask if we could spare a little nylon climbing rope. Sure, anything, we said, and ran to get him all the rope he wanted. After he'd spent most of an hour bandaging up his flying machine, the pilot stood up and affectionately patted the fuselage of his ailing friend. "She'll be O.K. till I can get her ski welded," he said, not too convincingly.

With a sigh Cassidy climbed into the cockpit, checked his instruments, fired the motor, then gunned the prop. Nothing happened. The plane's tail was stuck under a crust of wind-packed snow. Following his instructions, we positioned ourselves on the tail and under the wings. As Cassidy opened up the throttle we yanked upward on the tail and rocked and shoved forward on the wing struts. Suddenly, the plane lurched ahead and began racing away with a cloud of snow billowing out from the backwash of the prop. As the roaring vehicle bounced frantically down the uneven surface of the glacier it appeared for a moment that the wings were actually flapping. To our astonishment the plane eventually rose smoothly into the air. Cassidy circled us once, tipped his wings, and disappeared to the south. Less than two hours after Cassidy had left

Sheldon arrived. Without ceremony, he and Pirate loaded Farine's body into the plane. The next moment they were gone. In his shirt pocket Pirate had our statement for the press. It read: "On January 31, 1967, Jacques "Farine" Batkin, mountaineer from Paris, France, died in an unroped fall into a crevasse while attempting the first winter ascent of Mt. McKinley. Jacques Batkin died in the pursuit of a winter ascent, in which he truly believed. We will continue the attempt with his spirit and presence very much in mind."

On Pirate's lap were the letters we had written to our families. More than the press release, and more than what we had told each other, the letters revealed our attempts to articulate our tangled emotions and our reasons for not quitting.

I wrote to my wife:

. . . Farine will be urging the seven of us up every pitch of ice and rock that lies ahead, and at the same time reminding us to look at the sun, the wind, the snow and stars that are all about us. And Mairiis, I hope his spirit will be with you and me whenever we walk in a forest to see if the catkins are out or to pick mushrooms, or when we hear the wind through spruce trees or watch clouds breaking away from a storm. . . .

Gregg sent the first section of his journal out with Pirate. Written as a long letter to his wife, it reflected his day-to-day search for the courage to overcome his grief and lead us through whatever lay ahead:

February 1:

I don't know what to tell you, Honey. Everyone wants to go on, and now I agree with them. Certainly I couldn't desert them at this point. I cried, my God how I felt. I got quite carried away compared to the others. I said I didn't want to go on with the climb, probably for selfish reasons; I felt responsible.

His death is a terrible thing, but should it alter our purpose? I don't know. I know many people will condemn us for going on. I know many mountaineers will condemn with good reason this avoidable accident, but I can't really see how our quitting now would help. I hope you can understand. This accident will make us much more cautious and we will go slowly and carefully. I don't know if I want to go for the summit myself, but I must support those who do. . . . Farine was a mountain man who lived for the mountains. Compared to him, I don't belong.

February 2:

This climb is still a dream. I couldn't believe it prior to the climb and reality still hasn't hit. . . . The rest of the climb will be O.K., if the weather holds halfway decent. I'll hardly be a tiger from here on up, but at least I can be a help.

February 3:

. . . As you can see, the shock of Farine's death has worn off. I am glad because it was really hell for a while.

By evening clouds had appeared and it had begun to snow lightly.

John's Fall

SNOW ABSORBS SOUND. If there is no breeze, a glacier can become nearly soundless. When we woke to discover the Kahiltna covered with several inches of fresh snow the quietness was so complete that I believed my ears detected a faint ringing in the empty air.

We lingered over breakfast, wondering what had happened to our Pirate in the outside world. No one was anxious to begin climbing, but there was no real reason why we shouldn't put ourselves to some useful activity. It was after ten o'clock before we left to ferry up some food and gear from the cache about three miles across and down the glacier, where Sheldon had landed some of our supplies. Gregg and John snowshoed steadily ahead while Shiro and George waited patiently for me to film them skiing through the fluffy snow.

The sun, almost breaking through a gradually shifting overcast, filled the sky with a soft, yellow light. Occasionally a break in the clouds would brightly illuminate a small area on the glacier. As the clouds moved, the patch of light on the snow would change shape and drift across the glacier until it faded away. When the clouds grew thicker only an eerie, subdued light worked through the overcast. It was warm, +5°, and snowing lightly.

After filming a close-up of the skis cutting sharply through the powder snow, I waved George and Shiro on ahead, holding my camera in position to shoot their sweep across the glacier. I was following them through the camera lens when Shiro suddenly stopped and yelled, "Accident!"

A mile or so across the glacier someone was waving his arms and screaming. Either Gregg or John must have fallen into a crevasse. George and Shiro skied madly toward the lone figure. I hurried back for Dave, who was still in camp.

"God, not again!" was the first thing Dave said.

As we ran to the scene of the accident, it seemed that we were reenacting that race we had made down the glacier only five days before. Again, one person was kneeling close to the snow, shouting into a hole in the glacier.

It can be amusing to watch someone trying to run in snowshoes. His feet fly out to either side, his balance is easily lost, and, if he can keep up a fast pace without falling, the bindings usually loosen until one snowshoe is flopping uselessly. Not only did Dave and I see no humor in our clumsy flight over the glacier, but it seemed we were traveling impossibly slowly.

Finally reaching the scene of the accident, we saw Gregg kneeling by the crevasse. He looked and said, "My belay caught John before he hit the bottom. He's O.K."

John's fall had ended abruptly about forty-five feet down. His first reaction had been to try to climb out, but the walls around him were smooth ice and nearly four feet apart. He'd managed to push against one wall with his hands or back, but he'd been unable to get a grip on the opposite wall with his snowshoes. To relieve the tension of the rope, which had begun restricting his breathing as it had tightened around his middle, John wedged one of his ski poles across the crevasse and balanced most of his weight on it. Perched in this position he had casually taken a few photographs and munched a chocolate bar while waiting for his rescuers to arrive.

After George and Shiro had arrived, another rope had been lowered to John so he could attach his jumars to it and ascend. Unfortunately John didn't have jumars with him. He had tried prussik slings but, though this technique works well in theory or under ideal conditions, John had found prussiking a waste of energy; the fixed rope was too slick with water and ice for his prussik knots to catch.

John had been in the crevasse about three-quarters of an hour before Dave and I reached the scene. We lowered him another rope to enable him to try the Bulgari method of ascending out of a crevasse. At the end of both free ropes (the original climbing rope was still tight around his middle) John tied a loop large enough for one of his boots to fit into. With his boots firmly set in the loops, he put his weight on one rope while from above we pulled the other rope up a foot and a half. When John shifted his weight to his other foot, we pulled up on the rope he had just lightened. He rose only a few feet before the ropes wound around each other. It became difficult for John to shift his weight, and almost impossible for us to raise either rope. John struggled up two or three more feet; then the ropes jammed completely.

To give him some temporary relief we had to lower him all the distance he had fought to gain, and then some; we set him on a narrow ledge of ice that sloped downward off the wall of the crevasse.

Above, on the surface of the glacier, we looked at each other and at the growing confusion of ropes; they were strung between snowshoes, ice axes, and skis planted in the snow to anchor them, and they wound in kinks and snarls around our feet in a disorder that would have been comical had not so much depended on the ropes. For several awkward moments we stood speechless, waiting for someone to suggest what we should do.

"Let's haul him!" Gregg said.

Bending close to the crevasse, Gregg called down to John: "We'll have you hauled out in a minute"; his strained voice betrayed his mounting anxiety and must have been little encouragement for John.

George and I had taken a moment to photograph, but we forgot our cameras to concentrate on the rope. Dave carefully watched us find our positions on the hauling rope; nervously, his eyes searched for a flaw in the elaborate system of ropes supporting John; satisfied that they were securely anchored, he braced himself for the pull. Shiro didn't speak, but his face was drawn tight with concern. When George's eyes met mine for an instant we quickly looked elsewhere.

Resting more than fifty feet down on his ledge, John did something of which we were unaware. He knew that the rope would tighten around his middle once we began hand-hauling him up. Fearing that this constriction might cause him to pass out, he untied the one rope he was attached to and retied it, somewhat loosely, across his chest, just under his armpits.

Four of us were braced in position on the rope twenty to thirty feet back from the crevasse. Gregg, still stationed next to the hole, called out the command to begin. We pulled. With the first heave John didn't budge. With the second one he came up a few inches.

"Heave! One . . . two . . . three . . . heave!" We shouted out the signals with Gregg. Gradually John came up.

We had to rest after every fifth or sixth pull; progress was slow. During one break to catch our breath I was close enough to the crevasse to hear John's muffled voice: "Please hurry! I'm very weak!"

Gregg could hear that the rope around John's chest had begun to restrict his breathing. We continued to pull; as he neared the top of the crevasse, we could all hear him gasping for breath.

Then a problem developed. The rope began cutting into the snow at the lip of the crevasse. We had placed an ice axe between the rope and the snow to prevent this, but while we were pulling the rope had slipped off the axe; nothing restrained it from slicing into the snow.

With John's weight on the rope we were unable to place anything else between the rope and the lip of the crevasse. Since he was less than ten feet from being out, we decided to risk forcing the situation by hauling even though the rope would continue to cut into the snow. We heaved on the rope; it sliced deeper into the snow; John hadn't moved. We had made a mistake. The rope had cut its way three feet into the edge of the crevasse. The hole that John had made when he had fallen was his only way of escape; but that hole was no longer directly above him. The slicing of the rope into snow had pulled him away from the hole. Our efforts were now pulling him away from the hole, lifting him up into the snow roof of the crevasse.

Four of us held John where he hung, while Gregg tried to enlarge the hole. With his axe he whacked away chunks of snow. They hit John as they dropped into the crevasse, but there was no other way.

"I haven't any strength, Gregg," we heard John say, "I think I'm going to faint."

"John!" Gregg's voice sounded nearly as weak and desparate as John's. "Don't give up, buddy! We're bringing you out!"

Gregg struck away frantically at the opening with his axe. John didn't complain as the snow tumbled onto him; but he had begun mumbling to himself—we took that to be a bad sign. The four of us were stunned; all we could do was hold the rope, watch Gregg, and listen to John. Even as Gregg enlarged the hole, I knew that wasn't a solution because the rope would cut in again as soon as we began pulling. There had to be something else we could do.

"Please get me out. If I pass out, the rope will slip over my arms. I'll fall."

Gregg turned to the four of us with a compulsion to tell us what was painfully obvious to everyone: "Guys, we've got to get John out! We can't lose him now! God, he might die in our hands!"

"Please. . . . I can't. . . ." John became incoherent at the end of the rope. Only a few of his words reached us clearly. ". . . slipping . . . rope's. . . . I'm seeing red. . . . Gregg! . . ."

I saw Gregg's glazed eyes just before he buried his face in his hands.

"Oh, no. . . ." George, all the muscles in his huge body straining against the rope, began moaning. "Oh, no, oh, no. . . ."

"Shiro!" I yelled. "Go down to hold him!"

Shiro was running toward the crevasse before I'd finished saying that he was the lightest and could best help John inside the crevasse.

Dave managed to free a rope for us to lower Shiro on.

"John, John," Gregg yelled into the hole. "John, can you hear me? Shiro's coming!"

Shiro rappelled over the lip. We heard nothing from John. No one spoke. Shiro had disappeared from sight, but his panting and strained grunts told of his efforts.

We waited for word from Shiro. John's life depended on Shiro's quickness with the ropes and on John's ability to keep from passing out completely, if he hadn't already.

At length a simple command from Shiro's steady voice came up out of the crevasse: "O.K. Pull!"

We whooped joyously and began heaving on the rope that held John. He felt like a dead weight. We pulled. From below, Shiro was shoving John toward the opening. Gregg helped guide from above. I watched the rope inch up out of the hole.

We heard John's voice, then I saw Gregg grab an arm. We strained against the rope; suddenly it went slack. John was out!

"Thank you, thank you, thank you. . . ." Lying on his back, next to the hole, John was hysterical with exhaustion and gratitude. "God, you guys did a wonderful job. Thank you."

"Wow, John baby!" Dave shouted.

Gregg lay on the ice hugging John.

Shiro jumarred out of the crevasse.

John's face was pale, even blue in places. His ribs hurt; George thought a few were broken. One arm was sore. John said a sharp ache stretched the length of his back. But he was safe. His relief was complete; ours, however, wasn't. We knew we had bungled the rescue. We had placed John in unnecessary danger, almost lost him.

John had hung in the crevasse for more than three hours. I didn't know what we could have done differently, nor what our mistakes had been. Certainly the structure of the crevasse had complicated the rescue; but, anxious as I was to find a scapegoat to blame the troubles on, I knew it was useless to accuse the mountain because of our own failings. Why hadn't I thought of sending Shiro down sooner? Or why hadn't Gregg directed us more effectively? Why did he always have to hide his head when things got tough?

"Man, Art, am I glad you thought of getting Shiro down there!" Gregg said putting his arm around my shoulder.

"Yea, you bet," I said, glaring at him.

Gregg drew away from me with a hurt look. It touched me, but I couldn't think of anything nice to say; I was filled with criticism and Gregg must have sensed it.

We picked up the scattered axes, snowshoes, and skis we had used for anchors. We coiled the extra ropes. George attended to John's aches in a fatherly way. I asked Dave to belay me to where my camera set a dozen feet away and hold the rope while I filmed the scene. He blew up.

"Hell, no! I'm not going to hold the rope to let you film this awful scene. Get your camera, and get it fast!"

I retrieved the camera without answering. I didn't say a word while I packed it away, but my thoughts were a one-sided conversation directed at Dave: Don't be so damn impatient, we all decided to make the film, I can't quit now just because you want to be uncooperative.

I gave up filming for the day because I had another, more important, favor to ask of Dave. After being on the glacier a week, my testing schedule called for a urine sample from everyone. Unfortunately, all the plastic collection bottles were at the cache we had been heading toward before John had fallen. Knowing that Dave was the only one who would have enough energy left to go after the bottles with, I asked him if he would accompany me to the cache.

"Damn it, Art!" Dave made no attempt to conceal his bitterness. "Why don't you think of someone else for a change? I'm cold and tired, and not just about to get your piss bags. Why don't you open your eyes and see how someone else feels?"

Silently, we turned toward camp.

About a hundred yards ahead of the rope Shiro, Dave, and I were sharing, John hobbled along at an uneven pace with Gregg and George at either ends of his rope. I wanted to feel elated for him. I did, but tied in behind Dave, having to watch his figure take step after step, my compassion for John was crowded out by a resentment at Dave's anger. His criticism had stung me; I wanted to rush up behind him to tell him it was unjust. I respected Dave too much to ever hate him; that would have been easier. I told my-self that I shouldn't let his words hurt me; he was most likely venting his own frustrations on me. But maybe I was rationalizing, resisting the thought that I was as selfish and inconsiderate as Dave seemed to think. Did Dave see me more clearly than I saw myself?

There was no conversation as we trooped back to the igloo. I was happy for John; though luck plays no part in mountaineering, I couldn't help thinking we were lucky to have John with us.

I was quiet all evening. No one cared to talk. The freeze-dried porkchops Dave cooked cheered me a little, but I felt lonely and discouraged by the apparent ineptness of our expedition. After one week we had succeeded in losing one man; another was off trying to explain that death to the outside. John and I had both nearly disappeared into crevasses. The expedition was bogged down by something. The altitude wasn't bothering us yet. The crevasses were troublesome, but there was more than that. It seemed we were struggling in a sort of quicksand; all our efforts were getting us no further up the mountain, only deeper into the vicious tangle of our frustrations.

Dave had passed me my dinner without saying a word or even looking at me. With our relationship already strained to the point where we couldn't talk to each other, I wondered how we could even contemplate the high climbing that would demand our close cooperation. Considering all our open friction, I thought it would be suicidal to continue the climb. Nobody was enjoying it anyway.

Gregg suggested that maybe our expedition ought to leave the mountain. The subject wasn't pursued.

John fell asleep first. Gregg turned in without writing about the accident in his journal; since he was still writing his journal as a letter to his wife, I thought he probably wanted to avoid alarming her with a description of what had happened that afternoon. With-out much success George tried to tease some cheerfulness back into the rest of us. Shiro alone appeared self-possessed and fully re-covered from the events of the afternoon.

Lying in my sleeping bag I watched Dave write in his journal. I had no way of knowing what he was writing, but I imagined all sorts of awful things that he might be recording:

February 5, P.M.: Art asks me to belay him out so he can pick up his camera . . . sure . . . and what's he do? Starts filming. Man, maybe my patience is low today, but I'm cold and hungry and blow up at him and tell him to forget his &?@¢$#%&¢@ camera, if he thinks I'm going to sit shivering and belay him! Well he comes back, then wants to know if I'll continue on up to the cache to pick up some urine bottles. I tell him to shove it. Honestly, for a sensitive guy, he has less consideration for others than anyone I've ever met.

I consider our party: Gregg's really unstable under stress. John is not physically powerful, and does not have a wealth of experience to make up for power. I don't think George would fare well either, though he is powerful if he is not handling his own weight. Art's O.K. Pirate's very sensible and strong, tho not experienced. Since he can *think* I'd match him against anyone. Shiro is strong for his weight, experienced, and very sensible.

Gregg is very silent, almost morose. He's not happy about the whole deal. He realizes he is not leading, that things just happen 'cause Shiro, Ray, or I get them going. He seems worried about our weaknesses, about his own responsibilities as leader.

Psyched-out

STIRRING IN MY SLEEP, I felt something icy slip down my neck. I turned my head away from the cold sensation, but in another minute more snow sifted through to rudely awake me. I rubbed my eyes, blinked them a few times, and saw in the dim light that our sleeping bags were covered with about an inch of snow. Every few seconds the impact of a gust of wind striking the igloo forced a light cloud of fine snow to blow in from the entrance. While we had slept the wind had found its way through the food boxes and stuff bags we had placed in the igloo's entrance as a defense against the storm we had seen forming the night before. Outside it was snowing heavily, and the wind held steady at twenty to thirty knots.

No discussion was necessary to decide to spend the day in the igloo. We didn't even bother crawling out of our sleeping bags when Dave came in from the tent to see if we wanted anything to eat. A breakfast of mush followed by tea woke me up just enough to begin reading *The Agony and the Ecstasy*. With the book and a box of raisins by my side, I managed to settle into an indifferent sort of contentment.

Gregg absorbed himself in a book about Slocum, the first man to sail around the world in a small sailboat. This was an adventure Gregg dreamed of trying with his wife. Every few minutes he would suddenly sit upright to read aloud a passage that inspired him—the hero weathering a storm, or bartering with natives of a remote island. I thought to myself how much easier it seemed to be for Gregg to picture himself at the helm of a small boat crashing through a sea of towering waves than to buckle to and give us the

leadership we needed to get up McKinley. I didn't enjoy considering my old buddy so despairingly; to divert my attention from
Gregg and to pass time I kept my face buried in my book.

Though John's ribs and the muscles on the left side of his back
were painful, he wielded our glop ladle to carve a series of Romanesque designs on the inside of the igloo entrance. With exaggerated
dignity he delivered a short lecture on classical subarctic ice
sculpture in which he raised the question that may very well come
to stupify archeologists a thousand years hence when, prowling
about the terminal of the Kahiltna Glacier, they discover a
Romanesque arch preserved in the ice. Their question will be: How
did a band of Romans come to build an ice house on this Alaskan
glacier?

When we prompted John to reminisce about his childhood, he
talked of trips to the seacoast, woods, and hills, where he poked
about for things that flew, blinked their eyes, and squirmed; once
he had found an earthworm he couldn't identify, and since no one
else could recognize the worm it became known in academic circles
as species *edwardsae*. John divulged that it was bugs that led him
to climbing; after frequent shin-scraping ascents of cliffs to capture
peculiar insects, John had found himself returning to the cliffs for
the sheer joy of dangling from ledges and scraping his shins.

Admitting that he had attained the modest fame of being the
world's leading authority on the saliva of bedbugs, John dismissed
recognition as an important factor in his present research and
climbing. Comparing the satisfaction he drew from his studies to
his enjoyment of mountaineering, he paralleled the long dreary
hours he spent peering through his microscope to the endless hours
of backpacking on an expedition. Once in a while his microscope
revealed something he was hoping to find or something altogether
unexpected, giving him an inspiration or new insight. John likened
these moments to the times in the mountains when he had just
completed a demanding climb, or when the wind rushed across his
face with an unusual freshness, or when clouds breaking away from

a storm fused and scattered the sun's light into glorious hues and dimensions.

John retired to sketching scenes of the igloo and glacier when Shiro came in from the tent and began singing Japanese songs. His voice sounded so wistful and the songs so soft and lyrical that I suspected he was singing them with his wife Sachi in mind.

George sang Russian melodies, some boisterous, others playful. Translated, one of the tunes described George's dream of living in a large country house with farm animals in a meadow and deer and other wild creatures in the forest.

From the bottom of his rucksack John dug out an ancient, tattered book of ballads, a relic of his student days, to teach us the words to some of them. Then Dave sang "Ghost Riders in the Sky" and "Seven Daffodils" over and over till Shiro and Gregg had memorized every syllable of them. That night I watched Gregg carefully penciling the verses into his journal for his wife:

> . . . I can show you morning
> On a thousand hills
> And kiss you and give you seven daffodils
>
> I do not have a fortune
> To buy you pretty things
> But I can weave you moonbeams
> For necklaces and rings.

During the day Dave and I had kept a safe distance from each other. No open antagonism had errupted between us, nothing I could put my finger on, but the closeness we had shared in the mountains in the past was gone. Feeling restless, I pulled on my parka and wind pants; I received a few questioning glances from the others, who were settling into their bags for the night, but assuring them that I just had to relieve myself, which was true enough, I crawled out the igloo's corridor and into the storm on my hands and knees.

Outside it was completely black except for Dave and Shiro's wind-whipped tent glowing orange-red from their reading candle and a muted white light filtering out through the entrance of the igloo and the chinked cracks between the igloo blocks. I walked away from camp until the tent was barely visible through the swirling snow. Facing the wind, my eyes watered even though I squinted. Snow flew into my face, and with each gust of wind I had to readjust my feet to keep my balance.

The storm was loud as it raced along the glacier, but far overhead, high in the darkness, I could hear the wind howling along the ridges we would be climbing on—if we could get up there. I stood still for about twenty minutes; I resolved to try to be patient with Dave and Gregg and with myself. Feeling much better than when I had come out, I ran back to the igloo, blocked the entrance with food boxes, slid down the corridor, snuggled into my sleeping bag, and was soon asleep, dreaming of a storm.

While I dreamed of gray clouds sweeping fast and close to the ground, the weather fronts were shifting above McKinley. When we woke the next morning the sky seemed cut in two; the edge of the storm lay over McKinley. As cold, dry, arctic air rushing out of the Alaskan interior met warm, humid air blowing up from the coast, colossal wind currents made the clouds boil above the peak. To the north it was clear; to the south a heavy front of clouds was packed up against the range.

It was almost noon before we began to dutifully transport more of our equipment up through the crevasse area where John had fallen. The fear that John's accident might be repeated by one of us was ever present. "Psyched-out" is a term often used by climbers to describe an exaggerated fear someone has for a climb or part of a climb; we were all psyched-out by the crevasse field. We proceeded extremely slowly. Probing ahead of each step with an ice axe, we discovered several crevasses just in time to skirt them.

Because John's rib and back still pained him we had wanted him to rest in the igloo, but he had insisted on carrying a load. We had barely managed to convince him he should not carry a full sixty pounds. Part of our concern for him was because we couldn't tell how badly injured he was. One moment he would stubbornly demand to pack a hefty load, and another time he would remind us of his pain. I thought he was probably suffering more than he let on.

John wrote in his journal that night, February 7:

. . . I had twinges of pain on my left side when I finally got up, and didn't look forward to crossing back to the cache, but did so, picked up loads, and brought them back through the crevassed area. Apprehension, fatigue, and stabs of pain.

Gregg also wrote in his journal before turning in:

. . . John is hard to predict—sometimes he is a bit cynical, but he is a fine tent-mate and he is on my side. He was very much out of condition at the onset, and still is having his problems. I'll have to wait awhile to evaluate him. . . . Shiro is really feeling bad. He has hemorrhoids, only far worse than I. They must be painful, yet he remains cheerful and packs more than his share. He leads his rope and does well; I like him.

On the morning of February 8 we tried to talk ourselves into changing our residency from the Kahiltna Hilton to the level area at 10,200 feet, just below Kahiltna Pass. Dave and I, agreeing on something for once, wanted to move, but Shiro argued convincingly that we ought to be patient for another day or two because it was snowing lightly and Pirate hadn't yet returned. We settled for shuttling up the rest of the provisions for the higher camps. Shiro, who kept an up-to-date inventory of the supplies distributed among our camps and caches, calculated that after one more day's haul we would have thirty days of provisions at 10,200 feet. We planned to take at least twenty days' worth of it on up to 14,400 feet, then pack no less than a ten-day supply of food all the way up to our projected high camp at 17,200 feet, where we would wait for the weather to let us attempt the summit.

Although we had lightened our packs to about fifty pounds each and thirty for John, they slowed our pace considerably as we pushed up the long slope to the 10,200-foot campsite. Fortunately, our enthusiasm picked up as we gained altitude. I told Shiro how relieved I felt to be climbing away from the Kahiltna with its deceptive crevasse fields. He nodded in agreement.

Two miles out of camp and about two thousand feet above it, the clouds began to thin around us and, as we climbed through them, the sky became brighter, it stopped snowing, and patches of blue appeared; before we reached the new campsite we were climbing in direct sunshine.

Where Dave and Shiro had cached five food boxes only four days before, we found the snow littered with torn plastic bags of jello and potato flakes, scraps of cardboard, and bits of candy, cheese, and beef jerky. A band of ravens indicated their annoyance at being disturbed by cawing indignantly as they flapped off over Kahiltna Pass. Not only had they pecked into the cardboard boxes to pilfer our food, but they seemed to have delighted in shredding the packing from our carefully wrapped supplies. Though ravens are notorious for their thievery among the caches of climbers in the summer, we had naively assumed that these bandits wouldn't be marauding about the upper reaches of the Kahiltna during the winter months.

"You pesky Japanese ravens!" George shouted after them, watching Shiro out of the corner of his eye.

"Look, George," Shiro countered. "They have eaten nothing but sausage—so particular; and they have scattered everything else— such poor manners! They couldn't be Japanese ravens. I think they are Alaskans; Americans, anyway."

John watched the birds vanish, then announced with a devilish intent in his voice that those ravens were going to help him even the score with certain of his colleagues back at the Center for Developmental Biology in Cleveland. John explained that his friends had amused themselves by pointing out that McKinley, especially in the winter, was a most inappropriate locale for an entymologist like John to go to on an expedition, because it would be impossible for him to collect even a single stray insect. To astound his colleagues with trophies from his expedition north, John plotted to bait the birds with chunks of sausage soaked in medicinal alcohol, then pounce upon them as they flopped and reeled about in their drunken stupor, and, finally, relieve the captured birds of some of the parasitic insects living among their feathers.

As John became carried away with his imaginative exercise, he decided it would be of more value to science, and easier, if he prepared a professional paper entitled "The Foraging Habits of the McKinley Park *Corvus Corax* (Raven)." He could note that the birds prefered sausage over anything else, occasionally fed on freeze-dried beef, and were highly motivated to destroy plastic bags containing cheese, mashed potato flakes, or jello. The great hypothesis that John intended to put forth in his paper would suggest that whenever the ravens residing near Mt. McKinley spotted a silver plane approaching the mountain from Talkeetna, they knew they had to wait only about a week for a group of considerate men to spread food along the glacier in nicely spaced deposits.

After burying all the food boxes under snow blocks to discourage the ravens, we descended for what we hoped was the last time to our igloo at seventy-five hundred feet. A thin haze of ice crystals and a few whisps of cloud, the last remnants of the storm, lingered in the sky to diffuse the setting sun into pastel yellow and orange light. John, almost skipping down the slope, hummed melodies from Handel. Shiro, Dave, and George whooped and yodeled as they skied swiftly down to the Kahiltna.

We knew Pirate would be watching the weather clear from the airstrip in Talkeetna. He might be with us by morning. The air was growing colder as Gregg and I approached camp; it was almost dark. Near where Farine had fallen Gregg stopped for a moment.

"Art," he said looking straight at me, "if it had been you instead of Farine who died, I just couldn't go on. I just didn't know him the way I know you."

In an instant my remaining resentments toward Gregg disappeared. The day of John's fall, which had aroused my bitterness toward Gregg, seemed very far in the past.

"Yea, it makes a difference when you know the person." I said. "And none of us really knew Farine, did we?"

The next morning a rainbow circled the sun and high over Mt. Foraker a sun dog, this one a concentration of ice crystals, caught the sunshine like a prism to refract it into a small red and green cloud. The day began quietly, but around ten o'clock the still air over the Kahiltna was split by the buzz of a plane, followed several minutes later by a series of growls and roaring laughter that echoed far down the glacier. "Ah aha . . . yaaa! All right, you guys, lets go!" Sheldon had returned our Pirate.

Tossing us fried chicken and cans of beer sent by George's wife and throwing down a stack of mail from our families, Pirate quickly related the troubles he'd had outside. The newspapers had pressed for the story an hour or two after he had arrived in Talkeetna, but Pirate, with Sheldon's help, had managed to sneak the body into the hangar and conceal it under a pile of camping gear. Pirate had immediately cabled the legendary French climber Maurice Herzog, asking him to notify Farine's mother of her son's death before she read about it in a newspaper. To make certain the story didn't leak out Pirate had at first let the press believe that he had left the mountain because he had had a fight with one of the other climbers. When he did level with the newsmen, they wrote accurate if somewhat sensationalized accounts of the accident. I only glanced at the news clippings Pirate had brought with him because the words seemed to be talking about people I didn't know and an event that resembled only the basic details of what we had gone through.

Pirate had run into diplomatic problems with the body. The

McKinley from southwest: (1) Upper Kahiltna Glacier; (2) Windy Corner; (3) 14,400' camp; (4) West Buttress; (5) 17,200' camp; (6) Denali Pass; (7) South Summit; (8) North Summit.

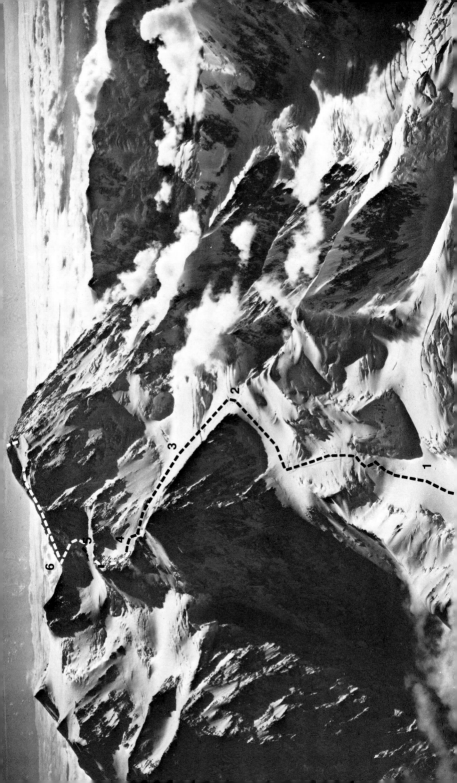

Shiro Nishimae, Art Davidson, Jacques "Farine" Batkin, George Wichman, Dave Johnston, Gregg Blomberg, John Edwards, Ray "Pirate" Genet.

Don Sheldon, glacier pilot

Base camp and igloo on Kahiltna

Gregg Blomberg

Dave Johnston

Ray "Pirate" Genet

Shiro Nishimae

Art Davidson

Jacques "Farine" Batkin

Tragedy of a crevasse fall

French Consulate said it had to have a passport before it could return to France; the passport couldn't be found. Someone had suggested burying it near Mt. McKinley, but no one could decide what type of clergy should give the service because it was not known whether Farine had been Catholic or Protestant or anything. The complications of setting the body in the ground had threatened to tie Pirate up for the rest of the winter, but fortunately, George's wife, Peggy, had taken the responsibility of settling these matters to allow Pirate to return to the mountain.

It was noon before we had read all our mail and eaten the chicken. The sky had become cloudless. Suddenly we realized there was nothing to keep us from moving up to the 10,200-foot campsite. As Pirate stomped about impatiently, the rest of us hustled our gear together. I hesitated packing away my physiological testing kit because there was one last thing I should do before we moved to a higher altitude—I needed to wangle a blood sample out of Dave. While I had drawn specimens from the arms of the others, Dave had been conspicuously busy elsewhere. In light of our recent disenchantment with each other it seemed useless, if not slightly dangerous, for me to risk asking Dave to give me some of his blood; but I plucked up enough courage to compose a calm little speech which I thought might possibly persuade him to bare his arm to my needle. I planned to explain how his blood would likely appear darker than when he had left for McKinley because his body was manufacturing extra red blood cells to protect him from the cold and thin air. In a whisper I rehearsed the exact tone of voice with which I'd deliver my pitch about science needing to know the exact red-cell count of his blood. I practiced maneuvering the tourniquet, syringe, and needle with professional style while saying in a reassuring voice, "Now, this won't hurt a bit." I found Dave in the igloo.

"Dave. . . ."

"No, Art, I'm not going to let you get me! I'd rather draw the blood myself than let you poke around with your needle."

I tried a smile as I pulled out a syringe to show Dave how harmless it looked, but before I could launch into my speech, Dave leaped to his feet.

"No, no, no!" He bolted out of the igloo, his head knocking down a loose snow block from the ceiling of the entrance as he escaped.

"Dave, wait!" I hollered at the top of my voice so he could hear as he ran down the glacier from the igloo. "I have an idea."

"I've had enough of your ideas! Forget about taking my blood!"

"I want you to take mine. Use this syringe to take a sample from my arm."

He regarded me suspiciously for a long moment before cautiously retracing his steps to the igloo. Growing a bit apprehensive myself, I took great care to explain how he should aim the needle toward my largest vein at just the right angle, then set it in with a quick jab and pull back gently on the syringe plunger.

I don't know who was shaking more as he brought the needle up to my forearm. I clenched my toes tight in an effort to fix a casual smile on my face. At the crucial moment I winced, and Dave involuntarily let loose a little cry of pain for me.

A minute later, when 5 cc. of my blood were transferred to a storage tube, Dave looked at me sheepishly. "Gee, Art," he said, "I guess you can take some from me now."

With Pirate back we felt fresher; it seemed we were making a new start. Our revived enthusiasm, along with an airdrop at 10,200 feet that Sheldom made for us, helped us move camp quickly. Thirty-six hours after Pirate had returned we were all comfortably settled into a small village of igloos we had constructed just below Kahiltna Pass. Our "iglooplex," as John christened it, consisted of two spacious—approximately eight feet by eight feet—snow houses for sleeping, a long connecting corridor for storing food and equipment, and one enormous chamber to eat in—it was large enough for the seven of us to sit upright on two snow benches, setting our feet in the aisle cut down the middle of our dining room.

On top of the center igloo Dave had placed a slender, four-foot slab of packed snow on its end, making the entire structure resemble a tiny Russian church. Inside, hunched over a candle, in the midst of a clutter of clothing, cameras, urine bottles, sleeping bags, parkas, snack food, paperback books, and testing equipment, Dave wrote in his journal; squatting in yoga position with a pink toothbrush sticking out of his mouth, Dave looked like just the sort of bizarre holy man we needed to look after our icy chapel. He wrote:

Clear at dawn, clear at dusk. I'm in a happy carefree mood today, singing songs, not self-conscious a bit. I think of helping Art film: don't mind at all stopping to film blowing snow and glazed drifts.

I was carrying my second biggest pack of the trip (sixty-five pounds), yet the day went well. My mind is free—and perhaps that is why I'm so happy. I found myself bursting out in song from time to time, just spontaneously, and it feels mighty good. Giving a little praise to each of the others sure made me feel good! Hell of a lot better than my usual old negative self.

At our 10,200-foot iglooplex the daily low temperatures averaged about −20° F., which was nearly 15° colder than the average had been at the 7,500-foot Kahiltna Hilton. A phenomenon called the "winter temperature inversion," along with the continued clear weather, was responsible for the colder temperatures. Around the approximately 1,000 foot base of McKinley the coldest air settles into the valleys and basins; the air becomes increasingly warmer up to about 8,000 feet, which is usually the top of the warm air layer. Above this level, which is the end of the temperature inversion, the air becomes steadily colder the higher one goes.

In the past I had often watched the Alaska Range from a distance in the winter as the alternate warm and cold layers of air in the temperature inversion created the effects of a mirage on a desert. I had seen the entire mountain massif change shape, appearing to have been replaced by a range of phantom peaks. The basic forms of the foothills had risen in a vertical distortion to one altitude, looking like enormous canyon walls. Normally insignificant high points on a ridge had thrown their image thousands of feet in

the air, giving them the appearance of the slender towers and pin-
nacles of Monument Valley. I'd seen ridges that had never before
existed appear, only to fade away as the air currents had shifted
around the mountain.

Undoubtedly, these mirages of the temperature inversion had
contributed to the mysteriousness of the McKinley winter which
had attracted me to the mountain in January; now on McKinley at
last, I was more than a little disappointed at not having seen a single
mirage. Evidently, one had to put some distance between oneself
and the mountain for the temperature inversion to make itself
visible. We did notice the inversion in the subtle ways that the
colder temperatures affected nearly everything we did. It took
longer to lace up our boots or tie into the rope because we had to
pause more often to warm our hands. At night in the eating igloo
we took turns marching in place in the aisle to keep our feet from
becoming numb. Snow and ice took longer to melt into water, and
any hot drink or bowl of glop lost its warmth in a matter of seconds.
To make our lunches edible it had become necessary to carry the
candy bars, sausage, and cheese close to the heat of our bodies to
thaw out their rock-like consistency. To guard our noses from
frostbite we began wearing our wool face-masks when there was
even the slightest breeze. Although I always wore nylon gloves
while I handled my movie camera, the tips of my fingers frequently
started turning white—the first sign of frostbite.

We took advantage of the days that broke clear one after another
to transport our supplies toward Windy Corner and beyond to our
next campsite at 14,400 feet. With the route growing steeper, and
many of the slopes wind-swept down to permanent ice, we replaced
our snowshoes with crampons; they lightened our feet. The crampon
points bit into the hard snow and ice, forcing the muscles in our
calves to stretch and ache pleasantly each time we lifted our feet to
take another step.

A hundred yards above the iglooplex we entered a basin strewn
with enormous blocks of ice which had broken off from the ridges

concealing this valley from the winter sun. The windless quiet, the shadows, and the ice blocks, many of them taller than a man and weighing several tons, filled this basin with, as John put it, "an unearthly, desolate solitude."

While I trudged through the monotonous hours of hauling supplies, I thought of this area as the "Valley of Silence," and indulged in a fantasy of imagining that the ice blocks, like Easter Island statues, were watching us. Some of the ice faces, aged by centuries of storms, appeared amused by our passage through their basin. Other faces in the ice were sinister; I felt their aloof, forbidding gaze as if they had some supernatural knowledge of our fate.

A few crevasses, mostly hidden, spread across the basin. Although we were constantly aware of their presence, only once did these crevasses trouble us. Dave slipped in to his waist, but managed to quickly pull himself onto the surface.

"Nice action, Dave," I called out, "but I didn't have my camera ready. Can you go back and try it again.?"

"Art," he said, laughing, "how come you and I are getting along better than we did down below?"

"I think we were bothered by those crevasses that kept reminding us of Farine," I answered.

"Hmmm . . . maybe so," Dave said.

Above the Valley of Silence, six hundred feet higher and nearly a quarter mile away, was a large shelf, exposed to the sun and giving a panoramic view, which became our favorite resting spot on this section of the route. To reach this tiny plateau we had to climb an ice slope steep enough for us to feel we were tiptoeing across an ice wall, yet gentle enough for us not to worry about falling. The shelf itself was like a niche in the sky. To the north we could look down four thousand feet, onto the winding Peters Glacier, or to the horizon across the sparsely wooded taiga and the treeless tundra. To the west stretched the Kuskoquim drainage, thousands of square miles of forest mostly uninhabited except for Eskimo villages scattered along the coast of the Pacific, three hundred miles away.

Below us, the thin line that was our trail threaded among the ice blocks in the basin. Above, a series of gullies packed with snow led to the last plateau below Windy Corner.

As we ferried our loads of supplies, weighing forty to sixty pounds, up past the eleven-, twelve-, and thirteen-thousand-foot points, each of us felt the altitude affecting our ability to work. We breathed harder, rested more often, and paced each step a little more slowly. John, worried about his performance, apologized profusely whenever he thought he was holding someone up, and forced himself to pack as heavy a load as the rest of us, even though his ribs and back still hurt. By evening he was invariably exhausted.

After being roped with John on one haul to twelve thousand feet, Gregg told Dave, "John was really going slow, but I cussed him out in a couple ways, and he did better."

"You think he's faking it?" Dave asked.

"Sure," Gregg said, "he has a lot more in him than he will admit. I know he can do better, and I know he will."

"Why the hell wouldn't a guy give his best?" Dave said, turning away.

Like myself, Shiro had been listening but had said nothing. I knew Shiro well enough to know he was concerned about John, and also about George, whose pace was becoming unsteady, but I never heard Shiro shout at anyone to climb faster or even suggest that someone's slowness was a problem. Shiro's way was to encourage gently. Always leading on his rope, he would set a pace that everyone could follow without straining themselves. In contrast, Gregg tried to drive John, and even himself, as fast as he could.

Pirate, always the first up in the morning, shouted us all on as if we were a team of worn-out mules he had to whip up the mountain. We might have taken offense at his tactless coercion had he not appeared so comical waving his fist and bellowing, "Move, ya bloody beasts!"

Several times I noticed Shiro watching closely when Pirate was climbing on ice; knowing that Pirate had little experience with crampons, Shiro was always on guard to catch an unexpected fall. I admired him for looking after Pirate so unobtrusively that Pirate was never aware of his watchfulness.

Shiro took care of us on the trail, but it was George who became our mother hen whenever we were in camp. At least a couple of times every day he would ask each of us if we had a headache, or how we had slept, or if our appetite and digestion were still normal. The few times he received a complaint, George looked hurt, as if he felt personally responsible for that person's ailment, and he'd rummage for the right pill through the huge, disheveled duffle bag that served as his medical kit.

Of all of us, Dave suffered the most peculiar effects of the altitude. He started climbing faster, and the faster he climbed the more impatient he became with the rest of us who slowed him down. Below ten thousand feet, only Pirate and I had been able to match Dave's pace, but even Pirate had begun flagging just a bit, and I was little consolation for Dave because I continued to stop often to fuss with my camera and tripod.

Before dinner on the evening of February 13, our last night at the iglooplex, Dave pulled me away from the others to voice some of his discouragement with our group. It took several minutes for him to tell me in a roundabout way that he was afraid we were climbing too slowly.

Long after I had fallen asleep that night, Dave wrote in his journal:

Poor John collapsed on the ice when he reached 12,300 feet today. Did his crevasse episode really take this much out of him, or did he ever have the poop to begin with? I just hope his weakness doesn't endanger us up high. If weather and snow conditions are perfect, we'll be O.K. If not, I'll be wishing Farine were around to tie in with. Without him, who? Art has plenty of fight. George is medium-fast and strong. At only 12,300 feet Pirate is not as full of energy as he could be. Gregg is medium-fast, but in an all-out effort or emergency I don't know. Shiro is very sensible, but quite slow. I think his hemorrhoids bother him much more than he'll admit.

Time'll tell. If we ever run into a situation where *speed* is a requisite for safety—and man, it often is—why, we'll all be screwed.

First thing on the morning of February 14, we wished each other a happy St. Valentine's day. Then we hastened excitedly to pack up our personal gear. We were moving up to the next camp!

As we climbed through the Valley of Silence and up the ice wall, we caught glimpses of several small planes circling above, probably trying to locate us and mark our progress up the mountain. When George thought he recognized one of the planes as belonging to a friend of his, Gregg called us to a halt. He traversed several yards to reach a level patch of soft snow; there he stamped out a big heart. Staring up at the plane, he yelled, "Now drop the smoked turkey!" A turkey didn't fall out of the sky, but, undismayed, Gregg adopted, "Drop the smoked turkey!" as his customary greeting to every passing plane.

By four o'clock we had made it to our high cache on the 12,300-foot plateau, where we decided to camp overnight. We figured an early start the next morning would allow us to reach the 14,400-foot campsite with several hours of daylight left for building an igloo. John (quite tired again), Gregg, and I set up the tents and put the camp in order while the others carried their loads on as far as they could that evening. They agreed to cache their loads wherever sunset caught them and descend to camp just before dark.

However, there were two sunsets that evening. At this higher vantage point we observed the sun set into the southern flank of Mt. Foraker, remain hidden for several minutes, rise out of the northern flank of Mt. Foraker, then set again an hour later out over the Kuskoquim flats.

"John," I laughed, "looks like we've strayed onto the Little Prince's planet." I filmed the event.

By the sun's second setting the procession Shiro had led up the slope had disappeared beyond Windy Corner. It was well into twilight before they reappeared to jog slowly down to camp.

During dinner I detected hints that all had not gone well above Windy Corner. Dave said little things that revealed his underlying apprehension, like, "Man, we gotta get movin' up this peak!" and "We can't be stumbling around when we get up high!"

I noticed that George was unusually quiet. But there was no open discussion of any difficulties, and Shiro and Pirate seemed their usual quiet and noisy selves, so I was left to puzzle what, if anything, had happened up there.

All in all, it developed into the merriest night of the trip. The cold evening let us feel all the warmer as we drank hot soup and hurriedly gobbled down our glop before ice crystals could form on its surface. Our suprise came after Dave went out to take a leak and check the temperature.

"Wowee! It's minus forty-two degrees!" I glanced out of the tent to see Dave leaping about. "Kazowie! Hey, you crazy honchos, it's minus forty-two degrees!"

We shouted, and began singing nonsense songs at the top of our voices. Minus forty-two degrees—what an event to celebrate on St. Valentine's day. Our elation ran unchecked; little Shiro even started wrestling with George. This is what we had come on McKinley to find! We were getting into the cold temperatures at last.

"O.K., Art," Gregg said, pounding my back for emphasis, "now the real climbing begins."

Eventually, our excitement lost its momentum, and we settled into our sleeping bags for the night. Next to me I could feel George wiggling his toes and rubbing his feet together to warm them. Once again Dave stayed up late to write in his journal by candlelight:

February 14: This afternoon Shiro was gung-ho to make 14,200 feet, so we raced off—at a snail's pace. Once or twice I nearly exploded into a run. I just get so fed up with this plod, plod jazz. Seems we ought to push just a little down here to get our bods in shape for what lies ahead.

Shiro, George, Ray, and I carried up to Windy Corner. My nose kept whitening, so I donned a surgical mask, folding it in half so I could breath unhindered through my mouth. It was nice, hard cramponing on 20° to 30° snow. Often it was so hard that our crampon points couldn't bite in.

George, in front of me, stumbled a couple times, weaved a couple more. I gripped my axe tightly in arrest position. The obvious route, the one Shiro was taking, naturally lies along the sidehill, above the crevasses, then contours into a broad basin. But George suddenly advised we descend into the crevasse field. He said: "In summer it's deep powder here. Do you want to bet 99 percent of the people use the route down there?"

"George," I answered too hotly, "I don't care where 99 percent of the people go. It is obvious that there are crevasses down there and that the simplest route contours into the basin."

George then came to the point: "David, we're not all super climbers. We can't all carry heavy loads on steep ice."

I said nothing, but in a moment suggested we descend into the crevasse field and cache our loads. We do, tho Shiro wants to continue. To continue tired and bitter is really inviting an accident. I'm filled with half scared, half bitter thoughts about this trip.

If George can't handle hard snow, angle 25°, at 13,500 feet, what's gonna happen on the ice at 18,000 feet? Man, our chances of an accident are bloody good.

Back at camp my thoughts are taken up by outwitting ornery lanterns and stoves. Halfway through supper, I'm joking with George, bitterness forgotten. Fed and warm, my attitude concerning safety and party skill is one of apathy. "Aw heck, don't worry, everything will work out O.K."

I hope it does. Oh baby, I hope it does!

Excitement tonight! Our record low by far— —42°! Wowee!"

The Climb to 17,200 Feet

I PUT OFF getting up as long as I could.

Inside the tent it was −38°. Each time we brushed against the tent walls—it was impossible to move without touching them—we were showered with ice crystals. My clothes were so cold that it hurt my fingers to touch them. During the night Dave's tossing in his sleep had waked me several times. Now he complained, "Didn't sleep worth a damn . . . half chilly all night." George, lying next to me, was a huge lump of sleeping bag which occasionally stretched and groaned. I heard some shifting about and an occasional swear word from the other tent. Getting a stove going was an unpleasant thought: spilling gas on bare hands, fumbling with matches, watching a sputtering flame go out, cleaning the orifice, pumping up the air pressure, striking another match. I was relieved to see Dave reach for our cooking kit and, mumbling profanities through his beard, try to persuade the stubborn stoves to melt snow into the water we needed for tea and mush.

As both stoves began roaring healthily, Dave's bitching turned into Beatles melodies with improvised background accompaniment. Gradually the grumbling from the other tent changed to Russian folk tunes and classical humming. I began singing "Red River Valley" and "Tumbling Tumbleweeds." Someone else started through his repertoire of animal and bird calls. Chirping and whistling to greet the new day, I wondered how this peculiar flock had come to lose its senses. "Gads," said Dave. "If someone were to walk by right now. . . ."

Pirate and Shiro hustled us out of the tents into a breeze which, coupled with the air temperature, brought the equivalent wind-chill temperature down around —50°. We didn't have any breath to spare for singing as we clomped slowly up the ice toward Windy Corner. We had to avoid panting and deep breaths because whenever we drew in the extremely dry and cold air too deeply we felt a burning sensation in our lungs.

We were at first puzzled by the small rocks, some of them weighing up to four or five pounds, which we found scattered on the snow below Windy Corner; there seemed to be no place they could have tumbled down from. That they must have blown off the buttress, thousands of feet away, was dramatic evidence of the winds that sometimes funnel through Windy Corner. We considered ourselves fortunate that only a slight breeze wandered down to us.

Climbing in the shadow of Windy Corner, we anticipated the direct sunlight which was hitting the crest of the slope. When, more than an hour after leaving our camping spot, we stepped into the sunshine, it purged our lethargy and sent us scurrying like hungry ground squirrels among the outcroppings of rock at Windy Corner in search of food cached by previous expeditions. Dave scavenged the most delicious find, which we all helped him eat—Almond Roca.

Beyond the Corner, the breeze left behind, we became so warm under our sixty-pound packs that Dave, Pirate, and I eventually shed our parkas. It was an easy, gently rising mile and a half to the basin below the West Buttress ice wall where we planned to place our next camp at 14,400 feet. Dave and Pirate joked with each other. Gregg raved about the view of Hunter and Foraker to the south of us and the ice riddled with rock ribs that swept up from the basin ahead of us toward the summit; "Sure glad we can climb around that stuff," he said. Shiro and George puffed past Gregg, John, and me, who were roped together and bringing up the rear. Although the slope wasn't steep, John was finding it all he could manage. Every two or three hundred feet he had to stop to rest. When we did move ahead his feet were so unsteady that he often stepped off the trail into a foot of soft snow which demanded even more energy to plow through. Only a few hundred yards from the new campsite John shook off his pack and plopped onto it.

"Gregg, I'm sorry." John tried to speak clearly between his gasps for breath. "I just can't . . . go on . . . now."

"What do you mean?" Gregg replied. "You can't lie here."

"Maybe," John suggested, "I could rest . . . for a while . . . leave my pack here . . . then make it."

The tight expression on John's face spoke of his weariness and shame. Asking if he could leave his pack was a painful admission of failure; I knew it couldn't be easy for him to swallow his pride just to keep from delaying us. There were heavy, dark bags under his eyes; his breathing remained irregular long after Gregg and I were breathing smoothly. It seemed unfair that what most of us would remember as a pleasant afternoon was an ordeal for John, "the misery of the ascent," as he wrote in his journal.

As Gregg and I waited in the hope that John would recover in a few minutes, I thought of something John had said a few days before. In a more reflective mood he had spoken appreciatively of the exhausting drudgery of backpacking our supplies up to our high camp. He had mentioned that occasionally, while pushing himself up a slope, one forced step after another, thinking of nothing but the strain in his legs and back, his senses would suddenly clear, letting him perceive his situation with a new, fresher intensity. John had said this sensation usually lasted only a few moments. He thought perhaps his concentration on the physical effort cut away at his usual mental patterns to the point where for a few seconds he saw without an orientation or framework to define and organize what he perceived. John had put it something like this: "It happens to me at the most unexpected moments. When I'm completely absorbed in the dreary rhythm of plodding, no more aware of myself or my surroundings than some mule packing a heavy load, I'm sometimes surprised by what I can only describe as a sort of mystical clearness of perception."

Now, collapsed on his pack, John expressed only regret for holding us up. He said that he would just wait at this next camp while the rest of us climbed up to the 17,200-foot-high camp and then tried for the summit. Gregg and I hastened to tell him that it was ridiculous to think such a thing; but I was afraid that John would be unable to climb above this 14,000-foot basin.

We decided that for the time being John could rest where he lay; Shiro and I would return in an hour or so to accompany him through the crevassed area that lay between us and camp. As Gregg and I walked away toward the campsite, John gazed off in the direction of Mt. Foraker.

In this basin below the ice wall rising to the crest of the West Buttress we selected a campsite that we calculated to be out of reach of any avalanches that might shake loose after a snowfall. We hoped to construct two igloos before dark, but the task took longer than expected because the basin, partly sheltered from high winds, was carpeted with snow too soft to be fashioned into solid igloo blocks. We were forced to dig two feet below the surface to get snow of the right consistency. Later, after we had brought John up to camp, he and I quarried blocks; Gregg and Pirate transported them the dozen or so yards to the structures that Shiro, George, and Dave were piecing together. By seven o'clock we had finished one snow house by the light of our headlamps, but, tired and needing a good meal, we decided to close in the roof of the second igloo the next morning.

We might have read the sky more closely; a lenticular cloud had appeared over Foraker after the sun had set; a high, light overcast had been barely discernible in the fading evening light. The previous night at 12,500 feet it had been $-42°$, and now, at 14,400 feet, it was only $-20°$; the sudden rise in temperature was a sure sign of an approaching storm. By morning a south wind had picked up. Snow began falling before we set the last blocks in the roof of the second igloo.

For three days the blizzard pelted our basin with so much snow that visibility was restricted to less than fifty feet most of the time. Although the storm restrained us from starting up the ice wall, we were able to fetch up the food we had cached near Windy Corner. The blustery wind, never more than thirty knots, rarely less than ten, never really threatened us; at times it was even stimulating. Bundled up in sweaters and parkas and hidden behind wool face-masks and goggles, we confidently leaned into the wind to force our way from willow wand to willow wand. I liked the feel of the wind whipping our clothing and the rope that tied us together. I liked to quickly shift my stance to counter an unexpected gust that tried to unbalance and topple me into a snowdrift.

Once, as were heading straight into the wind, it struck me that the physical difficulties of climbing in this storm were a relief from the more intangible troubles we had been batting our heads against down below. This blizzard was something we could size up and pit ourselves against, while down on the Kahiltna the strain of the hidden crevasses, the accident, and even the uncertainty of whether we'd go on had confused us, and had made us turn against each other.

Had the wind blown harder or the temperature dropped another ten degrees we would have had to sit out this storm in the igloos. As it was, we became invigorated when we stepped out into flying snow each morning, and we filed back to the igloos each evening with a satisfying sense of fatigue. Although falling snow and clouds obscured the summit and the route to 17,200 feet, we began to be infected with summit fever. The end of our climb seemed to be within reach, maybe just a few days away.

On February 17 Gregg wrote in his journal:

We are all optimistic that if we can carry a load up to 17,200 feet tomorrow we can all move up the next day, Sunday, (with good weather)! That means Monday we might have the summit. Dave is in fine shape, Pirate and Art are in good condition too. . . . We could be through by the twenty-fifth and I could be home by the first. Man, that would be nice!

But the next day the storm quickened its pace to delay our climb up the ice for another twenty-four hours. On the morning of the nineteenth the snow flurries cleared and the clouds finally began breaking away. With blue sky and a thousand feet of blue-white ice reflecting the sun's light, Gregg paced and stomped wildly around camp to get us going. He gripped and fondled his ice axe in anticipation of whacking out steps in the steep ice. When John and Pirate had their packs filled with gear and their crampons strapped on tightly, Gregg led them off toward the ice, laughing and belting out choruses of "John Henry" as they left camp.

About forty-five minutes later I led a second rope up the slope to find Gregg furiously cutting steps up the clean ice of the vertical wall of the bergschrund (a crevasse on a slope or wall) that stretched across our direct line to the col a thousand feet above. I had never seen Gregg so joyous. Steep ice was his element, and he knew how to handle it. With only a few of his front crampon points sticking into the ice, Gregg balanced, steady and confident, on a delicate stance. He was swinging his axe with a powerful, smooth rhythm which sent ice chips flying each time the metal adze or pick struck the blue ice.

However, before I reached the bergschrund I noticed a snow bridge no more than a dozen yards away; it appeared to offer easy and safe access to the slope above the bergschrund. Cautiously, I stepped up to the bridge, tested its depth and density with probes of my axe shaft, then climbed over it. In two minutes I had by-passed the vertical section that Gregg was still laboring up. I belayed my rope-mate, George, across the bergschrund, and within ten minutes Dave and Shiro had followed our route over the snow bridge to wait with us at the bottom edge of the ice wall while Gregg finished climbing the steep ice. Dave said to no one in particular, "Looks like Gregg's climbing with his head in his pocket today." Shiro murmured, "Very strange."

Several minutes later Gregg's bearded face appeared over the upper edge of the bergschrund; his hair was disarranged and beads of sweat stood out on his forehead. He looked angry. Breathing

heavily from his exertion, he brusquely congratulated me for finding an alternative to the pitch he had just led. Then he quickly
turned his eyes to study the route above. The rest of us remained
quiet. Dave scowled. I couldn't think of anything to say that would
ease the tension.

Gregg knew he had made a foolish mistake and that we all
realized his desire to climb the vertical ice had completely blinded
him to the possibility of the snow bridge. It could have been a costly
mistake.

"Hey, Gregg." Shiro spoke out boldly. "This ice pretty steep
above. I think you better lead it."

"Yaaa, come on, fearless leader!" roared Pirate, who, like John,
was roped to Gregg and was scurrying over the snow bridge instead
of climbing the vertical ice. He added, "Take us up . . . ah haa!"
We laughed, and Gregg even managed a self-conscious sort of
chuckle.

Gregg carefully inspected the three old lines that previous expeditions had left fixed in place on this section of ice. He decided
two of them were unreliable, but after yanking and swinging on the
third he judged it safe for us to use as a hand line. With exaggerated
caution and a bustle of crampons, legs, arms, and axe, he started
up the ice. Often he had to stop to jerk the fixed rope free of a
thin layer of ice sealing it to the mountain; in another year or two
the rope might be frozen an inch under the surface. Gregg chopped
steps for the rest of us to follow in. He hammered steadily with his
axe. He stepped up, chopped a foothold, stepped up again, chopped
another foothold. He attacked the ice so vigorously, with such
determination, that I wondered if he was trying to make up for his
mistake. Maybe he was taking his shame and anger out on the ice.
In any event, the steps he made were good ones, large and well
placed; we followed without difficulty.

But George and John weren't anxious to continue on. The going
was slow. It was getting late, they argued. They cached their loads
at the bottom of the fixed ropes and returned to camp.

The rest of us stuck behind Gregg. When the fixed ropes ended a hundred feet below the col, he didn't hesitate to lead over the final stretch of ice, snow, and scattered rocks below the crest of the West Buttress. Gregg was working hard, but his climbing wasn't livened with the same enthusiasm with which he had started the day.

At last there was no more ice above us; we stepped out onto the col and sat ourselves upon some comfortable looking rocks. The thermometer read −32°, and we were beginning to feel the cold since we weren't moving. Dave noted that it was more than 40° colder than when he had stood at this same spot three years before. We had originally planned to pack up all the way to our next campsite at 17,200 feet, but no one objected to Gregg's suggestion that we cache our food boxes and call it quits for the day.

We wedged the supplies among the rocks and weighted them down with the few loose stones we could find. We backed down the hundred feet to the fixed ropes, then used the ropes to steady our descent to the bergschrund. With two long, well placed steps we crossed the schrund, as we called it, and hastened down into the basin. George and John had soup and an enormous tunafish glop waiting for us. We turned in before nine, hoping to get away early the next morning.

Perhaps it was a new storm, or perhaps the previous one simply socked in again, but in either case snow was blowing wildly when we woke. Though I overheard a little griping about the weather preventing us from climbing, I don't believe anyone was greatly disappointed by being forced to relax.

Waiting through the stormy hours in the same igloo, Dave and I, despite the underlying tension that lingered between us, cautiously began discussing our dreams of homesteading. We pictured an area that could be reached only by boat or plane and where stout cabin logs could be felled from a virgin spruce forest. We decided bear, and moose, and sea birds were necessary. Dave wanted a sod roof on his home so he could plant flowers on it. He wanted to be able to wake up in the morning and feel the breeze off a glacier, watch a bear rooting along a side hill, and be able to see a thirty-foot tide flowing into the fjords. Dave's words touched me; he didn't talk of escaping from people or society or such things, but of just finding a wild place to live in simply and rigorously.

Much of the time I kept to myself. For hours I imagined traveling through country with thick green foliage. I tried to recall all the streams I'd ever seen in my life; mostly, I remembered water that was sparkling in the light of a close summer sun. I thought of berries, and moss, and ferns. I spent a long time trying to remember every clump of wild alpine flowers I'd ever come upon.

Unknown to me, Dave wrote in his journal: ". . . Art's in good spirits. We get on O.K. lately. He's dreamy nights—stares for hours—like I am when on pot."

Through the storm Shiro read a book describing the hardships of a man and wife who set off to homestead in the bush and wouldn't give up their primitive way of life even after their cabin with all their belongings burned to the ground. As Shiro read, I sometimes heard him whispering to himself. Once I asked him what was up; he looked at me shyly and said "Well, I wish Sachi and I could homestead." I knew an expired visa would send him back to Japan as soon as we were off the mountain.

When I was giving the physiological tests in the other igloo, I overheard Gregg say he would be satisfied if we all reached Denali Pass. I asked him what about the summit. He said we'd try for it, of course, but that it was an accomplishment if we could just set up a camp at 17,200 feet. I would have liked to talk with Gregg alone, but I wasn't about to drag him out into the storm to ask him what had happened to his drive to reach the top. The subject was dropped for the time being, and I was left trying to figure Gregg out. Was he still partially paralyzed because of Farine? Maybe his desire to climb was slacking off. Or perhaps he was preparing himself to accept defeat in case we were forced to turn back short of the summit.

John had grown noticeably quieter than he had been in the lower camps. His back still ached, but he talked hopefully of at least attempting the summit himself. He said that the storm was allowing him time to acclimatize, that he was feeling stronger after each day spent at 14,400 feet.

At five every afternoon, Pirate, with almost a religious faithfulness, slipped out of the igloo he shared with Gregg and John to radio Anchorage with a portable line-of-sight unit. Below this camp he had been unable to establish contact with anyone, but from this basin he could get a direct line to Anchorage, where he received weather reports from newspaper friends of his. It seemed odd to me that if all he wanted were weather forecasts, he didn't just call the weather bureau. George feared that he was trying to make a splash in the local newspapers. I had heard George say several times that publicity worked at a cross purpose to the reasons he liked to be off in the mountains. Now he said: "I like to get away from it all; away from the pressures, away from the pretentions that people live with. There's no need to broadcast what we are doing. Let's just climb."

Since Pirate was the only one who ever bothered radioing out, it seemed slightly unreal to the rest of us when he would return to the igloo and tell us about talking with people who were going about their regular activities in Anchorage. No one encouraged Pirate to make the calls, but he enjoyed them so much that we didn't have the heart to ask him to stop. The weather reports weren't crucial because we could see the signs of an approaching weather front in the sky. Nevertheless, we all got excited over Pirate's weather report on the evening of the twenty-first; it called for several days of clear weather.

When the next morning dawned clear as predicted, Gregg, Pirate, John, and George moved out of camp at about nine to begin the 2,800-foot ascent to our high-camp location at 17,200 feet. Since they didn't plan to return until the summit had been reached, or at least attempted, they carried food, gas, two stoves, snow shovels, an ice saw, a four-man tent, over a hundred willow wands, extra sweaters, and their sleeping bags. The three of us who were remaining behind wished them luck; they said they would stand on the summit the next day if the weather held clear. Off they went, and soon they were no more than small specks on the ice wall. John had surprised us; he was up there, climbing the ice that only a few days before he had been certain he would never get up.

Shiro's cautious reasoning was keeping him, Dave, and me from starting up this day. Arguing for patience, Shiro had explained to Gregg and the rest of us that we needed to bring more food from the 12,500-foot cache to the high camp in order to have enough provisions stocked at 17,200 feet to wait out a prolonged storm. It had been decided that only three people had to make the final haul up from the 12,500-foot cache; Dave and I had volunteered to stay behind for a day with Shiro. Although we consoled ourselves with the knowledge that our sacrifice of waiting was helping to assure the eventual success of the party, we did feel a bit envious of the four who were climbing up as we lumbered down below Windy Corner for more supplies. There was no immediate danger in splitting the party; still, none of us would feel completely at ease until our two groups, without communication between each other, were again one group.

Late that afternoon, with the day's haul behind us, we threw down our packs in front of the igloos, and before retiring for the evening, our eyes searched the route to 17,200 feet for our companions; as expected, there was no sign of them. Within a few minutes we were squatting on our sleeping bags by the yellow light of a Coleman lantern with clouds of steam from our cooking pots rolling around the igloo.

"Of course, they have first chance to make the top," Shiro said, eyeing Dave and me carefully, "but maybe we can rush, light and quick, from here to bivouac on the summit." Dave nearly upset his soup. We looked at Shiro with disbelief. A bivouac on McKinley's summit in winter sounded insane. Shiro smiled slyly. "It would be sporting. What you think?" Dave just flopped back on his bag and sighed, "Wow!"

A minute later we were sorting out the food we'd take for our camping soiree up top. We portioned out oatmeal, soups, dried potatoes, powdered milk, fig bars, cheese, meat bars, sausage, and generous allotments of our treasured Logan bread and grandma's fruitcake, which had been baked by Gregg's wife and my grandma. For protection from the elements we decided to take a piece of the parachute; we figured an ice cave could always be dug if a storm came up. We filled our most reliable stove with gas, and measured out three extra pints of fuel. Shiro, not anxious to lug up his sleeping bag, asked if he could use my down pants to sleep in; I said, "Sure, and you can crawl in with Dave when you get cold."

The more we thought about it, the easier and safer a night on the summit sounded. Instead of hurrying down we'd simply crawl into our bags, except for Shiro, and wait till the first light the next morning. The most thrilling part of our plan was the thought of waking up, or simply getting up if we had been unable to sleep, on the very top of the continent as the sun rose.

We assured ourselves success with an ever-expanding confidence we didn't question. And we didn't doubt that the other four were settled in at 17,200 feet, ready for their summit attempt the next morning.

However, we were wrong. Gregg, John, Pirate, and George hadn't made it all the way to the high-camp plateau. It had taken them longer than expected to reach the top of the ice wall, and they had all, except for Pirate, become fatigued by the effort. The deciding factor in their decision to camp at 16,500 feet instead of going to 17,200 had been Gregg's right foot. It had become cold. The large toe on the chilled foot didn't rewarm when Gregg massaged it, nor when he pulled on an extra pair of socks. Camp was made at the col. Only after eating a hot meal and holding his foot against John's belly for more than an hour did Gregg's big toe begin to rewarm with sharp, tingling pains.

Gregg figured that his cold foot was caused by a tight-fitting boot, which had restricted the circulation in his foot while he had climbed the ice wall. Ironically, he had originally selected a pair of snug-fitting boots because he feared loose-fitting ones would affect his balance on the ice wall.

That night, February 22, well into our fourth week on the mountain, Gregg confided to his diary:

Oh, baby, I hope I've got it in me to do the summit. I am feeling rather depressed tonight. The rest days weren't good for me. All I want to do is get this thing done. With good weather in our favor we could be finished and out in a week. Nothing could please me more. . . . It won't be too hard a day tomorrow, but I don't look forward to it for some reason. . . . I feel like writing a lot; I guess to get up my courage.

It was 2:00 P.M. the next day by the time Shiro, Dave, and I finally tied into rope. The gentle ice immediately above camp passed quickly beneath our crampons. Five hundred feet up we turned to look down on the indistinct mounds of snow which were the highest igloos we had built on McKinley. Above us rose the longest stretch of steep ice on the West Buttress route; swept by wind and avalanches, its hard, blue surface was clear of snow. And somewhere far above, perhaps near Archdeacon's Tower or on the final ice wall and ridge itself, we imagined the other four slowly advancing on the summit.

Again we were wrong. As we climbed up the last fixed ropes, then reached the col and pitched the parachute over us, the other four were camped only seven hundred vertical feet above. They were all crowded into a single tent pitched near the western rim of the 17,200-foot plateau.

Gregg wrote in his journal on February 23:

Above it looks very forbidding and steep. I only hope we can make it. My feet really got cold today; John warmed them for me. It is −50° outside and our bags and everything are wet, but if we play our cards right we will have one more night here at the most. My right foot is numb in the toes; I think it is all right. . . . I am really hopeful that we will be done tomorrow.

For Shiro, Dave, and me, who had shivered the night through huddled under the parachute at 16,500 feet, the morning was a long time coming. Dave had shuffled different socks on and off his feet at irregular but frequent intervals trying to find a combination which afforded him maximum insulation without restricting his circulation. Shiro said not a word about how well he had slept, but his ordinarily youthful face had become soft and heavy. Since I had had difficulty keeping warm inside my bag, I couldn't imagine how Shiro could have slept at all without a sleeping bag.

But even more than about Shiro's sleeplessness I worried about his cough. Several times during the night I had heard the dry, cracking sound which I remembered from two years previously, when Shiro and I had climbed together on McKinley. On that expedition his spells of coughing had nearly forced him to return to base camp instead of continuing toward the summit.

After our rising ceremony of yawns, stretches, and curses at the iced-up nylon parachute we ate a fast breakfast of candy, cheese, and salami. The day had come for us to attempt the summit. We figured we'd be able to climb up to 17,200 feet in less than an hour. We'd chat with the other four for maybe a half hour, then be off for Denali Pass. Archedeacon's Tower, the summit, and our bivuoac on top of McKinley. However, as we crawled from under the parachute to stand in the open air, my confidence began to wane. A breeze stung our faces with the cold; we had to shield our faces from the slight wind. Dave checked his thermometer— —43°. It took each of us at least twenty minutes to tie our crampon straps because we could work with our fingers only a few seconds before they became numb and cramped from the cold. And though I stomped in tight circles to get blood rushing through my feet, I couldn't get the chill out of my toes.

We didn't get off to the early start we had planned on, and once we did begin climbing we moved up the ridge much more slowly than we had anticipated. We shouldered the same loads as we had the previous day, but they felt heavier; we had to stop to rest every two or three minutes. And always the ridge rose above us in a series of steps. We crossed a narrow ice ramp which led onto steeper ice sweeping up a hundred feet to a granite tower. Foot by foot, the distance to this massive rock was covered. I felt unusually tired; I was forever losing my breath; my legs didn't seem to have any energy in them. Why was the altitude affecting me so much? It hadn't bothered me like this when I had climbed higher on Mt. Logan or on the volcanoes of Mexico.

Above us loomed the rock tower, a monument to the mountain's indomitability through the storms that were ravaging this ridge before the first Asians immigrated through Alaska. Fortunately, we didn't have to climb the tower itself but could skirt below and circle to the left to gain access to an ice slope scattered with boulders. We moved ten feet and stopped. We climbed twenty feet to the next boulder and halted. We gained another ten feet, then rested again. I was not quite dizzy, but my ears were ringing slightly and my head felt light. I laughed to myself at the thought of my red-bearded, begoggled, down-hooded head floating off over the Alaska Range like a circus balloon.

I began to suspect that maybe my legs and head weren't ready to climb on toward the summit that afternoon. When, at length, we gained the crest of the boulder-strewn slope, Dave threw off his pack and drooped himself over a rock. He pulled off his goggles and face-mask. "How ya feelin'?" I asked.

Squinting in the harsh sunlight, Dave mumbled that he had one of those headaches when your brains seem to be loose and rattling about your skull; he added, "My bod's as tuckered-out as it was three years ago on McKinley's summit."

Shiro coughed a couple of times, took a deep breath, and said quickly, with just a trace of sadness in his voice, "Well, maybe this is not a good time to push for summit bivouac."

With tired nods of resignation, Dave and I told Shiro that we agreed. For the time being, the summit remained unattainable; all our glorious anticipation of sleeping as high in the sky as we could climb vanished. We felt no shame for quitting because to stumble on in pursuit of the summit in our condition would have been foolish.

We wolfed down all the hard candies and crumbled cookies Dave emptied out of his various pockets. Then, with Shiro in the lead, we started to climb the last stretch of ridge that separated us from the 17,200-foot plateau and our four companions; we consoled ourselves with the belief that they had already made the summit. Slow but graceful, Shiro found his way along the very crest of the ridge. Sometimes our crampons scraped on rock, but more often they gripped into packed snow or ice. The ridge rose more gradually than it had on the lower sections, but I don't know that we climbed any faster; our decision to stop when we reached the plateau had taken away much of our impetus.

The ridge suddenly rose steeply for fifty or sixty feet. Above this last step would lie the relatively level plateau. We rested a few minutes before angling up on ice and small bits of rock frozen in place. It had taken us nearly three hours to climb from the col to the plateau, more than twice as much time as we had originally allowed for this section. Climbing close together, the three of us peeked over the edge at nearly the same moment. The plateau spread out before us, and no more than a hundred feet away, our familiar tent was pitched on the ice. Someone was pacing nervously around it. When he spotted us he waved once and began walking toward us. It was Pirate.

We expected him to run up to us, bursting with the news that they had reached the summit the previous day, but Pirate ambled quietly across the wind-swept ice, not even bothering to greet us with his customary chorus of growls and oaths.

"Did you all make the top?" Dave yelled. The three of us were ready to whoop and holler and leap and mob Pirate with hugs of congratulations, but Pirate's silence and then his few words cut us short. "Naw, we didn't even try."

We were stunned. We had been certain that at least Pirate and Gregg would have made an attempt. Someone should have tried for the summit during the two days of clear weather.

Motioning us toward the tent, Pirate told us how the cold and altitude had forced them to camp the first night at the col. He said John had fought every foot of the way to make it to the plateau, and that Gregg and George had gone all out to make it this high.

Dave unwrapped the cord that bound the entrance to the tent. We wiggled in. Gregg, John, and George, still in their sleeping bags, were delighted to see us, but after the initial greetings they seemed to find it difficult to appear cheerful. Their drawn features made them appear like invalids recuperating from a prolonged illness. It seemed to me that John had aged several years since I'd last seen him.

Neither Shiro, Dave, nor I mentioned that we had planned to bivouac on the summit; that was forgotten, never to be mentioned again. We listened to George say we'd be lucky if anyone made it to the summit. And we heard John tell us we'd have to try in the next few days because he should be back in Cleveland within a week. Gregg fluctuated; one moment he was fired with determination to make the summit, then he'd say something like, "Well, we can be happy we got this far."

Someone began brewing a kettle of tea. The ice in our large pot took twenty minutes to melt into water; the water took another ten minutes to warm up enough to draw the flavor out of our tea bags. Eventually, and with a rather forced casualness, Gregg mentioned that his foot might be frostbitten.

We looked at Gregg's right foot. His big toe was slightly purplish. George said that only the skin was affected and that if Gregg consumed huge quantities of liquid and was careful not to lace his boots too tightly, the damaged tissue would not prevent him from trying to climb to the summit.

But there it was—frostbite. I couldn't help wondering if this was just the beginning. Gregg's foot could become worse. Who would be next? This slight freezing had happened below our high camp; what might happen above where it would certainly be colder and windier? For a moment I experienced a keen awareness that up here the cold, surrounding us like a living thing, was waiting patiently for a chance to slip into our bodies.

We had read about frostbite as a hazard of high-altitude climbing; it had been a word we had casually thrown around in conversation. For me, the sight of Gregg's discolored foot had made frostbite something real.

Before we had drunk the teapot dry, Shiro, in the gentle but forceful manner that made us look to him for leadership, insisted that a better camp must be made without delay. "This tent is exposed to wind," he said. "We forgot to pack up those nice warm igloos we built down below." Because the surface of the plateau was too hard for cutting igloo blocks, Shiro suggested we chop out an ice cave.

Taking the initiative, Shiro untagled himself from a pile of food, cooking gear, and an untidy assortment of legs and arms to crawl out of the tent in search of a site suitable for a cave. A few minutes later he located a cornice and began burrowing into it. Like a wave of snow and ice, this cornice had been fashioned by the wind to resemble a breaker about to crash landward. The cold had caught and held this surf of the storms suspended above the precipice of ice and rock that fell away nearly three thousand feet. Shiro had begun tunneling a few feet from a blunt, eight-foot column of rock that thrust out from the base of the cornice.

Pirate and Dave stepped in to relieve Shiro, who had become overwhelmed by an attack of coughing. It was several minutes before he managed to force away the coughs and catch his breath; he lay back on his pack. His forehead was knotted into an expression I had never before seen on his face. Through his well-guarded emotions I thought I glimpsed anger at his affliction, and perhaps for not being as big and strong as Dave and Pirate. I had noticed that Shiro always tried to do as much of the strenuous work as anyone.

With their long arms wielding an axe or a shovel, Dave and

Pirate tore into the cornice. Their red and black beards iced up solid from exhaled moisture. Often they stretched back on the ice to gasp for breath. Sometimes Shiro or George would relieve Dave and Pirate briefly. I caught myself thinking how much faster the cave would have been completed if Farine's heavily muscled arms and shoulders had been in there digging. For almost two weeks I hadn't heard his name mentioned.

George and John stationed themselves at the entrance of the excavation, which still appeared more like an enormous, oddly shaped gopher hole than a mountaineer's ice cave. They shoveled or kicked loose snow and chunks of ice three feet west of the entrance, where the debris cleared the edge of the plateau to drop the three thousand feet to the basin we had just climbed up from. We would have to be careful getting in and out of our new home lest we too take the plunge back down to the 14,400-foot igloos.

Instead of helping to mine out our new home, I excused myself from the physical labor to go through the physiological tests with Gregg and to clean my cameras. The others, except for Dave, who mumbled a bit under his beard, accepted my reason for spending the afternoon in the tent. I did need to do some testing, but the truth was that I felt too weak to be of much help, and I didn't want the others to know I was feeling bad.

After testing, Gregg and I whiled away an hour or so talking strategy. How many days could we wait for a chance at the summit? John had to get back, but we did have a five-day supply of food in addition to a five-day emergency reserve which we'd break into only if a storm clamped down on us. We concluded that we had a maximum of six days in which to gather our strength and wait for optimal summit-assault weather.

Barely an hour before dark Gregg and I heard the others call that the cave had been completed. We left the tent to move into the cave. As I walked the thirty-odd yards to our new home I had to stop twice to rest. Since the ice was mostly level, I knew I shouldn't find it this difficult to cross over to the cave. Something was wrong with me. John spotted me panting and leaning against a rock; he asked how I felt. Muttering something about the fantastic view from this spot, I tried minimizing my dizziness.

Inside the cave, tucked deep into my bag, I felt better, well enough to help cook supper. I convinced myself that I'd be feeling strong by morning. The hot soup warmed our chilled and tired bodies. It was a little too cold, −51°, to be comfortable, but it felt good to be bedding down only a day's climb from the summit.

Alone

I SLEPT POORLY, and the tossing I heard through the night indicated that the others were also managing to get only short spells of fitful sleep. I was wakened by a gentle rattling of pans; Shiro was starting breakfast.

Our camp came to life more quietly than ever before. After our usual yawns and questions about the weather we sat silent over our oatmeal. The altitude had been working away at us during the night. No one was well rested. We had no energy to spare for joking and idle conversation.

The first person out of the cave shouted back that it was too windy for a summit attempt. The weather we feared most was the violent wind, which can rise within an hour's time from a gentle breeze. When masses of wind begin blowing over McKinley some wind is always forced through the passes and cols at velocities which have been reported at 150 mph and more. We were especially cautious about venturing out from this high camp because only a thousand feet above, and right on our route, was Denali Pass, the most notorious wind slot on the mountain. Up high in winter even a 50-mph wind could destroy a climbing party, because at $-50°$ a 50-mph wind creates an equivalent wind-chill temperature well below $-100°$. None of us had ever experienced conditions like that, but we expected that if the wind caught us above this camp there could be no retreat except to dig under the ice and sit it out.

Even if that morning had been calm, I doubt that anyone would have been ready to try for the summit. We were simply too tired.

Until I left the cave to relieve myself there was nothing to do with the day but settle back into our sleeping bags to wait for a morning without wind. I crawled out from under the flap of parachute that covered our cave's entrance without any premonition of what was coming. As soon as I stood up the cornice swung out from under my feet and the sky seemed to break away from the earth's grip. I leaned against the rock column to keep from toppling over the edge and breathed deeply many times before my head began to clear.

I sat still till I thought all the dizziness had left me, then tried to swallow a vitamin pill. The stubborn capsule stuck part way down my dry throat, and in seconds I had spewed my breakfast onto the snow. My head began aching. I felt sweat on my forehead. Little waves of nausea swept over me and I decided to squirm my way back into the cave on my belly.

There was no need to discuss what had to be done; we had no choice. Everyone but Pirate and George prepared to descend. At 14,400 feet I'd have a better chance to recuperate. As everyone hustled around me, I overheard someone say that if we didn't get off in an hour or two I might have to be carried down—I shuddered at the thought of being lowered down the ridge rocks and then the ice wall. Gregg decided that four people would be enough to get me down if I passed out along the way, and somehow it was decided Pirate and George would remain at our high camp so that at least two people would have a chance at the summit in case the rest of us never returned to this plateau. Hopefully, we'd be back up in two days, but there was no way of knowing.

Dejected, my head throbbing, I rested while the others hurriedly broke camp. I hated to think that I wouldn't be able to try for the summit myself. And, as my fears raced on, I pictured myself having to be airlifted off the mountain by helicopter. The worst torment was that the others were being forced to descend because of my sickness, my weakness.

To cheer me up John and Dave said they could use a rest at 14,400 feet themselves. Gregg, worried about his foot, told me he welcomed the chance to pick up some more socks at the igloos. As Shiro shoved my things into my pack, he reassured me that a single night at 14,400 feet would clear up the type of altitude sickness I had. George added that he didn't think I was suffering from anything as serious as pulmonary edema, and that I would be fit to give the summit a try after a few day's of rest.

"Day after tomorrow," Shiro said "you'll be back here." He winked at me. "Everything be O.K."

"You bet, Shiro." But I hardly believed it. I wanted to shrug off their reassurances, but at the same time I wanted them to comfort me.

We roped up. Shiro and Dave were on my rope; I went first. If I slipped, they would be behind me to hold my fall. I stepped down over the rocks and ice much more slowly than I had coming up the other day. Whenever the ridge began swaying, I leaned against a rock or on my ice axe until my dizziness cleared away.

The ridge was the most demanding part of the descent. We edged our crampons from ice to rock to loose snow. My legs were unsteady. I concentrated on my balance and on where I'd next set down my boot. I crept along the snow ramps, which now seemed to be impossibly narrow catwalks. I accused the gusty breeze of trying to trip me up.

Three or four times I asked Dave to secure himself and belay me over a tricky spot. I noticed his eyes following every movement of my feet. It was reassuring to know that his strong hands and arms were holding the rope.

We rested only a few minutes when we reached the col. Hastily, we clipped into the fixed ropes and continued down. Several hundred feet below the col I realized that the breeze was no longer prying at my balance. Already the air seemed to be thicker. I felt stronger. Perhaps it was only psychological relief that made me feel better; I was happy to be off the ridge.

Despite the rest stops that came every few hundred feet, our descent down the ropes was rapid compared to our travel on the ridge. All at once we were off the ropes and walking toward the igloos. Shiro got me into a sleeping bag. Dave passed me cup after cup of hot milk. I nibbled on some cheese and salami. Before the main meal was cooked, and before I had a chance to sit back and worry about my chances of going up again, I was asleep.

I didn't stir until laughter woke me around mid-morning the next day. When I grumbled about the racket the others were making, someone repeated Gregg's story about his first job; in a soap factory he had accidently emptied a several-hundred-gallon vat of shampoo onto a street, causing traffic to jam up behind a cloud of suds and bubbles.

I discovered I could laugh again, and, what's more, it seemed that I'd been given a new body during the night. My head was clear; I could think faster than I had been able to up above the previous day. My muscles felt so good that when I stepped out of the igloo for a breath of fresh air I had an urge to sprint across the basin and back. After gulping down a huge breakfast, I became restless for action. No one was more surprised than myself that I seemed to have recovered from my bout of mountain sickness.

Before I had awakened it had been decided that we would indulge in a lazy day, marking it off to time needed for acclimatizing. As the hours of reading and storytelling passed, I realized that since we had been up to 17,200 feet and back together, a new warmth flowed between us. We thought fondly of Pirate and George stuck together at our high camp; John observed that neither of them had been seen cooking in the nearly four weeks we'd been on the mountain; Gregg took bets as to which one would break down to mess with the stove and pots or whether they were both sitting up there getting hungrier as the day dwindled away.

The night came and went, and the next morning was mostly gone by the time Gregg and John stirred themselves to begin the climb back up to 17,200 feet. Shiro, Dave, and I were happy enough to loaf a while longer in this basin's relatively thick air; we planned to follow at about three in the afternoon, which would put us on the ridge in the light of the full moon that was due to rise a little after 6 P.M. John and Gregg had disappeared above the col when the time came for the three of us to start out. We roped close together, not more than twenty feet apart, so we could chat on the way up. As we toddled leisurely out of camp Dave suddenly stopped to cup his ear. In a moment he pointed up to the rocks on the edge of the 17,200-foot plateau. Straining my eyes, I could barely make out a tiny, orange speck which had to be Pirate. A thin, unintelligible call wafted down to us. Shiro said "Well, I bet he's saying, 'ALL RIGHT, YOU GUYS, LET'S GO!' "

Dave and I had to laugh at soft-spoken Shiro's attempt to sound like the Pirate. We figured that George and Pirate hadn't gone for the summit because the previous day had been a bit windy and they couldn't have gone today and be back already.

I filmed our approach to the fixed ropes with back lighting from the setting sun. By the time all three of us were on the fixed lines, twilight was being replaced by the darkness that was settling in briefly before the moon rose. We lingered, talking about nothing in particular, until the highest points on Mt. Foraker were illuminated with silver light. We climbed slowly at first, not anxious to reach the crest or the camp, but content to watch the moon rise.

As the light spread down the ridges of Foraker, onto Crosson, Hunter, and the Kahiltna Peaks, our pace quickened; too much excitement filled the air for us to climb slowly. Eventually, even the rocks atop the ice wall were lit by the moon we couldn't yet see directly. In our minds we began to climb faster than the methodical falling of our feet on the ice and our laboring lungs permitted. Above us shapes of ice and rock, silhouetted against the empty sky, appeared to be celebrating the arrival of the full moon. The rope tied us together physically, and Shiro's pace bound us together with its steady rhythm. At one point, high on the wall, we paused on our stairway of niches in the ice to observe a sight never before seen from this vantage point—the full moon appeared from behind McKinley's southern flank to light, each in its turn, the sweeping ice and rock couloirs and columns of the range.

Reaching the pass, I became intrigued by the patterns of moonlight among the rocks jutting out of the ridge's crest. To the north rolled away an expanse of low, silver clouds, broken only by two hills rising into the moonlight like a pair of white whales surfacing. To the south the low clouds rolled away unbroken to the horizon. Resting at the col, our eyes traveled over endless variations of ice and rock that held a fascination not apparent in daylight.

"Wow," Dave murmured, breaking the silence. "This makes all the work worthwhile."

"It's a little cold." Shiro beamed as he spoke. "Maybe we go on."

Dave checked his thermometer— −38°. He looked fondly toward Foraker. "We best be movin'."

Reluctant to leave, I asked if it wouldn't be just as safe, since we would need headlamps to continue up in the shadow of the ridge and had only two between the three of us, if I slept here and joined everyone at 17,200 feet in the morning. Though they must have guessed I was rationalizing, they agreed to let me wait alone until it became light. Both Dave and Shiro knew me well enough to know I wanted to be by myself for a while.

I watched their dark forms merge upward into the shadows. For a moment the black rocks glistened with white light from the passing headlamps. After they had disappeared I listened to the squeaking of their crampons into the ice. Occasionally, I heard a faint call: "To the left," "Loose rock, Dave." When there was silence I relaxed, turned, and gazed again out over the Kuskokwim.

The two white whales were still frozen in their arch out of the sea of ice fog and clouds. Long, snow-covered ridges of the McKinley massif flowed into the fog like white rivers into estuaries of darkness. I pictured the little animals that would be awake below the surface of clouds; ptarmigan and hares, moving with the quietness of the snow, would be hiding in their whiteness among the drifts, listening for prowling foxes and coyotes. Down there were streams half-choked with ice, winding across the tundra, with grayling responding to their currents in that unimaginable darkness beneath the ice.

I caught myself letting loose a long "whooo—hooooo" like the arctic owl. I listened for an echo, but my voice had disappeared into the still air. Farine would have enjoyed this night. In a few hours the moon would set; in a few days, summit or no summit, we'd have to pack up and be gone from these mountains. I called out again, this time like a wolf. Then, though afraid to face it, I turned my head toward the moon, and howled as loudly as I could.

Just at the moment I realized my hand holding the ice axe was shaking, I suddenly became self-conscious and hoped no one had heard. Howling at the moon was expected of wolves and coyotes, but not of a mountain climber. I glanced about for a place to sleep.

I chose to spread my sleeping bag on a tiny patch of more-or-less level snow barely three feet from the edge of the ice wall we had climbed up. I scrounged along the crest for loose rocks, and when I'd gathered a dozen I placed them between my sleeping bag and the fifteen-hundred-foot drop; should I start to slide or roll in my sleep I knew I'd wake up as I bumped into these fist-sized stones. Curled deep into the folds of down, delighted to be only an arm's length from the edge, I fell asleep with that particular satisfaction and relief which can come from securing yourself from danger.

A stiff breeze, gusting along the ridge, increased the chill factor until the cold penetrated my sleeping bag and woke me. I looked out of my bag at the pale morning light; the sky was clear but too windy, I thought, to start for the summit. I dozed for another hour or so before coaxing myself out of the bag to dress and head up to the plateau with a fifty-pound load of food and personal gear. Because I was governed by the heavy load to a step, two-second rest, step sort of plod, over two hours passed before I rounded the rock tower near the top of the ridge. With a clear sight of the ice wall rising to Denali Pass, I spotted two black specks high on the ice. I realized the wind had died down. The specks moved. The others must be trying for the summit, I thought.

I had been left behind. They had probably waited as long as they could before starting up without me. I could blame only myself for not being with them. My pace quickened, but after a few steps it occured to me that if I exhausted myself by trying to rush I'd ruin the slim chance I had of catching up with them.

In about twenty minutes I reached the camp, but by then the two figures on the ice had disappeared over the lip of Denali Pass. No one was in the cave. I had to decide whether to accept the risk of climbing to the summit solo. Reason told me it was foolish to try it alone, but how could I sit in the cave the rest of the day? Perhaps the altitude's effect on my brain helped twist my logic, which was already bent by my determination, because in the space of five minutes I managed to convince myself that there was a reasonably safe compromise between sitting idle in camp and bolting off after the others. I would start up alone, but the moment I felt the least bit uncertain of my footing on the ice or sensed that a crevasse might possibly stretch hidden in front of me, I'd turn back.

Despite the necessity of taking off without delay, I crawled into the cave to spend precious minutes getting the stove started to melt the water I needed in my system; fortunately, it lit quickly. I forced myself to wait until the water was warm before gulping it down; it would have been wasteful to warm it with calories in my body. I snacked on sausage, Logan bread, and some of my grandma's fruitcake. With my pockets stuffed with odds and ends of food that needed no cooking, I scrambled out of the cave. Throwing a minimum of bivouac gear into my pack I headed across the basin to the ice wall.

In a running dialogue with myself I repeated warnings to turn back the moment I became the least bit uneasy on the route. The ice steepened. A few willow wands that the others had managed to stick into the hard surface marked a twisting passage among several bergschrunds. My legs felt inexhaustible, and my senses were keyed up by the need to concentrate. I told myself again and again that there was no one to catch me if a poorly placed crampon upset my balance or if the previous day's nausea returned. I was determined to catch up with the others. I had to reach the summit.

I climbed as fast as I could, but the rest stops came more often as I worked my way up the steeper ice toward the top of the wall. Halting for a moment only a hundred feet below the edge of the pass, I caught myself half hoping that the others wouldn't reach the summit today. I felt ashamed. Could I really be climbing with such disgusting selfishness? I disliked admitting it, but, at the moment, I was being driven up the route by the fear that I would be disgraced by being the only one not to reach the summit. Just a few hours ago I had felt the selfless joy of watching the moon rise without thought of success or failure.

For what seemed like hours I stood on the shelf I had chopped in the ice. I didn't care to climb up and was too listless to start down. I wondered how the others struggled with their pride. Pirate appeared horribly vain at times; as George was always ready to point out, Pirate seemed to thrive on attention. But I thought he didn't climb for acclaim as much as to satisfy his energetic nature's need for action and adventure. As for George himself, though he always shied away from publicity, I knew he was a proud man, aware of the image he presented to others. Since Dave and Gregg often spoke of improving themselves, I figured mountaineering accomplishments probably boosted their self-esteem, yet I was sure they both derived an immense joy from climbing that was completely removed from thoughts of recognition. Shiro had a deep reverence for the mountains, but I'd noticed that he didn't seem to mind if people respected him because he had climbed many difficult peaks. John took delight in the moods of the mountains and in the comradeship of our expedition, and at the same time he applied himself to the ascent with an exaggerated need to handle his share of the work and prove he could do as much as someone like Dave, who outweighed him by forty pounds. But did it really matter whether pride was part of the reason why we climbed?

Though pride had fired me up to attempt a solo ascent this morning, I thought, as I had so often during the last few weeks, of another underlying motivation that had sent me to McKinley in midwinter. Cold and thin air at even moderate altitudes could incapacitate my father, whom emphysema had left with part of only one lung. Since a stroke had partially paralyzed my mother she could barely manage to step up onto a street curb. I hadn't told any of the others, but I somehow expected my attempt to climb up to this cold and highest point on the continent to compensate for their weakness. And I felt a need to assert my will to live through my climbing because my parents had tried, out of pain and a sense of helplessness, to kill themselves.

Still resting on the three-inch-wide ledge I'd chopped near the top of the ice wall, my thoughts wandered to a motivating force that seemed separate from my personal situation. I remembered my favorite fish. Its Latin name I've forgotten, but it is one that occasionally leaps out of its pond to rest awhile on a bank or in the branches of a tree. I doubt that the fish has the wits to understand why it tries to live in the air. An evolutionary force beyond its comprehension must compel it to jump into a new element. Sometimes I thought of our reaching up into the cold, darkness, and thin air of McKinley's summit in the winter as simply our way of obeying a force we couldn't understand.

My ankles and calves began to weary from standing immobile on my little shelf hundreds of feet above the basin. Cautiously, and much more slowly than before, I continued up the ice. After a few steps all the troublesome reflective thoughts receded. I climbed at ease; the unrestrained passion that had started me up the wall had been replaced by a lighthearted sense of well-being. I'd just take a look at the pass, go up to meet the others as they came down from the summit. It would be fine if I reached the top, but not necessary. I'd go as high as I could.

A slight breeze drifted through the pass; it struck me as a much more pleasant spot than its reputation for miserable weather had made me expect. Above the route was mostly clouded in, but by following the marks that the crampons of the others had left in the snow and ice I found my way up among several outcroppings of rock. The higher I climbed, the poorer visibility became; I considered turning back several times, but the tracks continued to be easy to follow. About an hour above the pass, three figures loomed toward me out of the mist. Three others soon appeared.

Gregg was astonished to find me here. He said he knew me well enough to expect me to try it solo, but hadn't imagined I'd get this high. Disappointment was written on his and the others' faces, but I asked about the summit anyway. It pained me to hear Dave say that at a little above nineteen thousand feet they had been stopped by clouds obscuring the route. Realizing how foolish it would have been to grope blindly toward the summit, they had waited a half hour for the frozen mist to clear. When it didn't break away, there was no alternative but to descend. Enough energy had been expended in this effort to make most of us want a rest day to recoup our strength. Since a storm might hit before we were fit for another attempt, there was a good chance that this would turn out to be our last chance to go for the summit.

George's shoulders slumped; he didn't talk; his whole being appeared discouraged. In light of his earlier difficulty, I admired him for making it this far, but of course for George this wasn't far enough; he had come on the expedition to make the summit. His voice was full of hurt when he said: "Well, we've had it. Maybe Dave has the strength to climb up here again, but I don't think I do."

John looked more exhausted than discouraged. He had pushed himself harder to get this high than most climbers have pushed themselves in reaching the summit. I tied into one of the ropes, and, as we climbed down, I wondered whether John felt the sense of accomplishment he deserved.

As we approached the rocks, something about the pass looked unfamiliar. The rocks didn't look the same as when I'd climbed up. It took me a moment to realize that the outcroppings of rock appeared strange because the clouds were thinning, causing the rocks to stand out more clearly. Someone called to look behind us, at the ridge above.

The sky was clearing. Not a trace of cloud remained above nineteen thousand feet.

There could be no going back up this afternoon because we would need an hour or more to ascend the distance we had climbed down in ten minutes. Night was close at hand, only two and a half hours away—no one was well equipped for a bivuoac. We had to continue down. If they had only waited above nineteen thousand feet for another fifteen minutes, everyone, except perhaps myself, would probably have reached the summit.

Gregg and George cramponed down the ice ahead of me; John was tied in behind. The ice rolled down in steps, and on the steepest one John asked for a belay. Being closest to him, I was the natural one to anchor myself and hold the rope steady while he stepped down the tricky section. There was no rock or level spot on which to securely station myself, and the ice was too hard to dig my axe in. I told John that it was impossible for me to belay him, that he'd have to climb down unprotected.

Gregg and George, who had heard everything, told me that I damn well better give John a belay. George said it was unforgivable that I'd even think of letting John risk the chance of falling. Gregg told me I ought to stick at least the tip of the axe point into the ice and brace my foot against the shaft. I said, my voice rising, that it wouldn't work. Gregg told me I didn't know what I was doing.

John was so tired that he might easily have slipped at this point. If he did fall, we would most likely all be jerked off. George shouted at me to belay him. I refused but wouldn't give my reason for not even trying the method Gregg had suggested. I feared that if John depended on the rope with a false sense of security he would not try as hard to keep his balance and fight to arrest his fall should he start slipping.

I looked back up at John; his legs wobbled, but he faced into the ice and began climbing down. In a moment he was over it; our pace quickened. We belayed over the lip of the pass and once again further down the ice wall. Before long we had crossed the basin and were trudging up the short rise to the cave's entrance. When we unroped Gregg gave me a stony glance.

As we jostled good-naturedly for space inside the cave, the incident with John was mostly forgotten. The seven of us contended with a new problem—food. If we all waited for another summit chance we'd be out of food (except for the emergency reserve) in three days. Naturally, if only three of us remained, much less food would be eaten each day, allowing this group to wait as long as a week for a chance at the summit. But if only the three strongest remained, the other four would have to face retreating to the igloos at 14,000 feet, giving up their chance to reach the summit. Far into the night we tried to decide who, if anyone, should go down.

John was the only one to volunteer to descend; he said he was the weakest and since he had to get back to his university position, he thought he and maybe just one other person could leave the mountain before the summit was climbed. His offer made some sense, but no one liked the thought of John not being with us, nor the prospect of only two people descending the heavily crevassed areas around Windy Corner and down on the Kahiltna.

Shiro asked John why he was rubbing and fiddling with one of his ears. John said it had been chilled during the day and had hurt ever since he had warmed up inside the cave. George crawled over several of us to take a close look at John's ear; he flashed Gregg's headlamp on the side of John's head. After a few seconds he said it looked like superficial frostbite.

George turned to take a look at the raw end of Dave's nose, which Dave insisted was only peeling layers of windburned skin, and discovered that it too had been slightly frostbitten. Dave shrugged his shoulders and said he had always thought his nose was a bit long and that it would be fine with him if the tip fell off.

Gregg's foot appeared to be no worse and no better. The purple patch on his big toe had darkened somewhat, as expected, but the discoloration hadn't spread. Gregg said one injured toe wasn't going to slow him down; then he changed the subject.

I noticed for the first time that one of Pirate's thumbs was bound in wads of gauze and tape. When I asked him about it he grumbled something like, "Ah, its nothing." John told me the thumb had been gashed rather deeply.

All of us, except Pirate, took a sleeping pill. Perhaps I could have slept without a pill, but I did not want to take a chance on being half rested when we went for the summit. It annoyed me that we hadn't been able to decide how many and which of us would sit tight at this high camp until the time was right for a summit assault. If the next morning broke clear and windless, we'd have no dilemma because anyone feeling up to it could try for the summit. However, if the weather turned bad, we would have to face the tough decision of who had to descend. Since everyone but John appeared determined to have another crack at the summit, we would probably have to let the strongest make the attempt.

I had been almost as fit as Dave and Pirate before my bout of mountain sickness, and I felt strong once again. I had not experienced any further dizziness, but I feared the others might decide I would have to go down because I might be apt to become nauseous again.

After the candles had been snuffed out, I lay still, listening to the others breathing heavily and waiting for my pill to take effect. Occasionally I could hear a muffled cough from Shiro, who had buried his head inside his sleeping bag.

Darkness

SHIRO WOKE AT FIRST LIGHT and crawled across our bodies to reach the parachute covering the entrance. After a quick check of the weather he crawled back to his sleeping bag and announced softly to whomever might be awake that it was clear but windy.

We dozed in our bags, reluctant to leave their warmth for the chores of getting dressed, relieving ourselves, and cooking. Soon we'd have to decide who was going down, but for the moment I tried to go back to sleep. Even with my head inside my sleeping bag, I could hear the parachute flapping over the entrance; someone must have loosened it to go outside. I poked my head out in time to see Pirate hurrying back into the cave with some gas for the stove.

I hunched up against the back wall of the cave to give Shiro room to fill and prime the stove; after a few minutes of tinkering he had it purring softly. He melted some ice and made a pot of oatmeal with raisins. "Maybe wind die down," he said, "and we have chance for summit later in morning."

We ate. We listened to the loose folds of parachute flap in the wind. We got dressed, and eventually went out to relieve ourselves. Outside the wind blew less strongly than the parachute had made it sound; it even seemed to be slackening off. It was −43°. There was not a cloud in sight, and although the sun which was already hitting our plateau didn't raise the air temperature appreciably, it did warm us psychologically with its dazzling brightness.

"Hell, let's go for the summit!" Pirate was pacing restlessly in front of the entrance.

"We could climb to Denali Pass, turn back if it's windy, or go on if it's calm," Dave said.

Around our cave the wind had died down to an occasional light gust which would whisk loose snow along the frozen surface. Our eyes searched the ridges above for the blowing plumes of snow which are the sure signs of a high wind; we didn't see any. Why not try for the summit?

Our sleepy camp suddenly buzzed with excitement as we hustled to get our gear ready. George said he was too tired from the previous day to give it a try. John too was still worn out; he told us that if he went anywhere it would have to be down because his ear had become swollen during the night. Gregg could not make up his mind whether or not to come. Dave, Shiro, Pirate, and I hurried to depart.

Pirate's suggestion that we go extremely light was overruled by Shiro's insistence that we take sleeping bags, foam pads, and a stove part way up in case nightfall or an accident forced a bivouac. Pirate offered to pack up the radio—he wanted to call his father in Switzerland from the summit—but balked at packing the extra weight of a sleeping bag and pad. Gregg finally made up his mind —he'd go. Scoffing at the idea of everyone having to lug up a sleeping bag, he said that if we got stuck out for the night he and Pirate could crawl in with someone else.

I left my movie camera and film in a nylon bag inside the cave. Since our arrival at this 17,200-foot plateau, the camera's gears had frozen up. Several times I had warmed the camera next to my body only to hear the cold grind it to a halt soon after I would try to film. I experienced an unexpected relief in setting the camera aside. Not only wouldn't I have to bother freezing the tips of my fingers while I ran the camera, but I wouldn't have to worry about trying to record our climbing on film. No more observing through the lens. I'd just climb.

Shiro, the first to have his personal gear packed, selected enough food to last five days if a storm caught us. By ten o'clock everyone except Gregg was set to take off. Pirate and Dave grew a little impatient with him because losing any more time would hurt our chances of reaching the summit and almost preclude a descent without a bivouac. Gregg, bristling at their implication that he was a slowpoke, said that they could leave immediately and he'd follow shortly if someone would wait to rope up with him.

Which three should start off? Each of us were anxious to be on the first rope, and on the fastest rope. Shiro said to Dave, Pirate, and me in his usual unassuming way: "You three go now. You are strongest. I come with Gregg."

I tied into the rope behind Dave and Pirate, cinching several loops tightly around my waist. We shouldered our packs and grabbed our ice axes. Each of us wore goggles to cut the reflection of the sun off the ice; Dave, I noticed, had put on Farine's Himalayan glasses.

John and George shook hands with us and said, each in their own way, that they hoped we'd make it. They waved as we set out across the basin at a brisk, smooth pace. As the angle of the ice increased we climbed with slower, more calculated steps. The wind had all but disappeared. Through the dark lenses of our goggles the sky appeared a deep, tranquil blue. The basin receded below us; Shiro and Gregg moved as tiny dark figures on the whiteness of the ice. Behind them the sharp white forms of the Kahiltna Peaks, Foraker, and Crosson cut the sky, and to the north and west patches of low gray clouds drifted across the flat tundra. Our crampons gripped the ice, which rose steeply above us to Denali Pass and fell away below.

Cautiously, we climbed diagonally up the steep final hundred yards of ice below the pass. Finally reaching the level ice at the pass, we decided to wait for Shiro and Gregg, still a quarter of a mile below. Dave led us to the south end of the pass to look for a place to cache the food and sleeping bags. Finding a sheltered corner in an outcropping of rocks, we sat on our packs and nibbled on raisins and nuts while we waited. Before long the cold in the ice

reached through our packs to chill our bottoms. We had begun stepping in place to warm our toes by the time Gregg and Shiro appeared
over the rim of the pass; they climbed the gentle slope to our resting
spot very slowly. Anxious to be off again, Dave, Pirate, and I urged
them to quickly cache the emergency gear and set the pace on up the
route. Shiro looked tired. Gregg hesitated. "I don't know," he said,
looking down toward our ice cave. "I feel strong enough, but my
heart's just not in it today."

I couldn't figure out what was wrong with him; his lack of enthusiasm puzzled me. Lately he had seemed so indifferent to complet-
ing the climb that I wondered whether he was losing his old love
for climbing, or maybe the memory of Farine was bothering him. I
drew him aside and spoke quietly. "Gregg, after all the two of us
have gone through to get this far, we've got to go for the summit
together."

"No, you and Dave and Pirate can climb faster than I can," he said.
"Besides, we've got only three sleeping bags here, and it's going to get
dark before you return. It's really safer for everyone to have a bag, so
you guys take mine. I'll make it tomorrow." Gregg turned back to the
group.

I wondered whether Gregg really wanted to go down. He was right
in saying that it would be safer if all five of us didn't continue. In an
emergency the food we brought up would last longer if fewer people
had to depend on it. Maybe Gregg was simply making light of his
sacrifice by saying he wasn't feeling too hot. Even if his original
enthusiasm had faded, he had come such a long way. The summit was
close. He knew he could make it. But our safety was evidently more
important to Gregg than reaching the summit himself. We were silent
for a moment. Shiro spoke first.

"I think I'll feel stronger tomorrow," he said. "I'll come up with
Gregg and maybe John and George. Looks like the weather should
stay good."

It didn't seem fair that either Shiro or Gregg go down. Pirate and Dave both took turns trying to convince Shiro and Gregg to continue, but in the end we shook their hands, slapped their shoulders affectionately, and left them behind.

Dave remained tied into the middle of the rope, with Pirate at the opposite end from myself; they had asked me to take the lead. I set a pace considerably slower than I knew we could climb because I wanted to conserve our strength for later. Between each step I paused long enough to take one breath. After we had put about forty yards behind us, I stopped for a minute's rest. Looking back the way we had come, we saw Gregg and Shiro kneeling over the ice and rocks which we had decided would offer reasonable protection from a possible wind should nightfall force a delay at Denali Pass on our way down. To secure our bivuoac equipment they were piling small rocks on top of our sleeping bags and the section of parachute which Shiro had decided to bring at the last moment. Both Gregg and Shiro had spoken confidently of attempting the summit the next day, but all of us knew that on McKinley, notorious for its sudden storms, one could never count on the next day being clear.

I led slowly up the ice, around scattered outcroppings of rock, over slight rises of wind-packed snow, all the time keeping close to the crest of the ridge. The next time I halted to rest Gregg and Shiro had disappeared; they were either hidden behind some rocks or had already started down. The ice around us had a harsh and ragged feeling to it; the wind-carved drifts were not delicate and elegant as they had been down on the Kahiltna.

"How's the pace I'm setting?"

"O.K., Dad."

Minutes and hours slipped away as we gradually gained altitude. The high point of the previous day was reached; the sky above held clear and breezeless. I turned from the ridge to cut left across a basin. My eyes usually focused on the ice a foot or two in front of my feet, because the flat afternoon light made it difficult to see all the ups and downs of the ice. Suddenly a crevasse gaped in front of me. Our procession came to an abrupt halt. My heart pounded faster; I'd come within a step of casually walking over the edge.

The crevasse stretched the length of the basin, and we searched thirty to forty yards in each direction without finding a place we could easily cross. Eventually, I turned back to a possibility we had considered a bit dangerous when we had first seen it. A thin ice ramp ran down to a lower level—not the bottom—of the crevasse. The ramp merged into a horizontal snow-bridge which looked stable but didn't reach all the way to the other side of the crevasse. We would have to jump across a two-foot gap onto an ice platform of questionable strength.

Dave put me on belay. I tiptoed down the ramp, trying to keep as many crampon points as possible on its narrow edge. I stepped along the snow-bridge, studied the platform for a moment, then swung one leg across the dark gap taking care not to jar the ice when my boot touched the other side. The platform held; I scampered across and up the other side of the crevasse. Reassured that it was a safe crossing, Dave and Pirate climbed across with quick, confident movements.

Negotiating the crevasse had taken about forty-five minutes. The sun was now hidden from our sight behind the crest of the ridge, and toward the southwest the sky was filling with the first pastel yellow of evening. We hurriedly angled back to the ridge, but because of the altitude I soon had to gauge down our pace to allow two breaths between each step. Every thirty steps I'd pause to count out fifteen breaths before continuing.

Ahead of us Archdeacon's Tower arched gracefully into the sky. The scattered clouds we had seen drifting over the tundra had begun packing up against the foothills. Another bank of clouds had socked in around the base of the range to the south and west. They weren't alarming because we had often watched storms gather and then spend their force at lower elevations while McKinley's upper reaches remained clear.

I began forcing our pace up the ridge. Not a word had been said about the approach of evening, yet it was obvious we would soon have to decide whether to climb on after the sun set or hightail it back to the cave. We climbed steadily, but just as steadily the white glare of the sun diminished to yellow, then to orange as the sun slipped into the dusky haze above the horizon. In the emptiness of the thin air the sky seemed especially enormous.

Our ridge gave way to a basin rimmed with smaller ridges. Archdeacon's Tower rose off to our left. A higher ridge, perhaps the summit ridge itself, appeared in the distance. Pirate shouted for me to hold up a second.

"Man, we're getting close!" Dave said.

"Yea, and it's getting dark," I replied.

"Hey Art, why don't you take off your dark glasses?" Pirate laughed.

Sure enough, with the goggles off the sky was lighter. However, the sun remained an orange ball suspended beyond Foraker. If we went on, we probably wouldn't reach the summit before nightfall. I asked Dave what he thought. He said a night out wasn't going to kill us. Pirate growled his agreement. I told Dave that I'd be glad to let him take the lead; I felt good when he said I was doing fine and ought to stay with it.

A few minutes after we had begun climbing again, we gained the crest of a low rise, then headed across a small basin toward the crest of another rise. The landscape rolled and rose around us like a sea of enormous, frozen swells. Each of us concentrated on the contours and variations of the ice, because we needed to inscribe the pattern of our route onto our minds to help guide us down in the dark. The only trail we would be able to follow by the light of our headlamps consisted of our crampon marks in the snow and ice.

I plodded more slowly than ever up the slope of ice which hid the summit ridge. When I reached the crest only a broad plateau lay between us and the ice wall which rose straight to the final ridge. Suddenly, nothing was hidden! All the ice lay clear and sharp before us! Our remaining uncertainty vanished! We were going to reach the summit! For the first time in all the years I had been climbing, tears rolled down my cheeks as I looked toward the summit of a mountain.

Dave climbed up to me with a big grin on his face; he grabbed my arm and shook it in his excitement. Pirate reached us out of breath, mixing growls and laughter with his gulping for air. In our minds we had already climbed to the summit. I wiped the tears from my cheeks before they had a chance to freeze.

"Art! Do you see the spires?" Dave waved his arms, "Oh honcho boncho!"

The western edge of the horizon was serrated by the jagged, black forms of the Cathedral Spires. Until now they had remained hidden from us behind the sprawling southern system of Foraker. The previous summer Dave and I had climbed together in the spires, precipitous peaks of smooth, granite walls—like Yosemite's —rising straight out of the glaciers which riddle the Kichatna Mountains.

"Yea Dave, do you recognize Kichatna Spire and Gurney?"

We had climbed and named Kichatna Spire, the highest of the range; we had tried to climb Gurney, but the days had grown short in September, and we had run out of time. Only Dave and I shared a memory so sacred to us that we hadn't mentioned it during all the days our friendship had been strained. The last day on Gurney just the two of us had climbed together. There had been a hot sun, but the weather had turned, and as clouds had boiled up through the passes below and then around the summits above, bright-yellow light and dark shadows had raced across the smooth walls of the Spires. We had descended, leaving our ropes fixed to the rock and ice, with every intention of returning to them when the weather improved. But we had never been able to climb back up to our ropes. The image of those ropes fixed in place had remained vividly in my mind, and now it evoked an immeasurable sadness.

The three of us ate some cheese and sausage. Dave pulled a sack of gorp out of one of his pockets. The varied evening colors in the sky and the vastness of the ranges of hills and mountains half obscured by clouds reflecting an orange-gray light gave an unearthly quality to everything we could see. The incredible stillness, immensity, and remoteness of the world that only the three of us inhabited gave me the notion that we were stopping for a moment in a fairytale. Something magical about the ice and rock and sky seemed about to disappear. I tried to grasp an impression of the forms and colors around us, because I feared they would suddenly vanish, to be recalled only with the vagueness of a dream half remembered, like a memory from earliest childhood.

We stretched our legs, which had stiffened during the minutes we had rested. I led us quickly across a plateau covered with wild ice drifts, unsettling evidence of the power of the wind's architecture.

Once we were on the ice wall, our progress became almost imperceptible. I was breathing four or five times between each step; after fifteen steps I would have to pause for about half a minute. I angled up to the left to skirt several bergschrunds. The ice beneath our crampons changed from a soft pink to a delicate purple as the sun set.

For the moment we didn't think of reaching the summit—it was too far away—but only of making it up the wall. Between steps I fixed my eyes on the ridgeline at the top of the wall. Step followed step, and suddenly, to my surprise, there was no more wall. I waited for the others to gain the summit ridge, then we rested several minutes before starting off again. Because the ridge rose much less steeply than the wall, I could set a faster pace, but my impatience to make the top, mixed with my weariness, disturbed the even steadiness with which we had climbed the lower sections. Pirate called for an extra rest stop; I figured he must really like his father to lug that heavy radio up here. Dave nudged me to start on again. Perhaps we should have taken time to put on our headlamps because we were climbing the ridge in the last moments of twilight, nearly an hour after the sun had sunk below the horizon.

Except for a faint blue which lingered in the west, the sky had become completely dark by the time we neared the top of the ridge. We had to carefully notice where to place our boots. A rest stop came every seven or eight steps. Behind me, Dave and Pirate were dark forms swaying against the grayness of the ice like dim shadows. No one spoke; occasionally the rope tugged me gently from behind.

The ridge ended; it simply faded into a shallow depression. To my left and right I could barely make out the lines of slightly rising ice against the sky. While I wondered which direction to head, Dave came up beside me. He said it rose to the right. I asked him to go ahead. Close together, grabbing up coils of rope in our hands, the three of us crept along the ice crest. A stiff breeze came up from the south face, which now fell away to our right and in front of us. The crest wasn't knife-edged, but we treated it as if it were because in the darkness we were unable to see the ice beneath us. Dave stopped by an aluminum pole sticking out of the ice. It took me a moment to realize that this was actually the summit marker. We grabbed each other in a three-way hug. We shouted and slapped each others' shoulders. We had made it!

We had looked forward to the view from the summit, but there was only darkness in every direction. After a few moments, Dave spotted a faint glitter of greenish lights way to the south. "Wow!" he sighed. "They look like specks of phosphorescent plankton in a black sea."

It seemed unfair to me that all we could see at the end of our journey into this wilderness of ice were the lights of Anchorage. It was as if we had never left them at all. And that aluminum rod planted in the ice annoyed me, not because someone had been here before, but because it struck me as a gross gesture of conquest.

I gazed off into the different quadrants of the black sky, trying to imagine the wild grandeur of the landscape that was hidden in the darkness. It was hard for me to picture where the ridges and glaciers ran, and my attention shifted back to that cursed aluminum pole. I wanted to forget it and enjoy these moments, but the altitude had weakened my ability to concentrate. I thought of how the aluminum ore had been dug from the earth, alloyed, molded into a shaft, carried to the top of the continent, and sunk into the snow and ice. How absurd it all was. Of course, it was simply a snow picket that another expedition had carried for safety, then left on the summit as a sign of their passing.

Pirate asked who had put the pole here. I shrugged and tried not to think about it. I said, "Look, isn't it funny that there are no stars out?" A high haze must have developed since the sun had set. Dave called my attention back to the lights by saying he noticed that curious effect of vision which made them appear brighter when we didn't look directly at them but slightly off to one side. Faint as it was, the cluster of lights gave off an illusive warmth. The green glow was almost pretty. I dreaded the thought that in a few days I'd be back among those lights, or the lights of Fairbanks; nevertheless, I began thinking fondly of people I'd see again. "Yup," Pirate barked, "there's my gal's porchlight!"

"This breeze must be about twenty knots," Dave figured.

The wind lifting up from below had begun to chill us through our parkas; we retreated the seventy-five feet back along the crest to the little hollow. On level ice again, we put on our headlamps. Dave read off the time: three minutes after seven. He checked the thermometer: −58°F. I said "Let's be moving."

Pirate set the radio on the snow, but all his twisting of dials, shaking, and rattling, cursing couldn't coax even a healthy static out of the tubes and speakers—it was too cold.

Dave dug a small pit in the ice to bury an assortment of mementos people had asked him to place on the summit; he tossed in a seal of the State of Alaska, and a cross from the diocese of which Hudson Stuck, first climber to this summit, had been archdeacon. Then, to my amazement, I watched Dave pull out of his pocket something which I thought had been lost long ago. As he placed Farine's hat in the ice, the inevitable images flicked through my mind. What were Dave and Pirate thinking? I didn't know.

While Pirate tinkered with the radio and Dave fumbled in his pack to find a flag from John's mountaineering club which had once been taken to the summit of Mt. Everest, I grew more anxious to descend. I urged them to hurry up. Pirate told me to take it easy. I felt an irrational urgency to start down. When Dave said I was acting almost paranoid, I realized I was sort of frightened. But of what? It seemed we shouldn't stay here any longer than necessary. We had a long, difficult descent ahead of us.

Pirate finally gave up on the radio; flashing my headlamp toward him, I saw how disappointed he looked. Suddenly I saw him, not as our tough old Pirate, but as a kid thinking of his home a long way off. Dave said, "O.K. Art, lead us down."

Confidently, I started down the ridge. Our headlamps illuminated about ten square feet; beyond this area everything was black. As expected, the route was traceable only by our bootmarks in the snow. Wherever the loose snow thinned, I had to stop to search for the next mark in the snow. Over and over I warned myself to forget the summit, to forget my relief. It's just beginning, I told myself. I tried to bolster up all my powers of concentration.

We stepped over the edge and down the ice wall, where only tiny niches revealed where our crampons had bit into the ice. If I lost the trail, we might wander to the right, where the ice was too steep for us to climb, or stumble across one of the bergschrunds. Each of us was well aware that, should anyone slip, we would all tumble down through the darkness to the basin five hundred feet below.

About a third of the way down the wall my eyes began watering from staring at the ice; I stopped to rest both eyes and legs. Looking out into the unbroken darkness which surrounded us, I was seized by the sensation that nothing at all was out there, that the night was empty and there remained only our three headlamps in the blackness which seemed complete.

With extreme caution, we continued down. As the ice became less steep, we moved more quickly. We didn't stop when we reached the bottom of the wall, but quickened our pace across the plateau. Once I lost sight of our tracks. I thought "Thank God for the rope!"; since I was connected to Dave who was still on the route, I could retrace my steps back to him and pick up our previous tracks again. We moved on.

My legs were beginning to feel weak and shaky. I asked whether I was going too slowly. Dave and Pirate assured me they would rather not go any faster. I began resting every few minutes. Several more times I lost the trail; each time I was able to return to where Dave had stopped and find it again. In many places the marks in the snow were barely visible even when we stared directly at them. With the greatest part of the tension behind us, weariness was overcoming our ability to concentrate.

When we reached the crevasse that stretched across the lower basin, I was suprised that we were crossing it much more quickly than we had in the daylight. We wound down the ridge and among the outcroppings of rock. Our memory of the route told us we were almost at the spot where our bivuoac equipment was cached.

After a few more minutes we stumbled onto the sleeping bags covered with the parachute and weighted down with rocks. Should we descend all the way to our cave or sleep at Denali Pass until dawn? Dave wanted to go on. Pirate, fully bushed by this time, said he would just as soon rest the few hours until it would be light. I argued that we shouldn't risk the steep ice in the dark while we were so tired. Dave insisted we get it all over with, but in the end I persuaded him that it would be safest to spend the night at the pass. Soon we were lost in the dreamless sleep of exhaustion.

March 1: −148°

Note: The expedition is split between Denali Pass and the 17,300-foot camp. With no means of communication, each group has no way of knowing what is happening to the other group. The narrative follows Dave, Pirate, and Art at Denali Pass, while diary entries written by Gregg, Shiro, George, and John during the isolation imposed by the wind record the course of events and the trend of their emotions.

17,300 FEET: GREGG, JOHN, SHIRO, GEORGE

Gregg's diary:

A frightening thing is developing, but let me start from this morning. Shiro got up early, and although there was some wind we decided to give it a go. We started off with Shiro and George and John and me roped in twos. From the time we started it was apparent we wouldn't get far. The winds aloft were howling. After a few hundred yards John pooped out, and I went ahead to tell the others. When I caught them George unroped to go back with John, and I roped in with Shiro. The idea was to go up and see that the others were all right. When we approached the pass it was evident why the others had not descended. The wind was howling like crazy. I tried to lead up to the pass but was turned back by the wind. We then traversed to a spot that we thought was directly under their bivouac site. Shiro went up and tried twice, but the wind was so fierce it was impossible. The wind was coming from our direction, and if we went one step too far it meant not getting back again.

Shiro tried another place . . . the same. . . . We retreated rapidly. Once, when Shiro had come back, I asked him what he saw. He said: "Three sleeping bags. They are in their sleeping bags." When we were just about back in camp he told me all he saw was one sleeping bag, lying up against the rock and flapping in the wind.

Shiro surmises the three are on the leeward side of the rock, covered with the parachute, with possibly two in one bag. All I know is that they must have made it back to the bivouac site, and are in a bind. If we could have reached them—they were less than a hundred feet away—we could have told them that the wind wasn't as bad on this side of the pass. We could have told them to make a try.

It's a bad situation . . . winds up to a hundred miles per hour, possibly more. It's a whiteout up there. . . . I pray at this point that they make it through. . . . They must make it through.

Much later Shiro confided: "When I saw only one sleeping bag I was certain they were dead. I told Gregg I saw three. He is very emotional. I thought maybe dangerous to alarm him. He might lose his mind."

DENALI PASS: ART, DAVE, PIRATE

The wind woke us. The wildly whipping parachute billowed and snapped with reports like those of a bullwhip or rifle. The wind blasted against the rocks we were nestled among with a deafening eruption of noise; crosscurrents in the storm fluctuated its pitch to a groan or a prolonged whine. A dull, aching pressure along my backside was the cold, pressed into me by the wind.

I twisted in my sleeping bag to grope for the loose section of parachute thrashing me from behind. The moment I caught it my hands were pierced with cold; groggy with sleep, I'd forgotten that the nylon, like everything else outside our sleeping bags, was about −40°. The cold sank into my fingers while the parachute, jerking and cracking erratically, resisted my attempts to anchor it. As soon as I managed to gather the slack material under me, the weight of my body holding it down, I shot one hand under an armpit and the other into my crotch for warmth. I was out of breath from the effort.

Drawn tighter, the parachute made less noise, and I was able to relax for a few moments. My fingers, aching inside from being deeply chilled, began to gradually rewarm with strong tingling sensations. I pressed the length of my body against Dave to be warmer on that side, and I felt Dave shift inside his bag, trying to press against me. I snuggled close to him and lay quietly for a long time, hoping I'd fall asleep again, as if not thinking about the wind and cold would make them disappear.

I couldn't sleep, and the wind only grew more vicious. I tried to ignore the cold along my backside, away from Dave, but when the first shiver ran through my body I turned to check the sleeping bag where it touched my back. To my horror it was no thicker than its shell, two pieces of nylon. The wind had pushed the down away. I could hardly believe it possible that the parachute, designed to resist wind, was letting the wind and eat through it and into my sleeping bag.

The parachute began cracking again. "Oh, hell," I mumbled. The cracking meant a portion of the parachute had broken loose again. Feeling I didn't have the strength for another attempt at anchoring it, I curled up in my bag, shivering occasionally, waiting for something to happen; I didn't know what. After what seemed like several minutes but was probably only a matter of seconds, I heard Pirate trying to tie down the parachute.

"Art." Pirate's voice sounded far off and unfamiliar. "Help me hold it."

Hearing his voice made me realize that the three of us had been awake for more than an hour before anyone had spoken. Burrowed into my sleeping bag, I didn't want to budge from its security, false as it was, for even a moment. While I was deciding whether to help Pirate or prolong my rest, I felt Dave get to his hands and knees and begin wrestling with the parachute, which was now pounding his head and back as it billowed and cracked back in rapid succession. Yanking and cursing, Dave managed to pull part of it around him again, only to have it whip off as soon as he settled down into his bag.

"Look, we gotta get outa here!" Dave yelled.

"Where? We'd never make it down!" I said, grabbing onto the piece of parachute that Pirate was clinging to. "Maybe it's a morning wind that'll die down."

"Morning wind?" Dave looked at me with disbelief. "It's a bloody hurricane, you fool! I'm checking the other side of the rocks."

"Awwghaaaaa. . . ." Pirate growled, staring up into the wind.

Instead of getting completely out of his bag, Dave tied the drawstring at the top tight around his middle. With his legs still in the sleeping bag and his arms free, he lurched toward the crest ten feet away. I was horribly apprehensive. If he lost his grip on the rocks he could easily be blown off the mountain. On the other side we'd never hear him again if he called for help. How far was he going? Maybe he'd be hidden behind a rock where we wouldn't be able to find him if we needed his strength. Besides the logic of my fear, I recoiled emotionally against Dave's leaving because it seemed to break our trust; it violated a fundamental law of survival—stay together.

"Dave," I cried. "Wait! I think it's safer here."

"Stay if you want!" he hollered back. "This wind's bad, and I'm gettin' out of it!"

"Where are you going?" Dave didn't hear me. "It's exposed over there!" He had disappeared over the crest.

Since my mittens were too bulky to grip the parachute, I pulled thick wool socks onto my hands; my fingers were nearly numb already. I was astonished as I looked up to see Pirate holding the parachute with his bare hands. Just as I yelled at him to get something over them, one of my socks started to slip off. Pulling it back on, I shifted position, and the wind seized the wind parka I had been sitting on. Inside its main pocket was the tape recorder I had been using for the physiological testing, but at that moment I was much more concerned about the loss of the half dozen cookies I'd stashed in the pocket. One moment the parka had been next to me, then I saw it whirling through the air, fifty, a hundred feet up, sailing in the direction of McKinley's summit.

With Dave gone, his loose end of the parachute caught the wind, and this threatened to rip the entire piece of nylon from our grip. We gave up trying to wrap the parachute around us; the pull on our arms wrenched our whole bodies as we clung to it to keep it from escaping. The parachute was our only shelter.

"My hands are bad!" Pirate's voice was weak, almost a whimper. His face was drawn up into a hideous, painful grin. Ice caked his beard.

"Bring them in!" I yelled, though his head was only inches from mine. His fingers felt like chunks of ice against my stomach.

"They're stiff!"

"Move them!" I reached for a better grip on the parachute. It slipped. I lunged. Pirate caught it as it whipped past him. He winced in pain.

"Aw, the hell with it!" Pirate sighed. As he let loose, the parachute twisted through the air. It snagged on a rock. I saw it starting to rip, then it was gone.

For the first time I noticed the sky. It was a blue wall, smashing into the mountain. Thin pieces of cloud shredding—everything grew blurred. My eyes were watering and stinging from squinting into the wind. Compared to anything I had ever experienced, this wind was like another element. It was as if gravity had shifted and, instead of holding us down, was pulling us across the landscape.

Pirate began digging his hands in under my parka. The top of my bag had fallen open to the wind. As I pulled it shut, I fell against Pirate. We grabbed each other.

"Hold onto me!"

"Art, let's get into one bag."

"How? There's no room. . . . Give me your hands." I felt his icy fingers grabbing the skin around my middle. My bag had opened again, and to keep the wind from getting to me Pirate pushed himself over the opening. I just leaned against him, trying to catch my breath. Shivering, teeth chattering, my whole body was shaking with cold.

"Pirate, it's no good!" Wind was coming into my bag. We were both losing our warmth. "Each in his own bag . . . it's better."

"I can't feel my fingers!"

"Put 'em between your legs!"

"I don't want to lose my hands!"

I remembered Dave. If it was less windy on the other side of the rocks, he would have come back to tell us. If it was just as windy, I thought he would have returned to be with us. Something must have happened to him. But maybe he had found a sheltered corner. How could he abandon us?

"Pirate, let's try the other side!"

"Naw . . . the wind's everywhere!"

We huddled together, hunched upright in our sleeping bags, wedged tightly between two rocks. Whenever we relaxed the wind caught us, started us sliding along the ice which gradually sloped away, and forced us to push and fight our way back up into the rocks. Leaning against Pirate didn't make me any warmer, but it was comforting—I wasn't alone. We didn't talk. I could breath more easily with my head inside my bag. I wondered what the others were doing down in the cave. Shiro's cough, Gregg's foot, John's swollen ear—it was too frightening to think about.

Beneath me I felt the ice sliding. Slipping onto my side, I brought an arm out in time to grab Pirate's knee. I pulled myself back against the rocks. My arms trembled from exhaustion. Pirate stared blankly out of his bag. His head turned slowly toward me with a groggy nodding motion. Was he slipping into a stupor? I wondered whether I looked as awful.

"It's no use here," I sighed.

I could barely keep myself up against the rocks. There was nothing I could do for Pirate. Maybe Dave had found a safe spot. I had to check the other side of the rocks, but that would be deserting Pirate. Yet there was no way I could help. How could I just leave him? I had to do something for myself!

"I'm going over." He didn't move. "Pirate," I yelled, "I'm going after Dave!"

His head shook from side to side as he half mumbled, half shouted, something I couldn't understand. I grabbed at the rock above me and pulled myself up the slope. Another rock; its sharp cold cut through the wool socks. Another pull. I reached the crest. To my tremendous relief I saw Dave crouched on the ice only about fifteen feet away. His back was toward me.

"Dave!" He couldn't hear me. I worked a little closer to him. The wind threatened to throw me off the crest. Beyond lay bare glacier where I'd never catch anything to hold onto if I was blown from the rocks.

"Dave!" This time he turned and saw me. I was out of breath and must have been gasping as much as yelling. "Is it better where you are?"

"What? . . . It's the same. Go back!"

I didn't want to go back, and waiting here on the crest was impossible because it was completely exposed to the wind. Before I'd decided which way to go, a cross-current gust caught me. I grabbed for rocks. One came loose. I caught another one nearer Dave. Somehow the sock on my left hand had blown off. I shoved the bare hand into my sleeping bag. The other hand held onto a rock. The wind flung and tossed my body as though it were weightless.

My right hand ached with cold from gripping the rock, and my forearm began cramping from the strain. I couldn't go back into the wind, but neither could my right hand cling to the rock much longer. The only other rock I could reach was three feet to my left, near Dave. My numb right hand had become so dead that I couldn't feel the rock it held onto. My shivering body seemed on the verge of going into convulsions.

I tried to think. If I lost my grip, I'd be blown across the ice. My mind was racing. I had to grab for the rock near Dave with my left hand: it was bare, no mitten or sock. It would be frozen. I had to. Suddenly, my bare hand shot out to grab the rock. Slicing cold.

I saw Dave's face, the end of his nose raw, frostbitten. His mouth, distorted into an agonized mixture of compassion and anger, swore at me to get a glove on. I looked at my hand. It was white, frozen absolutely white.

I pulled my body onto the rock. Dave was only five or six feet away on the ledge he had chopped in the slightly sloping ice.

"Christ, Art." His voice cracked. "You froze your hands!"

I pushed off from the rock, letting the wind throw me against Dave. He flung his arms around me. All I could do was lie across him, wheezing and shaking, trying to catch my breath.

"Man," he said, "we gotta dig in!"

17,200 FEET: GREGG, JOHN, SHIRO, GEORGE

John's journal:

The pass was roaring windy, and we had our first real concern for the summit party. . . . Change of wind. Raven flew down buttress! Hypothesis concerning summit party: perhaps they had not gone to the summit the previous day, and had gone today. . . . Weather worsening rapidly all afternoon. Flying clouds, but mountain looked magnificent all afternoon. Blue shadows, yellow snow. . . . Shiro saw one sleeping bag against the bivouac rocks. At the time Gregg thought Shiro had seen three, but had misheard under the roar of the wind, and was rather profoundly disturbed when back in camp Shiro said he had seen only one. . . . Very tired and anxious for the three. I am pretty sure they will break out despite the weather and come down tonight despite the whiteout. If not, we are in serious trouble indeed.

Sheldon flew in late this afternoon, low around the igloo, with landing lights on. Some discussion as to the significance of this flight, but probably a reconaissance before the storm. Had Ray been in radio contact with Anchorage and given an emergency to Sheldon, or was this flight on his own or on someone else's account before the onset of the storm? George very apprehensive about storm. Solemn. There is not much we can do about it but wait for the others to move down. But if they don't? I have no great apprehension for the three above yet. I think they will fight their way down, that is, if they are all well. Art's altitude sickness? But then we may have seven days before Sheldon can take us out

Gregg's diary continued:

It's evening. We all stayed in case there is a need to help one of the others down. The wind has descended to this altitude, and we are huddled in the snow cave with a large mouth covered by a tent, weighed down with rocks which we hope will hold. If they come down tonight, we will be crowded, but we will be a happy crowd. If they make it back tonight, we will descend tomorrow as quickly as possible. The wind is from the southeast, right into the tent, but it will hold unless things get worse. Those guys only had a bunch of lunch, one stove full of gas, a pot, their sleeping bags, and the parachute with which to cover themselves up

Please God, let us hear their voices. Let them descend unharmed. Give them a break in the wind and the wisdom and stamina to use it.

What can we do? I suppose the best is the prayer above. I am thankful that Shiro wanted to come down yesterday, or we would have probably been caught in the same trap. How proud and stupid we all are.

Edi [Gregg's wife], you can't imagine how I long to be in your arms, to lay my head in your lap while you stroke my hair. This is nothing new. I have been longing to be with you since I started. I think you can tell by this journal. All my love, honey. Don't worry. I'll still call you about the fifth of *this month*. Good night. Pray for a happy morning.

With the provisions and personal reserves they have they could probably last two more days at the longest, but practically speaking they must make it down tonight or tomorrow morning at the latest. If they had only known today that the wind wasn't as bad on this side of the pass. Oh, pray to hear their voices urgently wanting to come inside.

On the bright side, they are the strongest of us. Dave and Art have plenty of experience. Ray has good sense. They're all tough as nails. With a tiny break in the wind, they can't help but make it! Thank God the wind is dying down here, and pray it is there. Oh Lord, what anguish we are all suffering for our friends' safety.

DENALI PASS: ART, PIRATE, DAVE

Dave cradled Pirate's feet against his belly and massaged them gently until they began to rewarm.

"Dave," I said, "you know you saved us out there." My words sort of hung in the air. They sounded hollow, and Dave bit at his lip self-consciously. I didn't say more, but my eyes followed Dave with admiration and a kind of love as he tucked Pirate into his bag and then reached for the stove.

For more than an hour I had clung to the ledge on the ice, feeling the frostbite blisters swell on my hands and watching helplessly while Dave dug a cave in the ice. Just before he had completed it, Dave had collapsed from exhaustion; by then Pirate had pulled himself together, and despite his hands and feet, which were beginning to swell with frostbite blisters, he had somehow made it over the crest to finish hollowing out the cave. Dave had recovered enough strength to help me through the small hole in the ice which was the entrance to our new home.

Now inside our cave, Dave leaned on his elbows, and steadying the stove with one hand, he prepared some food with his free hand. In this cramped chamber under the ice cooking was more miserable than it had ever been in the last four weeks; Dave had quietly accepted the job because his were the only hands capable of working the stove. At least he had found some good food to fix—four pound-and-a-half cans of ham, bacon, and peas which had been cached by a previous expedition among the rocks we had bivouacked against. Since our pot had blown away, he heated the ham in its own can, then used the can to melt water in.

Flattened against the wall while Dave cooked in the middle, I realized how small our cave was. At the wide end there was barely enough room for our shoulders, and at the narrow end our feet in our sleeping bags were heaped on top of each other. Because of the rocks behind us, Dave and Pirate had been unable to make the cave long enough for us to stretch out completely. Over our feet the ceiling was about a foot and a half above the floor; toward the larger end there was just enough height to turn or lie on our sides with one shoulder touching the ice on the floor and the other touching the ice on the ceiling. We were quickly learning that our every movement bumped the next person. This cave certainly wasn't pleasant or comfortable by ordinary standards, but it kept us safe from the wind, and that was all that mattered, for the moment.

Dave looked for his journal and found it missing. We had lost too much to the wind—the use of four hands and two feet, an incalculable amount of body warmth, two packs with half our food in them, the parachute, my wind parka, and— perhaps our greatest loss—the foam pads which would have insulated us from the ice and helped to keep our bags dry. Yet we felt secure. We were supplied with enough gas to make water for another day, maybe two more days if we stretched it. With four lunches left, and three remaining cans of food, we needn't worry about starving.

That night ham and hot water were a feast, not filling, but delicious nonetheless; it was our first warm food since leaving the cave down at 17,200 feet more than thirty hours before. My hands had become so inflexible that Dave had to place each bite of ham— there were five of them—in my mouth, then tip the can to my lips to let me drink. Eating made us giddy with pleasure and almost got us feeling warm.

We were actually exultant, not from any sense of conquering the wind, but rather from the simple companionship of huddling together in our little cave while outside in the darkness the storm raged through Denali Pass and on across the Alaska Range.

We agreed that the wind coming out of the northwest was funneling through the pass at least 130 miles per hour. We remembered that a wind of such velocity, combined with the $-30°$ $-45°$ air temperature outside our cave, created an equivalent wind-chill temperature somewhere off the end of the chart; the last figure on the chart was minus 148°.

"One hundred and forty-eight degrees below zero."

It was frightening to say, but the worst was over, we thought. In the morning the wind should slack off; we would descend, greeting the others at 17,200 feet with the news that we had made the summit; we would get off the mountain and go home. We wanted to believe the climb was over, that in a couple of days everything would be warm and easy again. Yet the wind, howling and pounding the slope overhead, reminded us that we couldn't move until it died down. We talked of the cave as our refuge, but the suspicion that we were being held captive in the ice must have entered each of our minds as we fell asleep listening to the wind.

March 2: "Light breaks where no sun shines."

Gregg's journal, 9:30 A.M.:

The nightmare goes on. They didn't show up last night. I can't believe this is happening. While they are still strong they must make a break for it, all three slowly. They must try. It is windy and white out this morning, very bad conditions. The irony of it: they are only one thousand feet above us, yet we can't help them.

John's journal, A.M.:

A filthy day in the snow cave. I tried to sleep as late as possible. Roaring wind clapping and fraying the tent that covers the cave entrance, pulling it out from the stones that we used to seal it around the entrance. Shiro first active, made late breakfast. Not much conversation, but concern for the three above. Wind up there still roaring terribly. In our relatively sheltered cave—a lull in the sound of a great wind roaring toward us, then flap, crack, snow blowing in. But this must be a fraction of what is going on above. Much discussion later in the day as to what should be done. . . . During the night our tent kept giving away. Each time Shiro went out into the mess and put it right: fantastic. Cooking is very difficult, and we probably didn't have enough fluid. Anxiety increased as the day advanced and no one came down. We extended the snow cave to accommodate seven comfortably. We kept saying there was no chance of their coming out in the appalling wind, still a giant roar from the pass. To sleep, grimly.

Gregg's journal continued:

We are all sleeping. To be awake is to think about it as I am, and it doesn't help to think. If only they keep their senses about them, and try together.

Lord, I wish this nightmare would end. What a terrible ordeal they must be going through. If they come down in proper daylight today, three of us can descend while one stays and cooks for them. That depends on their condition. If they keep their heads, lacing their crampons on tighter, and descend together, they'll be O.K.

The waiting is hell. The wind stops, and you listen for footsteps. I can't remember a more prolonged terror in my life. It is the damn quick changeable mountain weather that got us. When the wind dies down here, you can still hear it howling up above. . . . Nothing on the peak could hurt me once those guys come down.

DENALI PASS: ART, PIRATE, DAVE

Through the night I had slept restlessly, waking every time Dave's knees and shoulders pushed into me. Each time my mind started to clear, the thought that the wind might be down rushed up, but before I'd be fully awake the damnable roar would be running through my head. A shift of legs, or a roll to the other side —in any position the ice was too hard to be comfortable. Sleep made time pass, but the altitude caused a nervous wakefulness.

Staring at the ice, supposing the others were asleep, I looked forward to discussing a plan of action when they woke. Eventually their shifting to find a more comfortable position convinced me that they must already be awake. I asked, and they both said they had been lying silently for an hour or more. I realized there was nothing to say. It was horribly simple. We would have to wait here until the wind stopped, at least until it died down. One sleepless hour after another we listened for the first lull.

During the morning the wind remained constant. The fluctuations in its monotonous tone were so slight that it reminded me of the perpetual roar inside a conch shell—only much, much louder. Later in the day, extraordinary blasts of wind hit the surface of the ice overhead with enough force to actually shake the roof of our cave, causing loose ice crystals to fall from the ceiling.

There was no joking, no idle conversation, hardly any talk at all. We retreated into ourselves, silent, waiting, staring at the ice on the ceiling, staring at the ice on the sides of the cave, staring into

the darkness inside our sleeping bags. I tried to think construc-
tively, develop a plan or project for the next summer, but it was
useless. The altitude was heckling my mind—the same restless
lightheadedness that was keeping me awake also prevented me
from concentrating. Wandering thoughts always returned to the
sound of the wind, and to the dreary question repeated continually—"When will it stop?"

The only event during the day which aroused any interest at all
was our one meal, stretching from late afternoon till after dark.
Dave, manning the stove again, thawed and melted more than he
actually cooked. Patiently, he dropped chunks of snow and ice into
the can, watched them melt, added more snow and ice, and finally
—with what Pirate and I agreed was a stroke of genius—he
dumped in a package of gorp. When the grog became hot the
chocolate bits melted into a fascinating brew, filled with cashews
and raisins. Flavored partly with my considerable thirst, it was undoubtedly the best drink I had ever tasted. However, when I had
gotten my portion down, a curious, mildly unpleasant aftertaste
remained.

About an hour after the hot drink, Dave served the rest of the
ham. He heated it over the stove only long enough for it to thaw.
Warming it would have meant wasting fuel, which we would need
in case the wind held us here another day. Dave placed two pieces
of ham, each about the size of an apricot, in my mouth, followed
them with several slices of cheese and salami, and finished with
three pieces of hard candy.

After another hour Dave melted enough snow and ice to fill the
can with water. When it was warm he emptied a tiny can of
chopped pork into the water to make a thin soup. Before I drank
my portion I felt the need to relieve myself. Going outside was
unthinkable.

"Dave," I asked, "isn't there a spare can or a plastic bag we
can use for a pee bottle?"

"Nope, Art," he answered. "All we've got is the cooking can."

"Then what did you use?"

"Well," Dave started uncertainly, "I thought you wouldn't eat or drink if I told you, but I used the cooking can."

Now I recognized the scent or flavor that had remained as an aftertaste—urine. It didn't matter. I thought it should, but it just didn't.

After Dave poured the last of the soup into me, I prepared to use the can myself—inside my sleeping bag. This would be the first thing I had attempted to accomplish with my swollen fingers; it was a task that even under more normal conditions required considerable technique. An accident would not only be wretchedly unpleasant but disastrous as well, because the extra liquid in my bag would consolidate the down, thus ruining its insulation.

I listened anxiously as the can began to fill. The liquid level rapidly approached the rim, but in the nick of time I managed to maneuver out of what would have otherwise been a shameful and uncomfortable predicament and looked about for a place to empty the can. Not finding a suitable spot to my left and realizing Dave was guarding against my dumping it to my right, I raised the can precariously over my head and sloshed its contents against the ice behind me. Most of it melted in, but a little stream trickled under my bag. No matter, it would be frozen in seconds.

Dave calmly observed that my performance of holding the can was so skillful that I could damn well feed myself from now on.

I had heard Pirate's voice only two or three times throughout the day. Even though he lay along the opposite side of the cave, only four feet from me, I could barely hear his voice above the wind the few times he did speak. The altitude had cut off his exuberance and made him a slowed-down version of his old self. When I asked Dave whether Pirate was all right, he simply said that Pirate was worried about his feet, which had become worse than his hands. The swelling had levelled off, Dave told me, but most of his toes were insensitive to touch.

One particularly excruciating aspect of waiting was knowing

that the longer we were held down the worse our frostbite would be. As our bodies began to dry up as a result of an inadequate liquid intake, they became more difficult to warm. Dave's toes were cold, but he didn't complain because he thought that was a good sign; better that they feel cold than numb. Only Dave and I had down booties, yet we had to frequently wiggle our toes to keep the circulation flowing through them. I considered lending my booties to Pirate, but the thought of my feet freezing while I slept discouraged me.

My main concern was my hands, which were swollen to nearly twice their normal size. To flex the tips of my fingers I had to painfully clench the muscles in my hand and forearm. I recalled the last time I had played my flute before leaving for McKinley. I had carefully watched my fingers run over the keys; I had wanted to appreciate them in case I lost them, and at the same time I had promised myself that I wouldn't lose them. I had begun to fear that was exactly what was happening every hour I lay in the cave. I caught myself wondering if I would still be able to play my flute with the first and second joints of my fingers missing.

Our stomachs hadn't really been full since we had left for the summit. An empty sort of craving had settled into my belly; I hoped it wouldn't develop into the cramps which I had heard afflict people suffering from malnutrition. The others down below would be running short of food soon. Maybe they would have to retreat down the mountain. I asked Dave whether he thought the others had given up on us. He didn't answer; maybe he was asleep. Surely they'd come looking for us when the wind died down.

That night, long after it was dark, I found myself repeating the words of a Dylan Thomas poem: "Light breaks where no sun shines." Before I'd come on McKinley I had known the verses by heart; now I couldn't remember the first one past "Where no sea runs the waters of the heart push in their tides." Further on there was something about the things of light filing through the flesh. I couldn't remember. Just the first line—"Light breaks where no sun shines"—ran over and over in my mind.

I lay a long time in the dark, unable to sleep. The wind, a persistent, audible ache in our heads, had been with us for so long that its incessant sounds were like a silence that had settled over our lives. That silent, paralytic quality in the wind recalled images of unalterable bleakness; I remembered seeing the wind run through the broken windows of an abandoned cabin, the wind in the dried grass of a beach in November after the birds had migrated, the wind over the delta of a frozen river.

I couldn't remember what it was like not to hear the wind, but the three of us knew that if we heard it in the morning, our situation would become critical. There appeared to be only enough gas to melt one more can of water.

Through more than thirty six hours the wind had not even for a moment relinquished its hold on the mountain and on our lives. Surely, we reassured ourselves, the wind's force would be diminished by morning.

17,200 FEET: GREGG, JOHN, SHIRO, GEORGE

Gregg's journal, 6 P.M.:

It is nearly dark. Nasty weather all day. Too dark to write. O.K., I have a headlamp. Today was too bad for them to descend. If it is nice tomorrow, we will all go up to the pass. If not, John and I will try to make it to the radio at 7,600 feet. It would be a long day, especially in bad weather. Paul Crews is the rescue man to call in Anchorage, and Carl Brady has two helicopters that can land at Denali Pass. No matter what, the guys are in bad shape after three nights.

John and I will have to be careful. It's a long way down, and Windy Corner could be very bad. In addition there is the crevasse problem. I hate splitting the party when there are only four of us here. Please, God, can't this weather end? What a hell this has been, and is. If the weather lasts for two more days, Shiro and George should come down too! There will be no hope for those above. Please God, don't let this happen. I surely must be dreaming. Can't the weather break, and the others show up, no matter how badly off they are, and then we can all go down together?

John and I will just have to descend slowly and safely, even if it takes three days. Windy Corner might be rough. Matter of fact, it will be rough with these winds. Edi, please pray for me and for the others. Love, I need God's strength. All my love for tonight, and tomorrow, and forever, darling. Love!

March 3: "Pieces are coming off my bad ear!"

DENALI PASS: ART, PIRATE, DAVE

The infernal noise filled our heads.

The wind's vicious, I told myself. It's diabolical. Silently cursing it became a pastime. I tried to think of all the words that described its evil nature—fiendish, wicked, malicious. I called it a vampire sucking the life out of us.

But the wind didn't hear me, and I knew my words were irrelevant anyway. The wind wasn't malevolent; it wasn't out to get us; it had no evil intentions, nor any intentions at all. It was simply a chunk of sky moving about. It was a weather pattern, one pressure area moving into another. Still, it was more satisfying, somehow more comforting, to personify the wind, make it something I could hate or respect, something I could shout at. I wished I were an old Eskimo shaman, seeing devils and demons in the storm and understanding the evil spirits that lived in the mountain. I thought that a good shaman would know a chant that would chase away the wind. But I didn't know any magic, and I knew all my cursing was only an attempt to escape the simple facts; we had to descend, we couldn't descend in the wind, and the wind showed no sign of letting up.

We needed water most desperately. There was very little gas left in the stove; I wanted Dave to melt ice with it. I tried to think of the most pleasant ways of reminding him that we needed to drink, but whatever I said he growled at. I knew he felt the strain of having to do all the chores for Pirate and me. I felt too thankful, too dependent, almost too much at the mercy of Dave to pester him about the water. He told me that "later" he would melt some ice and thaw the bacon or peas, but gradually the day slipped by without our eating or drinking. Yet, if my hands had been all right, I would have put off the cooking the way Dave did because the altitude had cut away our motivation; it was so much easier to say "later" because, though we didn't really believe it, we always thought the wind might suddenly stop, letting us run down to the cave at 17,200 feet.

It was toward the middle of the afternoon when I heard Dave beginning to coax the stove back to life. He fiddled with it for several minutes without any luck, then decided to let it sit while he opened one of the large cans of bacon, ham, or peas.

It was the moment I had waited for all day.

"Which one do we want first?" he asked.

"Mix 'em all together," Pirate suggested.

Dave scraped the ice off the can of bacon with his knife, clearing the top so he could open it. I could already taste the bacon.

"Damn!" Dave swore in disgust. "Holes in the can! We can't eat the bacon! It's rotten!"

He reached for a can of peas.

It could certainly not happen again. Those holes had been an accident. Nevertheless, Pirate and I listened intently as Dave cleared the ice from the can of peas.

When only about half the ice was off, he swore again. More holes! Than he tried the ham, our last can. It was the same!

We sank back into a numb depression. For two days we had anticipated the flavor of the bacon. We had let ourselves dream of the juice of the peas in our mouths. Suddenly the food we had counted on was gone. The gnawing cramps in our stomachs weren't going to be quieted.

Immediately we were angry for being so cruelly cheated, but only after several minutes did we realize how the spoiled food had transformed our trial with hunger into a confrontation with starvation. We had almost nothing left to eat—three bags of gorp, a dozen slices of cheese, some hard candies, a little coffee, a three-ounce can of chopped pork, and maybe a dozen cookies. The combined calorie count of our remaining food was probably adequate for one person for one day. Solemnly, Dave divided a little less than half of the remaining food into three equal portions.

Although Dave battled with the stove long after his fingers were insensitive from handling the cold metal, he failed to get it going. There was so little gas left that he couldn't build up enough pressure to vaporize it. At thirty below the gas was sluggish—he had to give up. Just like the punctured cans of food, our last drops of gas mocked us with their uselessness.

Our one hope was a gallon of gas Dave had cached on the far side of Denali Pass when he had climbed McKinley in the summer three years earlier. It might still be there; Dave had spotted the bottle of gas the first day we had tried for the summit. He thought we should take a look, but no one volunteered to go out. He said he had originally cached the gas only about two hundred feet from where we lay. No one moved. Dave was the most fit to go out, and the most certain of the place it was cached, but the horror of entering the wind overcame the slightest inclination Dave might have had to go after it.

We tried to imagine what the others at 17,200 were doing. They had shelter, but only a limited supply of food. I remembered how a week or two before we had been concerned for the strength of John and George, about Shiro's cough and hemorrhoids, and about Gregg's unpredictable emotions in a crisis. Now they were entirely dependent on their own resources; and the three of us who had once been the strongest might soon come to depend on their judgment and strength to be rescued.

We hoped the others would not attempt anything rash for our sake—that the strain of their fear for us wouldn't break them. We thought of the gallon of gas. We imagined how delicious a cup of water would taste. We shifted our hips and shoulders to relieve the hard cold beneath us.

We talked very little. The grayness inside the cave faded into darkness.

17,200 FEET TO 14,400 FEET: GREGG AND JOHN

John's journal:

We decided that today, the third, Gregg and I should go down to 14,400 feet and then on to the radio to call for a helicopter overflight, or for Sheldon to fly over Denali Pass to drop fuel, etc. George and Shiro will stay at 17,200 feet to determine what is at the top of the pass as soon as the weather allows getting up there. We had a miserable breakfast, cleared the snow off our gear, and slowly prepared for the descent. Set out about noon into heavy wind. Said thanks to Shiro and good-by to George. Not a great deal of response from either—dozing.

Not too cold, much blowing sandy snow in eyes. Severe, buffeting winds down buttress made going very difficult. As usual, concern that the crampons would come loose, but they held.

Just near the gendarme above sixteen thousand feet Gregg wrenched his ankle. We encountered terrible winds here and had to cling to the ridge rocks to save from being blown off our feet. Sometimes the wind blew up, sometimes down, unpredictable. Very difficult to maintain balance. On hands and knees to the fixed ropes in a screeching wind. I anchored Gregg, but this was not much use since I had Dave's ice axe, which had lost its point. Shiro is using mine. A crosswind and a driving snow made traveling down the fixed line difficult, but we got down the line without many problems. . . . Gregg moved slowly on his bad ankle. The pace was just right. Both exhausted by the time we reached the igloos.

Pieces are coming off my bad ear.

Shoveled out the entrance, listening to the roar of the wind up at the pass. Went to sleep standing up, leaning against the door of the second igloo. But felt much better after meal. Sorted gear for descent. Crevasse problem worrisome, but only a few wicked places. Weather down here contrasts—whiteout, gentle snow, occasional wind.

Compare the three on the pass. They must be getting near the end now.

And George and Shiro in the gusty snow cave are only a little better off than if in a tent at the same place. Tonight the sack is damn wet from all the snow that came into the snow cave. . . . This lousy weather cannot continue much longer.

Gregg's journal:

John and I at 14,400 feet. They didn't come down last night. Nasty weather. Shiro got up to fix the hole over the tent three times. Really miserable. I was hoping I would find Dave, Pirate, and Art here; that somehow, descending, they had missed the high camp.

I pity all those above. At least a plane could land here. We can hear the wind above. We must try for the radio at seventy-five hundred feet and get help. I hope the others are still holding out. Shiro and George will make it. If it is clear tomorrow they will try to get to the pass. We have no idea how long the others can hold out.

We had a good meal with plenty of liquid. Didn't realize how badly off we were above. It was such a problem to cook that we let it go too much. With only two to cook for they will be better off. I wonder if the weather will clear tomorrow. Inside this igloo we are oblivious to what is going on outside. With a reasonable day and God's help we can make it to seventy-five hundred feet tomorrow. Descending seven thousand feet with a screwed-up ankle is quite a day. I dread the crevasses. They are my only worry at this point. I only know we must try to get help for those above. If we don't soon it will surely be too late. This is their fourth night.

The trip down today was quite windy and our eyelashes were caked up with ice, but it was a warm south wind, thank goodness, and when we got here we were astonished at how warm it was— −10°. I don't know how cold it was at 17,200 feet the last few nights, but it must have been about −30°. Maybe it was just because the wind wasn't blowing here that made the difference. If John and I make it to 7,500 feet tomorrow we will be safe. Then we will radio out, and as soon as Sheldon can come and get us, we can get a rescue in progress.

Edi, I hope you're not too worried. We have no way of knowing whether the outside world knows anything of what is going on. Ray had been contacting Radio Anchorage every night and then stopped. So chances are that people are worried about us.

I hope the light isn't too flat tomorrow. It was hard descending with my ankle because I couldn't see where I was putting my feet. One minute the ground was steep and hard, then flat and soft, then a dropoff, etc.

Shiro and the others are more optimistic about the chances of those up at the pass than I am. If only they had made a break for it the first day, they would have been all right. Every minute they wait, they become weaker and have less resolve to make a run for it. Yet they are all tough, and if Ray, as usual, takes the initiative, they could make it yet. Tonight the weather might clear. They have only a thousand feet to descend to safety. . . . A hell of a mess, and yet climbing McKinley in the winter is no harder than we anticipated. We just got a mess of bad weather breaks.

Well, honey, it's time to get to sleep. Big day tomorrow. Wish us luck. If we are careful and God is with us, we will make it.

March 4: Delusion

I woke elated. The wind had stopped. I heard a helicopter.

Just outside the cave I heard the steady whir. Gregg must have gotten a rescue started. It sounded as if the copter had already landed. People must be searching the pass for us. I was afraid they wouldn't find our cave; it was such a small hole in the ice. Maybe they'd give up and leave.

"Dave!" I rolled toward him. "Dave, do you hear the helicopter? We'd better get outside right away."

"Go to sleep . . . it's the wind."

"No! It can't be. It's too steady, too constant. It's a copter. . . . Dave. . . ."

He didn't answer.

"It's a copter," I repeated to myself. "It's the steady whir of a copter." I listened to be certain; but I wasn't certain. Maybe it was the wind; it couldn't be. I almost asked Dave to listen; but I knew he was right; yet I strained my ears for a voice, any sound that would let me believe there were rescuers outside.

There was only the wind.

After a long silence Dave admitted that he had been susceptible to my delusion; he had convinced himself for several minutes that the sound of the wind really was a rescue helicopter.

"But you know," Dave said, looking toward me, "it makes you feel kind of humble to know a helicopter couldn't possibly get to us."

Dave went on to explain how he felt good to know that no device of technology nor any effort on the part of our companions could conquer the storm, or even reach through it to help us. He said the three of us were alone in this sanctuary of the earth's wilderness, and that our only security lay in ourselves, in our individual abilities to endure, and in our combined capacities of will-power and judgment.

I said, "Dave, it may sound funny, but I feel closer to you than ever before."

Dave beamed and said "Yea, I know what you mean. If we can't fight our way out of this storm, at least we can stick together, and try to live in harmony with it."

I thought to myself how the storm itself was helping to protect us from its own fury. Ever since the McKinley massif had been thrust upward out of a flat land, the wind had been packing the snow and ice of Denali Pass into contours of least resistance. We were sheltered inside ice that conformed to the pattern of the wind. We had suffered and nearly succumbed to the storm that first morning when we had fought it head-on in the open, but now all the force of the wind only pounded more stability into the roof of our cave as it swept across the slope above us.

The altitude riddled our attention span into fragments of thoughts. Discomfort was the only thing on which my mind seemed able to concentrate. My lips were deeply cracked in several places. Moving my tongue along the roof of my mouth I felt clumps of dried-up mucus; other experiences with dehydration had taught me that if I didn't get water soon, the rawest areas in my mouth would begin bleeding. The ligaments in my legs ached as they dried up. It was especially painful to stretch or change positions; unfortunately, the hardness of the ice made my hips and back sore whenever I remained still for more than a few minutes. I complained very little, not because I was naturally stoic, but because there was no one to complain to—each of us experienced the same discomforts; pain had become a natural condition of our life under the ice.

I was probably warmer than either Dave or Pirate because their sleeping bags were icing up faster than mine. Every time Dave had cooked, steam from the warm liquid had been absorbed into his bag, where it soon froze. As the down had matted together, its resilience had disappeared. It was particularly unsettling when Dave pointed out a number of lumps of ice mixed with the down. I didn't see how his bag could retain any warmth. Pirate's bag was a little better, but his down was fast becoming clogged with moisture from his breath because, against Dave's advice and mine, he persisted in burying his head in his bag, where his exhaled moisture had no escape. All of us sorely missed the foam pads. Without them, we were only able to place a spare wind parka or pair of wind pants under our buttocks and shoulders, leaving the rest of our sleeping bags on bare ice.

Pirate's hands were swollen, but he said he was worried most about his feet. He asked about my down booties. Though he didn't say it outright, I could tell he wanted to wear them. I tried to ignore him, acting as if I hadn't heard. My feet were cold with the booties; without them I thought they would surely freeze while I slept, or even while I lay awake. I avoided thinking about it, but that was exactly what was happening to Pirate's feet. He knew I didn't want to give them up, and didn't ask again. As he kicked his feet inside his bag to relieve their numbness, I knew he must be thinking of the warmth of my booties. Pretending to be asleep, I tried to forget about Pirate's feet.

I couldn't remember how many days we had been in the cave. The day we had gone to the summit, then that first day of the wind, the day we ate ham, then a day without water—it must have been the fourth day, but I was uncertain.

Sometime during the middle of the day Dave rationed us each a fig bar and two hard candies. Sucking on the candies brought a few minutes of relief to the rawness in my mouth. I put the fig bar aside. I wanted to save it for later in the afternoon as a break in the monotony of hunger. After about an hour I couldn't wait any longer. I had looked forward to saliva coming back into my mouth as I chewed the fig bar, but the crumbs only stuck to the gums and roof of my mouth. With some effort I swallowed the sticky wad, feeling it tumble into my stomach, where it set off a series of cramps. The pain constructed a morbidly amusing picture of four or five hands in my stomach grabbing for the fig bar, fighting each other for it, tearing and ripping at it. After a few minutes the cramps died down and the usual steady ache returned.

Silently I cursed the punctured cans of food. Some careless climbers must have punched holes in them with their ice axes as they tried to chip away the ice that covered them. We all wished we had never seen the cans. Without them we might have been able to accept our hunger, but knowing that ham and peas, rotten as they were, lay within arm's reach while we were gradually starving was almost unbearable. The cruelest twist to the irony was the uncertainty; the canned food might still be good. Perhaps the food had remained frozen ever since it had been brought to Denali Pass. It was doubtful that there were any bacteria living at 18,200 feet. At least a portion of the ham, peas, and bacon might not be rancid, but to find out would be risking food poisoning.

Early in the afternoon it became obvious that we were going to spend another night in the cave. Even if the wind let up toward evening, we wouldn't have the time, nor perhaps the strength, to descend. We knew our dehydration was critical. We hadn't drunk a cup of liquid for more than thirty-six hours. Because our circulation was down we were all chilly inside our bags with all our parkas and wind pants on. Occasionally, I could feel Dave's body tense and shake with shivers. We needed water, which meant we needed gas—which we didn't have.

The only possibility was the gas Dave had cached at Denali Pass three years before. If one of us went for the gallon of gas, he might not make it back through the wind to the cave. The gruesome reality of this possibility had kept us from retrieving the gas, but there was no longer any alternative. One of us had to go for the gas! Who? I couldn't go because of my hands, so I lay quietly in my bag, letting my silence ask someone else to go.

Dave resisted the thought of his going. He had dug the cave. He had cooked for us when there had been gas. He knew his efforts had kept Pirate and me alive. And we knew it.

It wasn't right htat Dave go out into certain misery to possibly disappear in the wind. Yet, knowing Dave, I sensed he was struggling with his weariness and fear to find it in himself to go out. Since he was the only one of us who knew for certain where the gas should be, it was logical that he go. Neither Pirate nor I could ask him. Semiconscious from the altitude and the numbing hypnotism of the wind, we retained a sense of justice.

There was another reason we weren't anxious for Dave to go. He was our hands! We needed him to cook if we ever got some gas. We would need him to tie the rope around us and hold us on belay when we descended, whenever that might be.

Quietly—I don't remember hearing him say he would go—Pirate got out of his sleeping bag. When he started to pull on his boots, he found it difficult and painful to force his swollen feet into them. I offered him the use of my down booties. He took them and quickly had them tied on. Dave described the rocks among which the gas had been cached. Pirate pulled down his face mask.

The wind had become more erratic: there were gusts and then short—ten- to thirty-second—lulls of comparative calm. Pirate lay on his stomach, facing the entrance, listening for the lull that sounded right to him. A resigned determination seemed to be all that was left of his former fierceness. Suddenly, he gave a short and not too loud "Arahhaa!" and began squirming out the entrance, uphill, through loose snow. Dave and I cheered, not loudly, but with all our remaining enthusiasm. For a moment we heard Pirate placing the pack across the entrance again. Then the lull ended abruptly, and all we heard was the wind.

For the longest time Dave and I listened without saying a word. Ten, fifteen minutes passed. We knew Pirate should have returned, but we said nothing. He might call for help only ten feet from the cave and we'd never hear him. I couldn't help imagining what we'd have to do if he failed to return. Maybe Dave would make a try for the gas. Maybe the two of us would attempt to dash down from the pass. If Pirate didn't return within a few minutes there would be no reason to go looking for him. Maybe Dave and I would simply lie in the cave, waiting until Gregg, Shiro, George, and John could reach us, or until we passed into delirium.

We heard a movement at the entrance. Two immediate whoops of sheer joy expressed our relief. A flurry of snow, then a plastic jug shot into the cave, followed by an exhausted Pirate.

"Bad!" He was gasping. "I couldn't stand up, even in the lulls. Something's wrong with my balance." I had never before heard Pirate say anything was rough or dangerous. "I crawled all the way, clawing into the ice with two ice axes. I can't feel my feet now."

We had gas! We could drink water!

With a merriment we'd forgotten ever existed Dave melted chunks of ice and piles of snow. The first can of water, especially, smelled and tasted sweet; we did not remember that the sweetness was the scent of urine. Dave heated can after can of water till they became hot. We drank, and drank, and always waited for yet another canful. For the first time in five days we went to sleep with full stomachs. That we were only full of water mattered not at all —or so we thought.

My feet had become colder. I had to constantly wiggle my toes to keep them from becoming numb. Still, I was glad I had not asked Pirate to return my booties after his trip for the gas.

14,400 FEET: GREGG AND JOHN

John's Journal:

Foul and filthy day. No chance to move when we got ready the first thing, with the intention of using all available light to get to seventy-five hundred feet. I feel very restless and anxious to communicate with O.M. [John's wife] who will be concerned and worried with no information.

Pent up in igloo, I stood around almost all day, going out every half hour to look at the weather. I am unable to read, unable to do anything constructive. Gregg's ankle is bad. There is a whiteout, so we can't get down to give word of our situation. We go about our private tasks with little conversation, but are are both preoccupied with the three up top and now with George and Shiro since today is a whiteout and they can neither go up nor down.

Hell. Late afternoon, wind drops hope for tomorrow. Crevasses will be a bad problem. How I want to be off this mountain. This P.M. we talked nonsense conversation for a couple of hours, and felt better for it. We should have been doing it all day.

Gregg's Journal:

Damn, we are still here. . . . It is just too nasty out to move. If there were four of us it might be different. If a man falls into a crevasse with four around he is out and down the slope in no time. With two it is easily a three- or four-hour ordeal.

The route from here to Windy Corner has only a half dozen wands at best, which makes them of little or no use. If only the route were properly wanded from here we could go. We didn't get unpacked till 1:30 P.M., hoping for the slightest break in the weather. We will even go tonight if the weather is clear. Though the wind is still blowing, it does seem to be getting a slight bit brighter outside A good sign, I hope. John thinks we may be able to move in an hour, which would put us in the dark, but that's O.K. if it is clear. I would at least like to be past Windy Corner in the light. . . . I told you I'd call you on the fifth, and I intend to try to keep that promise.

John is nervous, but then so am I. I am only afraid that I won't sleep well until I am home with you. I hope we can seclude ourselves for a few days then. God, but I hope we can get to seventy-five hundred feet tomorrow. If tomorrow is a day like today, we will just have to try regardless. I'd like to see Shiro and George show up. With four of us I feel positive we could get down, no matter what the weather. . . . It is harder to sit than it is to move at this point. The waiting is more terrible than moving. But to move now might complete the destruction of the party. No, we must wait until we are reasonably sure we can make 10,200 feet at least.

I try hard to forget the situation that the three above are in, but it is a gnawing, sickening thought that won't go away.

The weather took a slight turn for the worse, but the wind has died. It is snowing heavily. I hope we are not in for a five-day snowstorm. That's all we need. I just can't describe how anxious I am to get down and out, but I know the others feel the same way.

Edi, I feel sorry for you. The injustice and worry this venture has caused you. All the work you did for it. If I do get safely back to you, the least I can do is not go on another. I promise you will be along on anything I do from here on. I think I've said earlier that this climb is a real lead into that simple, uncomplicated life we want. I do hope you are not too worried for me. . . . I will be safely home to you in no time. I love you and am full of good hope for the future. All my love. Good night.

March 5: "Hope gives out for the three above."

17,200 FEET: GEORGE AND SHIRO

George's report:

The wind is still making a noise like Niagara Falls, just like a big body of water going over the rocks. All kinds of things enter our minds, one of which is: what could we do even if we did find the three above and if they need help? Because of the altitude and the steep slope below Denali Pass we just don't think we could carry them down on our backs. It is a very helpless feeling and a helpless situation.

The time has become more or less critical, and we just don't have the slightest hope. We don't discuss it. . . . Invariably this situation is a transition between life and death; it is so difficult to imagine somebody who was with you such a short time ago and is helpless up higher and we can't help them. Invariably the picture of Farine comes to mind because it happened the same way. The night we left him on the glacier he was still Farine—warm—and the next day he was just a frozen body, like a piece of ice. Things like this go through our minds.

It was very unpleasant inside the cave because the wind was blowing right into the entrance and the cave was filling up with snow. There was really no satisfactory way to shield the entrance. We tried to install a flap and weigh it down with rocks, but a gust of wind would destroy it. . . . We were miserable; it required constant work to keep the entrance halfway covered. We decided to start down.

We felt good until we started drying our sleeping bags. Even with rocks lying on top of it, a gust of wind picked up my sleeping bag and blew it into the little bowl below us. I acted on an impulse. Realizing how serious the loss of my bag would be, I chased it down without crampons or an ice axe. It was just like grasping for a straw in the wind. I lost my balance. I slid about twenty feet down and hit my shoulder very hard against a snowdrift. I think I may have dislocated it; it is very painful. Shiro retrieved me. Luckily, I got ahold of the sleeping bag and saved it.

I have a horrifying, dull bone ache in my shoulder. Even with straps around my shoulder I don't have full use of the arm—not because something is dislocated, but because of the pain; with a certain amount of pain it feels as if it will just give out.

Our packs are quite heavy and the wind is severe, but we head down.

14,400 FEET TO 8,000 FEET: JOHN AND GREGG

John's Journal:

As arranged, the first one awake went out of igloo to look at weather. To my surprise and relief, found clear sky, blowing snow, the mountain back to the clarity of previous days. A quick breakfast, but much preparation, and away by 9:45. I fumbled with knots and had difficulty with frostbitten fingertips. Ear is raw. An overheavy pack—all Art's photography gear, etc.—around sixty-five or seventy pounds.

Did quite well to Windy Corner. Wonderful sunlight on Foraker and the flat land out beyond, rivers crisscrossing white. Roaring still over Denali Pass and hope gives out for the three above.

Quiet around Windy Corner, to our great surprise and relief. Pleasant down to 12,500-foot cache of ill memory. Goldline rope snaking over snow, blue wind trouser, white boots, whip of rope marks on snow. Gregg's ankle giving some trouble. A bad time on steep pitch above Peters glacier. I came off. Gregg arrested, then I slid again. No control with too heavy pack and general malaise. Strong words, then continued. Stopped above the crevasse slope, where Gregg wrote message for Sheldon on the snow. Namely: LAND AT 10,200 FEET AT 3 P.M. Down crevasse slope without problems. Fortunate. Passed the waiting snow blocks, mocking us, and into deep snow. Heavy plodding in still air and warm sun down to 10,200 feet. Knee deep powder snow into 10,200 feet by 1:15 P.M. Good to see the iglooplex once again. Quite unchanged, except for some additional snow. Gregg boiled up much water while I sorted gear. . . . Wrapped up the crampons with a sense of relief that I would not be on them again.

We left on snowshoes about 4:00 P.M., setting out for the base camp at 7,500 feet. Shortly out of camp we got into deep snow. It was nice to drop crampons, but it was rough to go straight into deep snow. Breaking trail was bad. Gregg started off, then I took over and led for about one and a half hours.

It was dark as we got over the brow of the run down to the Kahiltna. Two planes flew in, in the dusk, to the head of the Kahiltna and flew directly out. We assumed that Sheldon had come in to attempt a landing with another plane as escort but had decided it was too dark and returned. We traveled very slowly in the deep snow. Both with headlamps, both fatigued, somewhat bewildered and uncertain, but anxious to get to 7,500 feet. Step by step, sometimes falling into deep snow. Great effort to get up again. Some of the weight of the pack was due to a great deal of ice in the sleeping bag and the pack was badly balanced since this had to be carried up on top. It was difficult to get pack onto my back and sometimes required several attempts before it could be hoisted. It was very difficult to estimate position on the slope in the dark.

Finally decided to stop around 10:00 P.M.—not sure of our position. Are we above or beyond the 7,500-foot camp? I was extremely fatigued, and although Gregg made no comment he was also clearly, extremely tired. I could barely carry the pack another step. Gregg dug out a cave in very soft snow while I got billy (pot) and stove ready to make drinks. . . . The warmth helped with the wet sack. Into sack with boots on, and immediately to sleep. Not at all certain of the prospects for the next day.

Gregg's Journal:

We had no idea the snow down here would be so deep and soft. Even with snowshoes one goes to one's knees. We kept plodding along in the dark till 10:00 P.M. John lost his lunch someplace, so we had a piece of sausage each, and tomorrow there is a piece of chocolate each for breakfast. . . . It looks for all the world like it will be snowing and whiteout in the morning. If it is, we will play heck finding the igloo. We need a little more good weather before we will be safe. If the weather is bad we must try to manage our way back to 10,200 feet. If it is really bad, we will have to stay here. Dread either.

DENALI PASS: ART, PIRATE, DAVE

The gusts and lulls of the wind sounded hopeful when we woke to another cold, gray morning under the ice. The ragged end of the storm seemed to be blowing itself out, and had we been strong we probably would have tried to dash down from the pass immediately. Unfortunately, we had become so weak that the wind would have to be completely gone before we could descend with any confidence. Yet, regardless of when the wind disappeared, this had to be our last day in the cave, because by the next morning there would be no food at all. For the three of us we had only a handful of gorp, four slices of cheese, and three little hard candies. When this food ran out the cold would take over our bodies unless we could make it down. We lay silent and brooding in our bags; cheerless as our situation was, I felt a curious sense of relief that it was so simple—without food, it was either descend or perish in this wretched cave.

Pirate refused to believe what the wind had done during the night. On going to sleep, he had fixed a rope to the pack which closed the cave's entrance, then tied that rope around his arm to keep the pack from being blown away if a gust dislodged it. He woke to find both the rope and the pack gone. As the wind had begun packing the entrance full of snow, some loose, fine-grained crystals had sifted into Pirate's sleeping bag; the bag had so little warmth that the snow lay in it without melting. Pirate stared at the snow for ten or fifteen seconds, then mumbled hoarsely that he'd leave the snow in his bag because it might help insulate him. His reasoning sounded absurd. I thought of telling him to get the snow out of his bag as fast as he could, but it was easier to lie silent than begin talking. Then I began wondering whether Pirate might be right about the snow helping to insulate him—his bag and Dave's were now little more than matted down and chunks of ice held together by the nylon shell.

Even after Pirate placed his boots and the gas bottle in the entrance to block the blowing snow from sealing us in, snow still blew through every time a gust of wind hit the slope above. Because the entrance wasn't tightly closed off from the storm, a steady draft circulated the −35° air through our cave. With the chill factor increased, I began shivering again. This wasn't particularly painful, but it was unnerving to watch my body shaking uncontrollably. What happens after you lose control of your body? I thought of asking Dave, but said nothing.

My thoughts wandered back to my childhood. I recalled my parents saying that when I was first learning to walk I enjoyed toddling around in the snow naked. I remembered the times when I was eight and nine and we'd run out into the spring windstorms that sweep across the plains of eastern Colorado; with bales of straw we built shelters from the driving wind and dust, and considered ourselves pioneers. In those days it had been great fun to run shouting from tree to tree in a thunderstorm or when the rain turned to hailstones the size of marbles and golf balls. How had those games in storms led to the desperate mess the three of us were trapped in? All I wanted now was to be free of the fear of freezing and being buried under the ice. I started imagining what we'd look like frozen solid. The feel of my mouth on Farine's cold lips came back. I saw his last expression frozen in his cheeks and eyelids. How much of a body could be frozen before the heart stopped? Was I acting cowardly to think this way? It wouldn't happen to us, not to me; yet, there was the cold in our hands and feet.

To get these thoughts out of my mind, I asked Dave if it seemed to him that the gusts were becoming less powerful and the periods of calm longer. He said, "Don't think about it." But I couldn't help being attentive to every fluctuation of the wind, even though I knew as well as Dave that it was only depressing to hear every lull end in a blast of wind.

Only food occupied our thoughts as much as the wind, especially the food in the punctured cans. Those cans haunted us. I felt the little holes staring at me whether the cans were in plain sight or hidden under a sleeping bag or out the entrance. After Dave had emptied the cans of their contents, he classified most of the food as definitely rotten, but there remained at least a pound of peas and a half pound of ham that he thought might be edible. He even thawed and heated some of the ham. It didn't smell or look bad; still, it had come from a partly spoiled can.

"Aw, I'm going to eat it," Pirate insisted.

But we wouldn't let him. There was no question in our minds that, weak as we were, food poisoning would do us in. As long as we could just resist the canned food we had a chance; if we gave in and ate the doubtful ham and peas we might eliminate that chance. Of course, the food might be good, and it could easily provide the extra strength we might need to get down.

As our stomachs tightened with cramps and the deafening repetition of gusts and lulls whittled away our patience, each of us changed our minds about eating the canned food. One moment Pirate would declare he was going to eat the ham, and the next he would be restraining Dave or me from trying it. So far we had been able to check ourselves, but every moment of hunger increased the temptation.

We dreamed about feasts, banquets, exotic dishes, all our favorite foods. For what seemed like hours Dave and I listed every type of food we could think of. Sometimes we would be silent for ten or fifteen minutes, as if the conversation had ended; then as soon as I'd mention something like "crab," Dave would say "Wow, oh honcho boncho! I'd forgotten crab!" Another ten minutes might pass before one of us would remember a forgotten delicacy.

Once Dave said, "Stuffed green peppers!"

"Yea . . . with lots of raisins in the stuffing!" I answered.

We tantalized each other with difficult choices between different foods. "Dave," I asked, "would you prefer a mushroom pizza or a pepperoni pizza?"

"Mushroom, and if you could have one fruit, what would it be?"

"Awaarraghaa. . . . I want some bloody meat!" Pirate interrupted. There was enough gas to make as much water as we could drink; however, Dave had only enough motivation to make a minimal amount. As our dehydration continued, our frostbite became more severe. The swelling in my fingers had started to go down; I didn't know whether this was a sign of improvement or an indication that my body simply didn't have enough liquid to keep the swelling up. Much as I worried over the blisters, I realized they were my body's way of trying to save the tissue that had been frozen.

Dave couldn't feel the large toe on his right foot, nor parts of several other toes. There was so little he could do for his feet— rub them, wiggle the toes. He said they were becoming steadily colder. The scabby, frostbitten skin on the end of his nose was sickening to look at, but not nearly as frightening as the freezing that was beginning in his feet. The frostbite on his nose was isolated and had come about because he happened to have a long nose which protruded from his face mask, while the frostbite taking hold in his feet was not isolated; it was a sign that the cold was steadily creeping into his body. It was happening to each of us.

At times I was surprised that I wanted Pirate to continue wearing my down booties, which I had previously guarded so selfishly. I knew I hadn't overcome my selfishness; Pirate was sort of included in it. Since his feet had suffered on his trip to get the gas, I had felt almost as protective toward his feet as toward my own. Later in the day Pirate passed one bootie back to me. Perhaps one bootie each would not be a practical way to halt the freezing in our feet, but, even if it was only a gesture, it was still the most touching thing I had ever seen Pirate do.

The one advantage of being dehydrated was that we rarely had to jeopardize ourselves by urinating into the can inside our sleeping bags. Likewise, our lack of food had saved us from the ordeal of a bowel movement in the wind. Nevertheless, our hour of reckoning came. We had postponed the moment until it appeared we wouldn't be safe another minute. To go outside would be risking the possibility of contracting a humiliating case of frostbite while our pants were down. By comparison, it was almost pleasant to contemplate attempting the feat inside our sleeping bags. Dave's ingenuity developed a technique which produced little packages, nicely wrapped in toilet paper. With some coaching from him I managed to get my bundles safely wrapped and out the cave's entrance. However, Pirate, who hadn't been very attentive, got himself into trouble. Soon after he had completely disappeared into his sleeping bag we heard him begin to mumble and swear. When the shape of his sleeping bag began shifting frantically, we offered him some advice.

"Oh, you had paper?" he moaned. "I didn't know you guys had used paper."

During the first days of the wind, sleep had been an effective way of waiting. Now it had become a continual twisting of hips and shoulders away from the hardness of the ice, a twisting away from the cold that seeped into our bags from the ice beneath. None of us had even a momentary respite from hunger cramps and the cramps and aches in our dried-up ligaments and muscles. Nevertheless, wakefulness continued to be a worse kind of half-consciousness; pain was felt more acutely by a more alert mind, and we realized that we weren't dreaming, that we were not going to wake up to find everything friendly and warm.

At times I was unable to tell for certain whether I was awake or asleep. Dreams of Farine lying on the ice, of John calling from the bottom of that crevasse, of Shiro coughing, of our hands and feet turning black, filled my sleep and drifted over into the different levels of wakefulness that stretched through the day. Hours no longer existed. I once asked Dave how long we had been trapped under the ice; he said he didn't know.

In the afternoon, during one period of what I thought was clear-sightedness, it seemed as though the wind was finally dying. The lulls had become much longer, maybe as long as five or six minutes, and the gusts were less frequent and no longer hit with the force which had shaken our cave for so many days. I dozed fitfully, then woke in the dark to a strange sound. I was startled. To ears that had become unaccustomed to quietness, the silence sounded nearly as loud as the wind's roar had that first morning.

"Dave, the wind's gone! We can descend!"

"Yea man, I'm cooking us up a farewell dinner to this awful hole," Dave said. In a moment his headlamp flicked on and several minutes later I heard the cheery purr of the stove. It was all over, we thought; we had made it through. Our farewell dinner was a farewell to the very last of our food, to the cave, and, we hoped, to the wind. Dave passed the hot water and divided up the four slices of cheese.

March 6: "We try to avoid the sentiments of death."

14,400 TO 10,200 FEET: GEORGE, SHIRO

George's report:

We headed down; there was no trouble until we hit Windy Corner—then suddenly the wind was very severe again. We just barely made it down to the beginning of the basin below the corner. From there it was easier though it was late.

My personal thoughts were of being as careful as possible while trying to get down to the lower igloos. We almost didn't make it; the snow began blowing again—it was deep; going was slow—it was getting dark. We lost the trail; we didn't see the wands in front of us, so we walked ahead without our packs to find the igloos. After we reached the igloos we retrieved our packs. It was a good trick I learned from Shiro; if we hadn't done it I don't think we would have found the igloos, and a night out would have been very miserable.

Gloomy, very, very gloomy; it was a condition of despair under which we walked down. I'm sure Shiro had some discomforts, but they haven't been expressed. His dry cough had persisted at 17.3, but now at lower altitudes it is much, much better. His hemmorrhoids aren't bothering him, as far as I know; we are in such a state that things like that and my shoulder don't matter. I think we are susceptible to those minor things when we are idle, but they are really unimportant because our biggest problem is what has gone on in the past and what will go on in the future.

Looking at personal belongings of Art, Dave, and Pirate we just can't help discussing it again. There is a flicker of hope—as anyone would have hope—but logically we reject the possibility that any of the three could come down alive.

It just isn't real; it is very difficult to describe. Actually, the more we think about it the more agonizing it becomes, so in conversation with one another we try to avoid the sentiments of death. But of course, lying in our sleeping bags, all sorts of thoughts can't help but come to mind.

8,500 FEET: JOHN, GREGG

John's journal:

Crawled out of the sagging cave to find whiteout, wet stars last night. Ugh. At first not sure whether to forget about it and go back to sack, but finally woke Gregg. He was very tired and needed some prodding before he would take any interest in the bad news.

I found that I did have some lunch from the previous day left in my parka pocket. We had no meal the previous evening. Packed up without brewing, decided to look around. Difference of opinion as to position. I thought we were down, beyond the seventy-five-hundred-foot camp, judging by the seracs above. Gregg felt we were still above camp. The map did not help much since very few landmarks were visible in the whiteout. There was no wind, dense cloud, light snow.

We struck out from bivouac, south into deep snow without packs. Within about five minutes I saw a wand, only the top half of the flag appearing above the snow. This established us on the hill above camp. Gregg was right. We followed downhill approximately on fall line without packs and located two further wands. . . . However, we seemed still to be too far up the slope to have reached camp. Dumped packs at the flags and struck south on compass course into nothing but white. Waded through four feet of new powder, snowshoes sometimes going in deep, sometimes staying on the beginning of a crust, or sinking a few inches down. Visibility still negligible. Then to great delight found wands way ahead too.

Gregg's journal:

What a fight! Woke up in partial whiteout and spent till noon finding the igloo. Then went back over the knee-deep snowshoe track to get our packs. It was about all I could do.

Dug out the igloo when we arrived, and at least had some food. We didn't have a drink this morning, so we were really dehydrated. We only found four wands above the snow. The rest were buried. If it hadn't been for some long bamboo poles Ray picked up in Anchorage we would never have found this place. It was completely buried.

We spent some time dinging with the radio (used stove to warm it, etc.), but finally got through to Anchorage. I had them try to call you, Edi, but no answer. . . . I hope you are happy. Couldn't hear your voice, and so wanted to. I love you, and am so looking forward to our seclusion after this trip. Now you must know about the whole mess.

John had such a heavy load coming down yesterday that he fell twice. He slid more than anything. The second time I caught him with an arrest. He was above me with the first fifty-foot fall. He did a fine job breaking trail today, but is really pooped out toward this evening. Poor guy, really worked hard. He is not very strong but he tries.

Settled into my wet bag now. Worked at my black toe. Looks bad, but of course it will make it.

Sure glad we marked this camp with poles. Sure glad the radio worked. Good to get boots off after two days. Drank so much liquid that we're bloated, and yet we're still thirsty. Running out of tobacco fast. Lots of luxuries at this camp. Even a bag of whole-wheat flour, three pounds of bacon, brown sugar, milk, etc. Plenty of gas and matches. A really secure feeling for the first time in weeks. It's been five weeks plus one day.

It was a real ordeal coming down, and I am glad that phase is over. Seems they have a rescue all in order on the outside, just waiting to come in. Arrangement here has it that I will call at 8:00 P.M. and every other hour thereafter to notify them about the weather till they can come in. Happy the radio works. Helio will land here to pick me up while John gets stuff ready to go out. I'll go up with Vin Hoeman (who's standing by in Talkeetna), stop wherever Shiro and George are, talk with them (Do they know what happened up high?), then go up. On the way back down I hope we can clean camps, especially the 10,200-foot camp.

Bad weather is predicted for twenty-four to twenty-six hours. I hope it's a lie. Thank God we are here. I hope God is as kind to Shiro and George. I hope to the Lord the others are safe, but I can't imagine much hope for them after a week. . . .

DENALI PASS: ART, PIRATE, DAVE

In the gray light and quietness we anxiously prepared to leave the cave, but it took us several hours to get ready. Dave melted ice. Pirate was a long time cramming his swollen feet into his boots. My feet and Dave's weren't swollen, but during the night we had both lost feeling in several toes. With my hands still mostly useless, I relied on Dave to stuff my feet into my boots, then lace them up.

Keyed-up by our departure, we felt more alert than we had at any time since the first day of the wind. When I decided to give the mental tests before we went down, Dave helped me with the stopwatch and the sheet of subtraction problems since my fingers were unable to hold them. Dave said he was thinking as clearly as he ever had; the test results did not agree. It took each of us twice as much time to answer a series of subtraction problems as we had needed to answer a similar series down on the Kahiltna. Although this was only a rough indication of one way in which our logical thought processes were impaired, I made a mental note to be damn careful if we had to make an important decision.

But we weren't really worried. There was no wind. After sticking out the storm we felt there was nothing we couldn't do. In a few hours we'd reach 17,300 feet; we might descend all the way to the 14,400-foot igloos before night. It was going to be great to walk in on the others; they had probably given up on us by now. A new excitement quickened our movements. We were going down, going home! Dave was the first outside. With one word he cut short all our excitement.

"Whiteout!"

"Whiteout." The word hung in the air. We had never considered the possibility of a whiteout after the wind. Dave could see only twenty to thirty feet. A mile of ice stretched between us and the 17,200-foot camp if we took a direct course; but on the slope below us there were four or five square miles of ice, in the basin below there were another four or five square miles of ice, and the basin fell away through forty or fifty square miles of heavily crevassed glacier. Blinded by the whiteout, we might wander about the ice forever, or rather, until we collapsed, or walked off an edge, or fell into a crevasse.

We hoped the whiteout was merely a small passing cloud that would sift away in an hour or two. We dreaded to think of what would become of us if the whiteout proved to be the beginning of a week-long snowstorm.

I followed Pirate out of the cave only to see his hunched form stumble into Dave, who was also unable to straighten his back. For a moment I just watched the two lean against each other like drunks trying to maintain their balance. A mist of ice crystals crept silently over the rocks behind them.

With short, painful jerks of his head, Pirate twisted his face up to look Dave in the eye: "Dave," he said in a hoarse whisper, "I think I'm too weak to go down."

For the first time since the night we had pulled Farine out of the crevasse, Dave's face went blank with shock. In an instant his confidence had been broken. It wasn't only Pirate's words that had shaken him. In the half-light of our cave we had been unable to see each other's features clearly, but now nothing was hidden. Pirate's appearance was the most appalling. It was as if he had emerged from the cave twenty years older; his voice was that of an old man; his face was furrowed with lines we had never seen before; his eyes were faded and glazed and sunk back into their sockets.

I felt shaky getting to my hands and knees and was unable to stand on my feet without Dave's help. I tumbled over with the first step I tried, hitting the ice with my shoulder to avoid falling onto my swollen hands. None of us had a sense of balance. Our legs were dried up and, along with our backs, were stiff from lying immobile for days. We practiced walking, but it took ten or fifteen minutes of stretching and limbering up before we regained enough coordination to walk in a relatively straight line.

To be able to walk again was an achievement, but hardly a consolation, because even if the whiteout cleared, we didn't have nearly enough balance to climb down the hundreds of yards of steep ice that separated us from 17,200 feet. Yet waiting in the cave would be suicide, since one more day without food would certainly leave us without the strength to descend.

Dave grew nervous. Pirate leaned against a rock and mumbled to himself. Desperation made us begin to voice wild plans for escaping from the pass. We discussed the possibility of just Dave and I trying to make it out. Pirate said he'd wait by himself in the cave until we could get a rescue party to him; but of course assistance would not reach him for at least two days, and that would be too late. Once, feeling I was the strongest, I said I wanted to try it alone. I reasoned that if I made it down I could send in help, and if I didn't make it Dave and Pirate would still have a chance if the weather cleared.

How easy it might have been if I could have fully deceived myself. I knew my reasons for a solo descent were flimsily constructed excuses to conceal my desire to save Art Davidson above all else. I became afraid that my fear of our situation was stripping away my sentiments of loyalty to the others. I didn't want Dave or Pirate to see my ruthless self-centeredness. But then, wasn't this need to save myself a sense of self-preservation? And wasn't this healthy, even necessary?

As I began to feel panicky, my eyes glanced swiftly over the ice and rocks and at the whiteness all around us. Dave looked at me. Pirate appeared lost in his thoughts. I didn't know what to say. Despite the urgency of my desire to try it alone, that other sense of being unalterably bound to Dave and Pirate persisted. Maybe this inclination to stick it out with the others was only a reaction to loneliness, but perhaps it was a basic reaction I couldn't violate.

My fingers began to throb and my head felt light. I didn't seem to have control of my thoughts. I wanted to take off by myself, but I couldn't abandon Dave and Pirate. I had to save myself at any cost, but I wouldn't be alive now if it hadn't been for Dave and Pirate. What good was there in perishing together? If I had a better chance of making it alone, shouldn't I forget about Dave and Pirate and take off without them?

I felt I had to scream or run across the ice. To relieve my tension I looked at the clouds. I studied the different shades of grayness that walled us in. And it worked. My panic disappeared as quickly as it had rushed up.

Dave said we ought to hold off deciding what to do because the whiteout might clear. I nodded. Pirate looked at the hole in the ice that was our cave's entrance.

Clouds clung to the pass, filtering the sun's light into a bleak variety of flat grays and whites. An eerie quietness had settled over the mountain; soundless and still, it seemed impossible that this was the same pass the wind had stormed through. The sky that had been terrifyingly alive hung around us lifelessly. The entire range, which had seemed to be some sort of living being during the days the wind had howled, now was only a frozen waste of ice and rock.

Hiding under the ice from all the fury, I'd felt closed in, but this day, standing outside in the stillness of the whiteout, I began to feel brief moments of claustrophobia, as if I were being smothered along with the mountain and all the peaks around us. Standing on our patch of ice it seemed as if the whiteout had cut us off from the world. The sky was gone, and we had only our little island of light in this immense grayness.

Pirate said we had to do something. We continued to stare into the cloud, hoping it would break open to let us descend. *Hoping*— we had come to understand it so well that it had lost much of its meaning; but none of its appeal. I decided that to hope was to ignore the reality of our situation in favor of a wishful belief that some stroke of luck would befall us. No one could come for us through this whiteout. I berated myself for ever hoping, and warned myself never to hope again. Faith was what I lacked. I needed faith that this whiteout, like any stretch of foul weather, would eventually end; and faith that we'd have the presence of mind and stamina to take advantage of that moment when it came. I told Dave we'd be lost if we stopped believing in ourselves; he looked puzzled and said, "Huh?"

Several minutes later I realized I was once again staring at the clouds, hoping they'd part.

As we grew weary of waiting for the whiteout to clear we searched among the rocks for food—a cache someone else might have left behind or some of our own supplies that had been blown away—but found nothing. We stood at the edge of the pass, looking down toward the 17,200-foot camp. Through the grayness I tried to picture Gregg, Shiro, John, and George camped in the cave, waiting patiently for a chance to look for us. Then I remembered they would have run out of food by now. But surely they hadn't left us.

For many minutes no one spoke. All our mountaineering experience told us that we should not descend into the whiteout because we would almost certainly lose our way, or else, weak and without a sense of balance, we would fall. At the same time, we were certain of what would be in store for us if we waited in the cave.

Hours had slipped by since we had first crawled out of the cave. Although the lateness of the hour was beginning to force us to make up our minds, every alternative still appeared futile. It seemed absurd to choose. I thought that if we ever decided there was no chance at all of our getting down, I'd use my last energies to wander up toward McKinley's north summit.

I told myself that was another desparate thought that ought to be discouraged. Our situation demanded thoughtfulness which we weren't certain we were capable of. The most frustrating part of having our minds affected by the altitude was our inability to know to what extent we were affected. Probably the duller we became, the less we realized we were dull at all.

At length it became apparent that our greatest chance lay in trying to find our way down the ice wall, instead of waiting for the whiteout to clear. Besides, we were disgusted with the cave; Pirate said crawling back into it would be the same as crawling into our grave. By descending we would at least be active, be trying. Dave said we'd better get our crampons on. Pirate said O.K., and I didn't say anything.

Dave, with Pirate lagging behind, headed back up the fifty yards or so to the cave, where we had left our crampons. I waited near the edge of the pass because Dave had thoughtfully offered to bring down my crampons and gear after he was set himself. As Pirate passed the scattered ruins of a large cache, I called after him to ask if he had checked it for food. He said that he and Dave had looked all through it without finding anything edible. Nonetheless, Pirate plowed again through the rubble of a shredded tarp, pieces of wooden crates which must have been airdropped, torn clothes, silverware, all sorts of things we couldn't eat. I figured the cache was most likely one that Washburn had carefully prepared after one of his scientific expeditions, but twenty years of storms and curious climbers had left it a trash heap half buried in the ice. After a minute, Pirate stopped searching and looked at me without speaking. I asked if he had found anything.

"No." Very slowly he continued on up to get his crampons.

I stood in a daze, not wanting to do anything until someone came to take care of me. Staring at the cache, I remembered advice Shiro had once given me; since it was urging me to move, I tried to suppress the thought. Yet it nagged me: "When there is only one way to survive in the mountains, you must check every possibility to the very end in order to find the one that works." The cache was a possibility. Just possibly some food remained hidden toward the bottom of the rubbish; but the cache was forty feet away, forty feet uphill. I stood still, without the energy or desire to move. Shiro's words kept repeating themselves in my mind. I heard them in his soft accent: " . . . check every possibility to the very end." I resisted checking the cache; a waste of energy, I rationalized. Then, not realizing I had started, I was walking toward the cache. To get a grip on my ice axe I forced my fingers around the shaft, no longer caring whether my blisters broke—I was going to dig.

I whacked at the ice where it held the canvas tarp; my hands, revolting at the pain, dropped the axe. The tarp hadn't budged. I picked up the axe, and by the time I had swung a couple more times I was in a frenzy. I slashed and beat at the canvas frozen into the ice. I pried and yanked. Hitting with my axe as hard as I could, I must have struck a rock, because the axe's metal adze broke.

I became furious. I couldn't stop. I smashed at the pieces of wood, lashing out with my axe until I collapsed onto my knees. I was out of breath and dizzy, but as soon as my head began to clear I started swinging at the debris again. Still on my knees, I uncovered bits of rotten rope, pots, old socks, ladles, odd boots; and of all the absurd, useless luxuries there was even a colander.

I attacked the cache, driven by an obsession to reach the bottom of it. My hands throbbed with pain and my feet had become numb, but all that mattered was that I check every last inch of the trash. A rage drove me to see what was underneath. When I discovered another layer, I was careful not to destroy anything. I opened a box, but it was full of clothes.

I kicked some of the surface junk aside with my boots, then dug in again with my axe. Ice and splintered wood and strips of canvas were frozen around each other. I grabbed and yanked and kicked, and swung the axe, and eventually I reached another unopened box. I pried it open: more clothes on top, but underneath lay several cloth bags, small, white bags. Excited and exhausted, I felt my heart beating wildly as I fumbled to see what was in one of the bags. The drawstring came loose, and as I looked into the bag I'm certain I would have cried, if my body had had enough water to spare for tears.

Dried potatoes!

Farther inside the crate sat a box of raisins packaged in a wrapper that had gone out of style at least fifteen years ago! I found two more bags of potatoes and even uncovered a can of ham without holes in it!

We ate!

Dave enlarged the cave. Crouched on his knees the circulation to his legs was partly cut off. He mentioned that his feet were icy-cold below the arches, and mumbled about warming them on someone's stomach, but he didn't want to bother Pirate or me. I heard him ramble on to himself: "Oh, well, a couple toenails lost, nothing new. . . . It won't happen to you, Dave baby . . . don't sweat it. . . ."

Far into the night Dave brewed hot drinks and made quantities of raisin, ham, and potato stew. Life seemed easy again. Our cave was more comfortable and we had the security of knowing there would be something to eat the next day. We settled in, determined to hold out another week if necessary but hoping, as we had hoped for the last six nights, that we could descend in the morning.

March 7: Green Feet

I dreamed that a kindly man cut off my feet every time they grew too large. There would be several minutes of relief each time he sliced them off and set them on a shelf, but always my feet, glowing a bright chartreuse, would swell again to the size of basketballs and ache as if about to burst until they were cut off. I was lying in a small, dark cellar, and before long the shelves that lined the walls were filled with huge, luminous, green feet.

Dave woke me to say my tossing was keeping him awake. A sharp, pulsating ache made both my feet feel as if they were about to explode. They had become partly frozen while I had dug for the food. I wasn't sure whether they had thawed or frozen some more during the night. The only way to relieve the pain was to shift their position; sleeping, I had dreamed of each shift as a thoughtful slice of my friend's knife.

The wind was gone and the whiteout had disappeared. Soon we were all awake, eating, drinking, and wondering where we would meet Gregg, Shiro, and the others. Pirate tried to get us to laugh by saying they had probably scratched us off and flown on home. They must have descended to the 14,400-foot igloos for food, but I figured that they would be coming up to look for us and that we'd run into them on the wall below our cave or perhaps down at 17,200 feet. Dave, not quite so optimistic, said we wouldn't see them until we reached the igloos.

Two hours after waking we attempted to pull on our boots. Once I screamed out loud as Dave shoved and jammed my feet into my boots. Since Pirate's hands were as bad as mine, Dave had to help force his boots on too. When he got around to putting his own boots on, Dave had more trouble than he had with either Pirate or me. The ends of both his feet were swollen.

After crawling out of the cave, we bumped into each other and sprawled onto the ice as we tried to control the uncoordinated blocks of pain that were our feet. Every time one of our boots touched the ice a burning sensation shot up the calf. Pirate spotted a four-engine plane circling the summit. We were not just about to rush down onto the open ice toward 17,200 feet, where the plane could easily spot us. Before setting foot on the steep ice below the pass we had to learn to walk and climb on our injured feet. We stepped in place and practiced traversing a gentle slope. Unfortunately, walking downhill was the most painful and difficult because all our weight jarred onto our frozen and half-frozen toes. Dave strapped on my crampons, then helped Pirate tighten his. Because his were the only hands that hadn't been frozen Dave also took the important anchor position at the end of the rope when we finally decided we were ready to start down.

The ice wall fell away from the pass at an angle of thirty to forty degrees. At sea level we could have almost played tag on ice no steeper than this; however, at eighteen thousand feet we had climbed this ice gingerly on the ascent, when or legs had been relatively strong and our balance keen. Now, as we wobbled on spindly, dried-up remnants of legs, each step was near the limit of our capability.

"Don't charge off, Pirate!" I felt I had to warn Pirate, who was leading, to go slowly even though he only crept out onto the ice wall. We tested each position of our feet before trusting our weight onto them.

Because the wind had stolen our packs we had our sleeping bags draped around our shoulders; they hung to our feet, sometimes snagging our crampons, but it was the only way we could carry the bags.

"Slower, Pirate!"

The only thing certain about each step was the pain it would send through our feet. Step after step Pirate led us across and down the ice. The rope tied us together with only a psychological protection; if one of us slipped, we would all peel off the wall. A belay was impossible. If we did come off there would be nothing we could do to arrest our fall until we crashed into the basin six hundred feet below.

Pirate stopped.

"Oh, God!" I whispered to myself. One of his crampons had loosened. We were caught on the steepest section of ice. Dave and I chopped out small ledges to relieve some of the strain on our ankles. Pirate's fingers had been too stiff to tie his crampon laces when we had started, but now they had to bind his crampon to his boot.

Dave called anxiously at Pirate to hurry up. My ankles felt on the verge of buckling. Pirate grappled with the stiff straps, cursing at the cold cutting into his fingers—he had to handle the metal crampon with bare fingers. He knew everything depended on him. Should he lose his balance while tugging at the frozen bindings, all our efforts to hold out during the storm would be for nothing.

Pirate straightened; he grabbed his ice axe. I sighed with relief and turned to see Dave grinning behind me.

"All right, you guys. . . . We're goin' down!"

Tense with caution, we placed one foot in front of the other. Each step was carefully considered. The large military plane which Pirate had noticed earlier swung out over the Kahiltna. Even if the plane located us, there was no way it could help us now. We didn't see Gregg, John, Shiro, and George climbing up toward us. There absence began to worry me because I knew they'd be here to help us down the ice if they could possibly manage it.

"Slow down, Pirate!"

With the steepest ice behind us, Pirate quickened his pace. Actually, he was taking a step only every two or three seconds, but that seemed dangerously fast to me.

"You're gettin' us down, Pirate—you crazy honcho!"

Pirate paused to turn and holler, "Aaahaaaa. . . ."

The rough but level ice of the basin began passing beneath us. "We did it, we did it," I repeated to myself.

However, as the ice rose ever so slightly toward the rocks, our feet became so heavy that we were soon stopping to rest every seven or eight steps. The rocks appeared unfamiliar. When Dave motioned for Pirate to turn right, I said I thought we had to head for the rocks to the left. After discussing the difference of opinion for a moment, we decided that none of us were certain which particular outcrop of rocks the cave was next to. Tired as we were, it was discouraging to think we might go fifty or a hundred feet out of our way if we climbed toward the wrong rocks. We compromised by striking out in a line running directly between the two main rock outcroppings. Ten and then twenty yards of ice were covered; Pirate called out that he could see a bamboo pole sticking out of the ice. It looked to be about ten feet high. Since we had not brought a bamboo pole to this point, we figured a helicopter must have landed rescuers who had left the pole behind. But where were they now? Maybe the others had had an accident. Anyway, the cave had to be near the pole.

Weary and growing apprehensive, we slowly approached the pole. One moment it was hundreds of feet away, then we suddenly realized it was only ten feet away and wasn't a bamboo pole at all. It was simply a willow wand. Our eyes had fooled us. Somehow the altitude or our dehydration or perhaps even our lack of food had affected our sense of depth perception. It was particularly startling because each of us had been deceived in the same way.

We passed by the willow wand and approached the cave. Just before we peered into it, I was seized with a sudden fear that we might see bodies. They could have been trapped here and could have never made it down for more food. We looked in; to my relief the cave was deserted. In one corner a small pile of food was stacked against a stove. They must have descended thinking we'd never come down; yet on the slight chance that we would they had left us the most favored delicacies—sausage, cocoanut balls Gregg's wife had made, and some of the fruitcake my grandmother had baked for us.

While we ate, the circling plane spotted us. Then Sheldon's silver Cessna 180 appeared and flew low over the basin. We waved. He swung around, came in lower yet, and dropped a bag. I retrieved it. Bits of a smashed orange were scattered on the ice. I picked up a carefully wrapped kit but couldn't figure out what it should be used for. Although it was tempting to leave it where it had fallen, I decided the others might be able to determine what it was. I felt somewhat foolish when Pirate immediately recognized it as a radio; the altitude was affecting me more than I wanted to admit. Either our minds were too fuzzy to operate the radio or else it had been damaged when dropped, because we couldn't get it to send or receive.

Filled with food and a little water, we continued the descent. With extreme caution we inched our way down among the rocks along the ridge. We were climbing several times more slowly than we had ever ascended this section of the route. Reaching the fixed ropes, we lowered our bags in front of us to free our arms for handling the ropes.

Our feet suffered a cutting pain every time our boots hit the ice. It became almost unbearable for Pirate and me to grip the rope with our frostbitten hands. Once I slipped, and as I grabbed the rope to halt my fall I could feel the skin and blisters tearing across my fingers.

Near the end of the ropes we entered a cloud. Despite the white-out, there could be no thought of waiting because we had to avoid bivouacking for another night. Since Dave had climbed this part of the route more often than Pirate or I, he took the lead. We climbed down deeper into the cloud. The tops of the high ridges on either side disappeared. Somewhere ahead in the grayness were two igloos and our friends; beyond the igloos lay an ice fall of enormous crevasses. Should we pass by the igloos, we would walk blindly over the edge of a crevasse. The grayness grew so thick that from my position in the middle of the rope I could see neither Dave nor Pirate.

Dave stopped, then started again. My knees and ankles seemed on the verge of collapsing. Slack rope on the snow in front of me indicated Dave had stopped again. We were lost.

Gray cloud and gray ice appeared the same; the glacier and the sky had become one wall of grayness. Since we couldn't see the slope where we set our feet, I began stumbling onto my hands with a crunching of stiff, swollen flesh.

I shouted into the grayness that I thought the igloos were to our right. The rope jerked me to a halt from behind; Pirate must have fallen onto the ice. I heard him yell that we should head more to the left. Dave said nothing. I lay flat on the ice myself, waiting for Pirate to pick himself up and retighten a loose crampon. After several minutes Dave called, "Let's go!"; with considerable effort I got to my feet, and we started staggering on through the whiteout. As we passed through the endless grayness, I began to think we had already gone beyond the igloos. I tried to pull my befuddled mind together to be ready to throw myself onto the ice in arrest position should Dave plunge into a crevasse. I still could not see him, and the rope disappeared in the grayness about ten feet in front of me. We might have passed within ten feet of the camp without spotting it. As the snow became deeper, I began wondering whether the igloos would be buried. Dave plodded on.

Blind, and uncertain that my legs could manage another step, I let the rope running to Dave pull me on.

"Waahoooo. . . ." A call in front of me—unable to see Dave, I wasn't sure it had been his voice.

"Igloos!" It was Dave's voice.

With luck or an astonishing instinct he had led us straight to the igloos.

Dave waited for Pirate and me to appear out of the whiteout so the three of us could share that first moment of greeting the others.

Nearly delirious with relief and joy we shoveled the entrance of the main igloo free of some drifted snow, then pulled back the tarp which closed the igloo from the weather. We peered inside.

Darkness! The igloo was empty. We found the other igloo also deserted and dark. There wasn't even a note. Were we alone on the mountain? Where were they? None of us felt like voicing our disappointment that the others were gone, that they must have given up on us.

We attacked the food left in the largest igloo. Mashed potatoes, rice, jello, gorp, freeze-dried meat—never had food been so satisfying, but never before had our appetites been really insatiable. Long after we were full we continued to stuff food into our mouths—we had a compulsion to devour everything that was edible. It seemed irreverent to leave any food uneaten.

Despite the excitement of our feast, we ate quietly because we were weary and apprehensive about the fate of the other four.

March 8: Sunshine

We prolonged breakfast as long as possible. It was good to eat. And while we ate we inspected our purplish-black feet. Although the swelling began above our ankles, only our toes and patches on our heels were grossly discolored. The first attempts at forcing our misshapen feet into boots were so agonizing that we discussed cutting our boots to make more room. Pirate even suggested that we throw the boots away, bundle our feet in socks, and wrap them with cloth. Before resorting to this, we jammed, squeezed, beat, cussed, and eventually our boots went on. However, they fit so tightly that the pressure caused a constant throbbing ache.

Even though Dave's feet had become the most discolored and swollen, he said they weren't terribly painful. We wondered whether the parts that were numb might still be frozen, or whether the nerves had been injured.

We crawled out of the dimness of the igloo to squint into a blazing sun which hung in the sky beyond the massive upthrust of Foraker's ridges. It didn't seem to be a winter sun; close and burning, its hot light felt so tangible that we playfully snatched at it to catch a handful. The air temperature was $-16°$, but the sun warmed our cheeks as we lingered near the igloos. After those cold and dark days without the sun, we absorbed the sunshine with a thirst almost as consuming as our need for food and water. I couldn't remember ever being so at peace with myself. I thought all I would ever ask of life would be to let me feel the sunshine.

We saw it flash in the sun before we heard it. The jet shot low over the Buttress, shattering the still air with a blast that echoed off the ice around us long after the plane had disappeared. The jet must have cut around behind the Buttress, because after two or three minutes it reappeared to scream past again, this time at our level. We waved as the sleek form of glinting metal streaked by; it was more a conditioned reaction than a heartfelt greeting.

The four-engine plane we had observed the previous day thundered out from behind the southern flank of McKinley and teamed up with the jet in buzzing our basin. It seemed strange to be found when we didn't feel the least bit lost. As they rushed purposefully overhead, the planes aroused in us a sense of urgency. We became anxious to descend to the Kahiltna, where Sheldon could pick us up. We wanted to get down and out.

A stove, some food, and odd pieces of clothing were thrown into our sleeping bags. When we roped up, the tightness of the rope cinched around my middle felt pleasant. A feeling of security and confidence came with being tied together again. I took the lead; we set out.

Each time one of my boots set down on the ice I felt a grating sensation just above my toes. Pirate and I were certain our feet had thawed because with each step the soft, injured tissue ground against itself. Walking would have damaged the tissue less if our feet had remained frozen. Dave was afraid parts of his feet were still frozen. "Feels like the ice crystals in the frozen flesh are grinding against the thawed tissue," he said.

The jet flew away, but the four-engine plane circled ever closer. I wondered how we must have appeared to people in the plane. On the mountain's frozen vastness they must have seen us as tiny animated specks, linked together by a thread of a rope, hobbling along the windswept ice and stepping unsteadily through occasional drifts of soft snow. On one particularly low pass of the plane the deafening and dissonant vibrations of its four engines set off an avalanche of ice blocks from the crest of the ridge above and behind us. Loose snow flew in the wake of great chunks of ice, some of them smashing into smaller segments as they rolled and swung unpredictably down the incline. One block veered toward us. It was no use trying to run from it because there was no way of knowing its course or which direction to run; besides, it was catapulting—sometimes in the air, sometimes gouging through the snow—much faster than we could run. We watched the block crash into the level basin, slow down, and finally come to rest about thirty yards from us.

Dave voiced our irritation: "We might need to be rescued if that crazy plane shakes down any more avalanches."

I thought to myself how it seemed that the plane and the mountain had thrown some angry words at each other, and we'd been caught in the middle of their disagreement.

On its next pass, still lower and noisier, the plane dropped a small parachute, which drifted out over the crevasse field to our left and below. We figured it was probably an air-to-ground radio, but trying to recover it from the tangled icefall was unthinkable.

We limped on toward Windy Corner. Before us, Foraker and all the peaks along the Kahiltna rose abruptly and sharply into the clear sky. The ice and snow reflected a brilliant whiteness and the dark lines of rock stood out more boldly than I remembered. In this new clarity the rhythm of every sweep of ice became so startling and the mystery in the shadows so apparent that it seemed as if these mountains had never been explored, or climbed, or even seen.

The plane droned over us again to drop another parachute, which also landed among the crevasses.

Sometimes our crampon points snagged our sleeping bags as we dragged them over the ice. Whenever one of us stopped with crampon trouble, all of us stopped; when one moved ahead, we all moved ahead. I amused myself with the thought that the rope was the body of a long and skinny caterpillar, and we were the legs.

The few times we traveled more than a dozen yards without

someone catching his bag on crampon points I would halt our procession to relieve the pain in my feet. Resting, I'd shut my eyes and face the sun. Although its light was still warm, it didn't feel as tangible or alive as it had earlier.

After we passed beyond a slight rise of ice we caught sight of the rocks of Windy Corner for the first time in over three weeks. I felt more hurried. Each step was taking us down to Gregg, Shiro, John, and George. The closer we were coming to them, the more keenly I felt our separation from them. By nightfall we should be with them again; maybe Sheldon could take us out the next morning or even this evening if we managed to reach the iglooplex at 10,200 feet in time.

As we neared Windy Corner, the plane dropped yet another parachute, and this one landed only a few hundred yards ahead of us on the ice. When we reached the Corner the parachute still appeared to be about fifty yards away and somewhat downhill from us. I asked if we really had to go after it; Dave said he sure as hell didn't want to go out of his way to retrieve it. Pirate, who had said scarcely a word since leaving the igloos, told us the idea of accepting an unneeded rescue package did not appeal to him. I sensed that besides our weariness and pride in making it down on our own another factor was making it difficult for us to bring ourselves to go for the parachuted package: the parcel, whatever it contained, represented our first real contact with the outside world —it threatened the solitude that had become our way of life.

Nevertheless, we had an obligation to retrieve the package which the plane had gone to so much trouble to deliver. Pirate offered to go after it alone to save Dave and me from having to go fifty or so yards out of our way. We untied and let the rope fall onto the ice. Pirate headed off. After about five minutes he returned with a radio. He pulled out the antenna: "McKinley expedition to plane. . . . McKinley expedition to plane. . . . Do you read me? . . . Do you read me?"

Nothing.

"McKinley expedition to plane. . . ."

"Mt. McKinley expedition, this is Rescue 489. . . . This is Rescue 489 calling Mt. McKinley expedition. Over."

"McKinley expedition to Rescue 489. . . . We read you loud and clear. . . . Uh . . . what do you want? Over."

"What is your condition? Over."

Dave told Pirate not to mention our frostbite, and Pirate agreed that they didn't have to know about our hands and feet. I said it would be better if we told them now because they'd find out later anyway. Dave voiced his concern that they might become alarmed and attempt something rash. "Yea. . . ." said Pirate, "but Art's right." He handed me the radio.

"All O.K., except for a little frostbite," I announced to the plane. "We will climb down to ten thousand two hundred feet for pickup by Sheldon. Over."

"What is the extent of your frostbite? Did you reach the summit?"

We had forgotten that only the three of us knew whether or not we had reached the summit. But what did it matter? In the face of all that had happened in the last week, the pilot's question sounded irrelevant.

"Hands and feet a bit black and swollen. We climbed to the summit at seven in the evening about eight days ago; uncertain of exact date. Over."

As the plane flew behind the buttress the radio went dead. We could send and receive only while the plane was in direct line of sight with us. Since each pass of the plane allowed enough time for only two or three questions to be radioed from ground to air, it was more than an hour before we learned that Gregg and John were safe at the 7,500-foot Kahiltna Hilton. We were told that they could have been picked up the previous day, but that Gregg had insisted on staying on the mountain until everyone was accounted for. Although no one had spotted George and Shiro, it was thought that they were in the 10,200-foot iglooplex.

"McKinley expedition, this is Rescue 489. . . . Two Huey helicopters are enroute to mountain from Talkeetna. . . . Do you wish to be picked up? I repeat: do you wish to be picked up? Over."

"We can walk down to ten thousand two hundred feet," I radioed back. "But are helicopters already coming? Over."

"Helicopters are enroute from Talkeetna. They are already airborne. Do you want to be picked up? Over."

Again the plane circled behind the West Buttress and we lost contact with it.

I didn't know what we ought to do. "What do you think, Dave?" I asked.

Before he answered Dave glanced back up the way we had descended, then stared at the ice at his feet. He tapped one foot against the other. "Aw, let's climb on down," he said, looking up at me. "I want to surprise old Shiro and George. I'll bet they think we've had it."

"Yaaa," Pirate laughed, "let's walk down and scare em. . . . Arrr . . . aaghaa . . . hawyaaa. . . . George will think we're ghosts. . . . Aahaaa."

"Dave," I said firmly, "your big toes looked pretty bad this morning. Wouldn't it be better to accept the ride?"

"My feet are all right!"

"You know"—Pirate didn't look at Dave or me, but at the ice slopes winding down toward the iglooplex—" if we are flown out it'll look like we couldn't have climbed down. Everyone will say we had to be saved."

"As long as the helicopters are coming in anyway," I answered, "why don't we risk losing a little pride instead of a little more of our feet?"

"McKinley expedition, this is Rescue 489. . . . Do you want to be picked up? Over."

Another hour passed while we talked to the plane, a C130, and tried to decide whether to walk down or be flown out. The afternoon began slipping away. Suddenly Pirate said, "Hey, I hear a copter!" and several minutes later we saw two helicopters circling over the Kahiltna, close to the ice. The plane was radioing the copters and to Gregg and John, relaying messages back to us. When we were told that rescuers had come all the way from Seattle, Dave exploded.

"Damn, why did all those honchos have to come up!"

"We can take care of ourselves!" Pirate added.

For several minutes we discussed the planes and rescuers; it all seemed so unnecessary. Dave said, "Hell, I don't want to feel responsible for this commotion." Pirate told me to radio the plane that we didn't need saving, and that the copters could fly on home. I thought of sending the C130 a simple message to the effect that we had climbed the mountain, had sat out a storm, and were now going to climb down.

Voicing our irritation somehow made it begin to pass. I started thinking of all our friends and of people we didn't know who were trying to help us. On a previous McKinley rescue a search plane had crashed and the pilot had been killed; people hadn't forgotten that accident, yet still they were out trying to save us. And if the storm had lasted two more days, or if our hands and feet had been in worse shape, our survival might have depended on their efforts. When Gregg had decided we were dead or near-dead, the only thing he could have done was call in the planes and hope we'd be found in time.

The four engines of the C130 shook the air as the plane lumbered over us again; I shuddered at the noise.

The radio operator in the plane pressed us for a decision about flying out or walking down, but because we felt alternately irritated and thankful for the rescue it was 3:30 before we decided which way to leave the mountain; our decision was forced on us. Night would come before we would be able to reach the iglooplex; a bivouac along the way was a grim thought. Dave had noticed a plume of snow blowing off Kahiltna Pass far below us; a wind appeared to be funneling through from the north.

Communicating with the plane, along with our own indecision, had taken so much time that we now found ourselves dependent on the helicopters.

I radioed that we agreed to be flown off and asked for a weather prediction. The C130 answered that a ground blizzard had come up on the Kahiltna, causing the helicopters to have trouble landing. The forecast read: "A large front is moving in from the northwest. Winds in excess of one hundred miles per hour are expected within twenty-four hours."

The plane circled away. Dave checked his watch as twelve minutes passed before we were able to reestablish contact with the C130.

"McKinley expedition, this is rescue 489. Is it still calm at Windy Corner?"

A slight breeze had begun blowing around the Corner; I told the plane that the copter would have to get here soon because the wind was already starting up. The plane reported that because blowing snow was keeping the visibility on the surface of the Kahiltna near zero the copters were having difficulty maneuvering and could not start up immediately. A landing at 10,200 feet to check for George and Shiro had been impossible. The helicopter pilots didn't know whether they would be able to land at 7,500 feet for Gregg and John.

To warm our bodies Dave, Pirate, and I began stepping in place. Around us the breeze grew more constant and slightly more forceful. Even from Windy Corner, we could see that the snow plume over Kahiltna Pass had become enormous. We began hearing a deep, distant roaring of wind coming up from below. The mountain was waking again. A breeze sighed and whispered around the ice and rock behind us.

The C130 radioed that one copter had been able to land near Gregg and John's igloo, and that the other Huey had begun climbing to our altitude. The plane swung out over the Kahiltna; we glimpsed the helicopter circling up from below.

A sleek, gray, lenticular cloud, appearing from nowhere, now obscured the summit of Foraker. Snow blowing off the lower ridges of Foraker and Crosson marked the advance of the storm up the mountains. A high haze was seeping into the sky and the sun, lower and diffused, no longer warmed our faces. Our feet, which had been pulsating with pain for hours, felt better, but only because they were being anesthetized by the cold.

The helicopter was gaining altitude, but so was the wind. The C130 instructed us to be ready to leap into the copter if it could land. The wailing of the wind through Kahiltna Pass filtered up to us through the Valley of Silence, up over the ice wall and the tiny plateau that had been our favorite lunch stop. We decided that if the copter failed to land we would retreat to the 14,400-foot igloo to wait out the storm.

I wondered whether George and Shiro had any idea of what was going on and decided that they were most likely oblivious to everything but the pounding of the wind over their igloo. Dave said it was frustrating not knowing what condition they were in. Pirate figured they were probably sleeping through the entire rescue operation. Although they were probably comfortably camped in the iglooplex, each of us knew that something could have gone wrong with their descent. Dave remarked on George's earlier unsteadiness on the Windy Corner ice, and I recalled how racking Shiro's cough had been the last time we had seen him—over a week ago. If they had begun descending during the storm, they could easily have been blown off the Buttress. If they had tried to climb down during the whiteout, they could have blindly stumbled into a crevasse.

When at last the helicopter reached our altitude, it flew in tight circles around Windy Corner. We were unable to radio the copter directly, but the C130 persistently banked overhead to relay messages. We were told that at thirteen thousand feet the Huey was operating near the limit of its capability and that if it landed it might not be able to take off with our added weight.

The breeze around us had become almost a wind; the helicopter hovered unsteadily. As it lowered close—thirty, then twenty feet—over the ice, the wind-blast from its prop set off a cloud of snow that all but obscured the copter from our sight. We heard the whirling blades being revved up, then saw the helicopter rise above the cloud. It circled as the snow settled. Pirate waved it toward a flat surface. It hovered, then slowly came down.

All at once the machine was setting down on the ice, and we were rushing toward it. Our bags were shoved through an open hatch. The two cleanshaven faces looked strange. A voice with a southern accent said, You'll have to leave some of your gear, or we might not make it off."

We clambered through the door. Our sleeping bags were in. They contained all we had—except the rope.

Just as the pilot gunned the copter's motors and the windblast from the rotary blades sent snow flying across the ice and rocks we'd been standing on, I caught sight of our rope, lying loosely on the ice where we had unroped.

With the deafening roar of the straining motors, we lifted off. For an instant I pictured climbers reaching Windy Corner in some future season; they might find the coils of our rope frozen to the ice and wonder how it had happened that a rope had been left out in the open.

It seemed unfair that the rope which had tied the three of us together over so much ice had to remain on the mountain. We had depended on it to keep us together when we had descended from the summit in the dark and when we had stumbled through the whiteout. We had relied on the rope for protection on the ridge, on the steep ice, and among the crevasses.

We rose and drifted away from Windy Corner. "This is unreal," Dave whispered to himself.

A pilot asked if we were all right. Pirate mumbled, "Sure, we're O.K."

When the co-pilot asked if we needed anything, I said "Yea, three beers." He laughed and said he couldn't help us there. I shrugged and looked out the window; I hadn't really wanted a beer, and the conversation suddenly seemed stupid.

The pilots talked of all the folks that were worried about us; there was nothing we could say. Our copter circled, waiting to be joined by the one that had picked up Gregg and John. As we drifted west over the Kahiltna I hoped we wouldn't see that awful crevasse and the tiny hole in the surface of the glacier; yet I couldn't help looking down on the area of the accident. Fortunately, the surface of the glacier was hidden by the ground blizzard.

Once together, the two copters spiralled upward over the Kahiltna to gain altitude. We could not see John or Gregg, but knew they were inside the other copter, looking for us, knowing we were flying out with them. We were informed that the Seattle rescue party had been left at the 7,500-foot igloo to search for the last two members of the expedition, As the copters straightened their course to the southeast, toward Talkeetna, Dave said something about Shiro and George huddling together in the dimness of their igloo.

"There's quite a crowd waiting at the Talkeetna airstrip for you guys," said the co-pilot.

We caught only one glimpse of our route to the summit when the copters veered around the Kahiltna Peaks, and even then we were unable to see Denali Pass. The sky had become a deep blue; evening was settling over the range. The rock on the peaks appeared black; the glaciers, already hidden from the sun, were dark; but the ice fluting on the higher ridges reflected a delicate pink light. The low sun through the haze filled the west with soft, warm light which belied the fury of the storm that was mounting.

As we flew over a sprawling, corniced and knife-edged ridge of Mt. Hunter, Dave exclaimed: "Wow! I've been down there! That's the ridge I climbed three years ago."

We passed on, and over the foothills. We stared ahead to catch sight of the lights of Talkeetna out on the flat. The three of us said very little, and when we did speak we were suprised to find ourselves somewhat self-conscious; our voices sounded slightly un-familiar in this new situation.

"Sure wish we could have walked in on George and old Shiro," Dave said slowly. "We're leavin' too fast."

"Yaaa. . . . I know what you mean," sighed Pirate.

Only now that we were leaving did we begin to realize fully how isolated we had been, and how closely the three of us had been bound together; it would never be that way again. I kept seeing our rope lying discarded on the ice.

McKinley from south: (1) 14,400' camp; (2) 17,200' camp; (3) Denali Pass, ice cave; (4) summit.

Art and Dave

Ray "Pirate" Genet

Gregg

Ray

Dave

Art

Getting Back

THE HELICOPTERS CIRCLED once over the streets of Talkeetna, then lowered us into a pandemonium of friends, press, and curiosity-seekers. Gregg rushed joyously toward me, but as he grabbed and shook my hand, I involuntarily screamed and jerked it away. Before I had a chance to explain that my fingers were frostbitten, a cameraman pulled me and the other two summit climbers aside for a television interview. While we talked to the cameras Gregg and John stood forlorn and bewildered just outside the floodlights. We hardly felt triumphant for having reached the summit; but the summit did serve as an acceptable justification for all the commotion, and even for our having started up the mountain in the first place.

When the newsmen let us go we hugged and kissed our friends, some of whom had been camping in Talkeetna for three days, hoping we'd return. Someone passed a carton of real milk. Gregg threw his arm around my shoulder. John said that during the last few days he and Gregg had been so certain the three of us were dead that they had stopped talking about us and even avoided mentioning us in their journals.

When rescuers reached Shiro at the 10,200-foot igloo on the Kahiltna, his first words were, "Did you find their bodies? Were you able to recover the bodies?" Then, as one of the climbers recounted, "Nishimae's worried face at first went blank when he learned the others were safely off the mountain, then slowly changed to a look of sheer joy as he realized they were not dead."

Shiro departed for Japan three days after coming off McKinley. The rest of us returned to the Institute of Arctic Biology in Fairbanks for a post-expedition evaluation.

The scientists just shook their heads in disbelief at the human wrecks the mountain had sent back to them. They described us in clinical terms such as "obtundation" which denotes dullness or depression. They hooked our heads back up the the electroencephalograph and recorded mental patterns common for a person sleeping lightly. Physically we had set out lean and fit, with a very low percentage of body fat. After five weeks on the mountain Dave, Pirate and I had lost an average of 35 pounds each, a situation we set out to rectify with enthusiasm—the second morning back I had a regular breakfast plus 19 eggs.

We tended to our frostbite with considerably less relish. John's ear and Gregg's big toe healed up in about six weeks. Dave's feet kept him in the hospital for 45 days and in bed for another 16. The doctors learned to keep a close eye on him because twice he had snuck out of the hospital to roam the streets of Anchorage, looking for rock walls to climb. Dave eventually lost some toes, but his hands were ok.

I was restricted to a wheelchair for eight weeks and then to crutches for another six. To observe how the body would heal the frostbite naturally, the doctors left the blackened skin and flesh in place to see what would happen. After 14 weeks the decaying parts of my feet were beginning to smell pretty bad. So late one night, I took out a razor blade, sterilized it over a match and cut off the dead and rotting pieces. After this bit of midnight surgery, the doctors relented and finished up the operation.

Both of Genet's feet had frostbite, but the hospital couldn't hold on to him more than about three weeks. "You shouldn't listen to those doctors," he said. "I got the circulation going in my toes after those days of lying around the hospital by dancing for twenty-eight hours one weekend. You know, that's how you've got to treat frostbite."

We were informed that our estimates of the extremes of the storm had been conservative. The U.S. Air Force, Aerospace and Recovery Center placed the winds in excess of 150 miles per hour and the temperature at −50° which produced a wind chill temperature of more than 148° below zero.

Sheldon's own on the spot description of the storm ran something like: "Yea, I was hucklebuck'n on up there to take a look at ma boys, when I look out the window... Whoa... I seen this ridge just standin' still. I look down at my speedometer and it says 140 miles per hour. Yowza, I had to fly 140 just to keep even with that ol' wind."

A grim testimony to the force of the wind high on McKinley occurred the following July. A sudden storm caught seven young climbers between Denali Pass and the summit. The air temperature was warmer, but the wind blew with nearly the same force as the storm that Dave, Pirate and I experienced. The seven climbers died. Only three of their bodies were recovered. The leader of that ill-fated expedition, Joe Wilcox, survived. In the context of a study on the storms of McKinley he said that in the winter the three of us "...probably endured the most severe high altitude windstorm of any mountaineers who lived to tell about it."

Another comment on the conditions we faced came from Dr. Terris Moore, one of the pioneers of Alaskan mountaineering and author of *Mt. McKinley—The Pioneer Climbs:* "If my thinking and computations are correct, your winter expedition has made the highest climb yet into Alaskan skies: over twenty-three thousand feet..." Dr. Moore explained the difference between geographic altitude and the simulated or barometric altitude which indicates the thinness of the air. In terms of the scarcity of oxygen, our winter climb was evidently equivalent to ascending a 23,500 peak in the Andes or Himalayas.

Infinitely more difficult to define and gauge than the extremes of the storm or the beating our bodies took was the effect the experience had on our minds and outlook on life. Initially we all felt the jarring reentry to everyday life. During the first hours and in some cases days after we returned all of us experienced the sense of isolation and unreality which we were told is similar to severe psychosis. As George described it: "After the silence of the glacier; all the noises, voices and sights which rushed at us when we returned were overwhelming in their confusion... I had difficulty understanding what was going on."

Over days and weeks our senses cleared, our spontaneity returned. We appeared to be our old selves once again. And we began to get some perspective on what we had been through. Gregg wrote me a letter which made me appreciate his sense of leadership, and his courage to support it in an entirely new light. Gregg wrote:

> The expedition represented an obstacle to what I wanted to do with my time. By the time we actually got together, all my original desire to do the thing, and all the excitement and joy with which I had faced the thing earlier, had gone by the wayside in the process of getting it on the road. As a result, though in the final analysis I enjoyed the expedition, all I wanted to do was to get back to what at this time seems more meaningful to the continuing evolutionary process of my life. I am sorry if these feelings were terribly apparent. I didn't mean them to be. I am also sorry if, because of these things, I wasn't quite the leader you guys expected me to be...

After the expedition we each went our separate ways. I haven't seen Gregg since he said good-by to me in the hospital, but I often think of how he had led us through every hour of cold even though his heart was thousands of miles away; he had not wanted to make the summit himself as much as help the rest of us reach it.

Shiro returned to his wife and new baby in Japan. George went back to his clinic and John to his research at the University of Washington. As soon as his feet were healed, Dave headed off to Antarctica, where working with archeologists he stumbled across a rare fossil that was a key link in the theory of continental drift. Genet had become the Pirate, more boisterous and outrageous than ever; he started guiding on McKinley. Gregg returned to his wife and his dream of sailing. Within a year I had married, become a father, and could sense my priorities beginning to shift.

We headed back out into life somewhat altered and redirected. Inside, we were each a little different for our experience; but how it would affect the course of our lives we would know only after the passage of time.

We each packed our own lodestone up the mountain in the winter, and we each would offer different answers to the questions: Why do you climb? What did you get from the winter expedition? We solved none of life's problems, but I believe all of us returned with a new awareness of some of its realities. Each of us may have realized in his own way, if only for a moment, what Saint Exupery spoke of as ". . .that new vision of the world won through hardship."

Afterword

> Annapurna was a treasure upon which we would
> feast the rest of our lives. It was time to go on.
> There are other Annapurnas in the lives of men.
> —Maurice Herzog

IT IS NOW twenty years since we climbed McKinley in the winter. During this time I've often been asked what happened to everyone. Did we go on to other climbs? Did the winter ascent have lasting effects on us?

Over the years, I've often thought how those 42 days on the mountain in winter altered the course of our lives. And I've talked and corresponded with some of the others. So, in conjunction with the republication of MINUS 148°, I'll share some of our thoughts and look back at how that experience became part of our lives, and, for some of us a turning point.

Gregg Blomberg and Ray Genet had quite different reactions to the winter climb. Genet would be drawn into the mountains for the rest of his life, but for Gregg, this would be his last climb.

The impact of our experience on Gregg was revealed in a letter he wrote me many years later. "After 19 years I read the book (MINUS 148°)...I had not read it for all these years because I simply did not wish to relive the experience. The climb was a low point for me...Farine's death easily showed me that climbing was not important enough anymore to me to die for it. For the rest of the climb I was ambivalent about being there..."

When we think of great achievement in the mountains we usually recall how someone's driving desire to reach a summit forced a way over incredible obstacles. Gregg, I realize more clearly now, showed a more unusual and less obvious courage. Faced with the finality of our friend's death and wanting to stand not on the summit but in a sunnier place thousands of miles away, Gregg nevertheless stuck with us. It was his care for us that made him risk his own safety and endure all those uncertain days of cold and darkness. "I don't know," he says, "if I would have ever recovered if you guys had died up there."

Shortly after our winter climb, Gregg and his wife Edi got their sailboat. Although they didn't sail around the world, their boat brought them to peaceful Lopez Island in the San Juans off the Washington coast. There, on some land close to the sea, Gregg built a house, barn, and other farm buildings.

He puts up about 150 acres of hay each summer, keeps a large garden, and watches over about 85 fruit and nut trees. He and Edi have a daughter, Cedar, and a son, Zack. "The McKinley trip," he says, "was easy compared to raising kids."

As for mountains, Gregg writes, "Last summer I climbed Mt. Baker, my first time climbing in 18 years since McKinley. We have a view of Mt. Baker from our house and I had long promised myself a view of the farm from the summit."

"The only thing wrong with mountains," Gregg goes on to say, "is they are so far from salt water. In the last few years I have taken to sea kayaking. I built a traditional style kayak and a dugout canoe in the west coast or Nootkan style. I've become intrigued with the fantastic art of the coast aboriginals and we are now manufacturing tools for carvers and sculptors working in the tradition of the original Americans. I am quite pleased to be doing this work, and we are very happy living in this small and supportive community."

Genet, on the other hand threw himself into the mountains with a passion rarely seen anywhere. Before our winter climb, his brash and restless temperament had bounced him around from job to job and occasionally got him chased out of the country by immigration officials. In McKinley, he found an outlet for his incredible energy and an arena for his exuberant personality.

Pirate became the first full-time mountaineering guide on McKinley. Through Genet Expeditions, he helped dozens of others to realize their dreams of climbing the mountain. With his rallying cry of "to the summit," Genet pushed, cajoled, cursed, and did whatever necessary to get his clients safely up and down. As a guide, he would reach the summit more than 30 times.

In 1979, Genet teamed up with veteran dog sledder Joe Redington; together, they became the first to mush dogs to the summit. Such feats and his flamboyant personality drew attention, but it was the many times he risked his life to help others that endeared him to people. On one occasion, a military plane crashed near the summit of sixteen thousand foot Mt. Sanford. Conditions precluded a helicopter or regular ground rescue. Genet and another climber volunteered to search for survivors. Shortly after flying to the mountain, his companion came down with pulmonary edema and died before he could be evacuated. The military pleaded with Genet not to risk another accident, but Pirate prevailed, went back up alone and, in deteriorating weather, found the plane. An aura of heroic invincibility developed around Genet.

The legend of Genet grew, part of it coming from his way with the women. Decked out in a leather vest that flung open across his broad chest, carabiners jangling from his belt, he was macho to the core. The ladies loved him for it. On forays into Anchorage for provisions, he was known to breeze through a store and literally sweep some lovely clerk off her feet. "Ah ha... I'll take you up McKinley," he'd say with his thick European accent and that gleam in his eye. "Sure you can make it... you'll love it...trust me." The sweet young thing would be halfway to his cabin in Talkeetna before she'd begin coming to her senses.

Ray Genet lived life on his own terms: infecting others with his outlandish ways and his reckless abandon.

At the age of 50, Ray went on an expedition to Mt. Everest. He became sick in Nepal. Released from the hospital in Katmandu, he helicoptered to base camp. Without taking time for his body to recover, let alone acclimatize, he charged up to the high camps. It wasn't in his nature to turn back. Depleted physically, he somehow forced enough energy out of his body to reach the summit. On the descent, another climber was too exhausted to continue, so Ray, also near his limits, bivouacked with her. They died in the night, a short way below the summit of Everest. His body rests there to this day.

In Alaska the story of Genet's life and last climb filled the newspapers for days. He had become larger than life. People who had never met him loved him and mourned his passing. A hero had died.

But Pirate wasn't quite finished. Six months later, he made newspapers around the world under the headline—"GENET'S LAST JOKE." In the tradition of carrying little mementos to the summit for friends, Genet had taken up a young lady's phone number. So it was that the next climbers to reach the top of Everest found a note tacked to the summit— "for a good time, call Pat 907-274. . . ."

The winter climb also marked a turning point in the life of Shiro. He had been a fearless young climber, who would climb through the night and into the next day to reach a summit. He became an elder who, in the Japanese tradition, would not go for a summit himself, but draw on his experience and judgment to lead others. After McKinley, Shiro returned to Japan. He led a number of expeditions, including the first ascent of an extremely difficult Himalayan climb on which the summit climbers died tragically on their way down.

At home in Osaka, Shiro teaches English and, with his lovely wife Sachi, has raised a son and a daughter. His love for Alaska has never diminished and he's returned several times. "You are so lucky in Alaska," he says, "to have so much beautiful wild country. It is a dream land."

George Wichman stayed in Alaska, practicing orthopedic surgery and spending as much time as possible with his kids in that wild country. Their outings were not so often to the mountains as to the sea, particularly the remote bays and fjords of Prince William Sound.

When I asked George what he remembered most about our winter climb, he said, "Nothing really. My mind blocks out life's most unpleasant experiences."

With a little coaxing he recalled the "pristine beauty of the glaciers...
the shades of blue in the winter sky... seeing the northern lights from a
ridge high on McKinley." Then shaking his head slightly, George said,
"Art, the really horrible part was knowing you and Ray and Dave were
dying in the storm at Denali Pass and feeling so helpless. It was so hard to
turn and start down, leaving you up there."

Perhaps more than George or any of the rest of us, John Edwards was
haunted by ambivalent feelings about the winter climb and his role in it.
It was in a letter John wrote 19 years after our climb that I first learned
how he felt. "On the positive side," John wrote, "the experience of being
on that great climb was certainly a high point in my life, literally and
figuratively. I can look back on it as an experience few people ever know;
to have pushed to, and found the limits of one's physical and mental
endurance."

"On the negative side there were periods of self-doubt when I was
seized by recrimination for not having been a physically strong member
of the party. Did that reduce the effectiveness of the team as a whole? For
some years afterward, climbing was no longer a simple pure pleasure."

Had we known John's feelings, any one of us would have instantly
reaffirmed his contributions to the climb; his humor and strength of
character helped bond us together. Fortunately John didn't stay away
from the mountains. Over the years, he climbed all the volcanoes and
major peaks in Washington and made ascents in Europe and South
America, often accompanied by his wife Ola.

"The urge to climb has still been there," he writes, "but the stronger
thread of my mountain activities has been in Alpine ecology. Ola and I
have worked for over a decade on the plants and insects of the alpine
zone on Mt. Rainier. So long as my legs still work, and I can add collecting gear to an alpine pack, I expect to continue to explore the secrets of
the strange insects that live in cold places. A couple of trips to Antarctica
to pry into the private lives of its hardy insects also gave a chance to
wander in the mountains of Tierra del Fuego. I think the satisfaction of

this work, with the opportunity it creates to be in the mountains, if not on top of them, has exorcised the remaining demons of despair about my role on the McKinley expedition."

When I've seen Dave from time to time, he seems never to change. He's still that 6 foot 7 inch man-child, bubbling over with enthusiasm and friendliness. Dave's blessed with a delightful, romantic innocence that has never let him get too serious. Let others worry about careers and the practicalities of life, Dave was going for enchantment in the woods.

On his way back from a trip to Antarctica, Dave fell in love with a New Zealand girl. After meeting up again in Nepal, they traveled through Asia, Europe, and Canada. Dave and Sally got married and returned to Alaska to live in the woods near McKinley. Cutting and peeling his own logs, he built a beautiful log house—but, well, it wasn't quite on his land. The site Dave favored for his house was only a couple of hundred yards from what was officially available from the state. So Dave had thought "what the heck—nobody's going to mind out here in the woods." Unfortunately the state agency that had to deal with such things couldn't adjust its regulations to Dave's idea of where his house should be. A string of eviction notices followed.

There were a few anxious moments, but when his house site came up for grabs in a land lottery, dozens of Dave's friends entered the drawing. Surely one would draw his parcel and be able to give it to him. It worked and Dave got his land.

His house was secure, though a bit isolated, being three miles from the road with no running water or electricity. Nestled among a grove of trees, near a small lake and with a spectacular view of McKinley and the Alaska Range, it became a rustic sort of mecca. People sought out Dave for, in his own unassuming way, he had become a kind of beaming, oversized guru, always ready to fire up the sauna, take someone out on his favorite ski trail, or dispense his love for cold mountain mornings, little birds, wildflowers, warm toilet seats and such. Dave's joyfulness was very contagious.

His job as a seasonal park ranger gave Dave a decent salary in summer, and brought him opportunities for "good finds." One of his favorite responsibilities was emptying the campground dumpsters. He did a very careful job of it, rarely missing a nice little treasure that was hidden among less useful things. Once a friend came to visit when Dave was gone; so he wrote Dave a note and carefully placed it at the bottom of a promising looking dumpster. Sure enough, within a few days, Dave found the message.

Eventually, life in the woods lost some of its romance for Sally. She went back to New Zealand with the children. It was very hard for Dave; he coped as best he could, but a lot was missing from his life.

It was in the winter of 1984, Dave returned home from visiting his kids in New Zealand feeling the need to renew himself. He had a bold idea. He would climb McKinley in winter again, this time by himself. However, when he got back to Talkeetna, the aftermath of Naomi Uemura's tragic attempt of a solo winter ascent was unfolding. Dave decided to wait.

Two years later, Dave had a lot of things on his mind. There was a new lady in his life, Cari, a schoolteacher in Talkeetna. In spring they planned to climb and trek in Russia, China, and Nepal, ending up in New Zealand. He wanted to marry her, but he said: "Art, I've got to go get this out of my system first."

His plan: pack through the woods to the Kahiltna Glacier, get an air drop of food, then climb the peak and stroll on back to his cabin. (see Appendix)

Telling just a few people that "it's time I get reacquainted with an old friend," Dave slipped on his pack and quietly skied out from his backyard, headed for the mountain 60 miles away.

He planned to be by himself for over a month, surrounded by all the peaks, under the winter light and stars, climbing into that austerely beautiful world. "I'll return," he said, "and share my joy for it."

Before leaving, Dave had written down some of his thoughts on McKinley and his life.

Denali
Winter
Solo

Thought about it
        a year
Sometimes it seemed right
sometimes not . . .

But mountains have been my steady
        friends
Sources of inspiration
Mirrors of my soul
Once again I would look there for
answers.

I committed myself to the idea.

This time it would be solo . . .

This would be a test of just me.

It will feel good to return to this
Starkly beautiful world of
        deep blues
        brilliant whites
        thin air
where security lies in houses of snow.

In the hills I like myself . . . I
        reestablish some confidence, at
        least in winter mountaineering,
        and I don't at all get bush
        crazy in isolation . . .
                (no crazier than usual)
Quite the opposite
        I come alive . . .

> It's by getting away from life that
> we can see it most clearly. . .
>
> It's by depriving ourselves of the
> myriad of everyday experiences
> that we renew our appreciation for them:
>> people's smiles, water running,
>> children, warm rooms, trees,
>> unfrozen boots and socks, my dogs,
>> indoor toilets.
>
> I've learned from my experiences (in
>> the mountains) that I love life.

Like Dave, I returned from our ordeal in winter on McKinley with a greatly enriched love for life. I came to cherish a lot of things I'd previously taken for granted. Just being alive meant more than ever before.

Unlike both Dave and Ray, I found my life as a mountain climber slipping away after the winter climb. I would return to McKinley to lead a testing expedition for the Institute of Arctic Biology, but not to try a demanding ascent. The summer after our winter climb, my good friend Dave Roberts and I went out to a remote range of massive granite mountains we would call the Revelations. It was a great trip in a very wild place, but I could feel that old desire to go out and climb to my limits ebbing. The frostbite hadn't fully healed on my feet, so my climbing was more tentative. But other things inside were pulling me in new directions. I thought of the woman I had recently married, the child we'd soon have. How was I going to provide for a family? What was I going to do with my life? The next summer I was scheduled to go up to the Arrigetch in the Brooks Range with Roberts. We would be the first climbers to set foot among those graceful granite towers. I canceled out at the last moment.

I wouldn't go on another major climb or expedition. Nevertheless, the mountains, particularly McKinley in the winter, would remain a central part of my life. I'd find their meaning and treasure on different levels, at different times.

One path out of the mountains led me directly into conservation work. Reading the newspaper one day, I noticed that a lovely valley near Anchorage was going to be logged—clearcut right out of existence. I couldn't let this happen to one of my old stomping grounds. So I called a few friends who felt the same way. Within a few weeks we managed to halt the logging and were on our way to creating Chugach State Park, the state's first and the nation's largest state park.

Encouraged by this experience, I put my energies into other efforts to preserve wild areas. This country had been good to me and I wanted to give something back. When David Brower started Friends of the Earth in 1969, he asked me to work on Alaska issues during this period of great change. At various times I lobbied for legislation, wrote articles, testified at hearings, made documentary films, labored over land use plans— anything that might help the Alaska I love. There were high points, but overall the trend was discouraging: each year another chunk of untamed, wild Alaska was lost.

I tried to keep my life close to nature and was fortunate to find a magical valley, surrounded by rocky peaks and alpine meadows, filled with wildflowers and little streams. With my wife Mairiis, I built a log home in a clearing in the birch and spruce woods. There in the mountains, we began to raise two fine boys, Arlyn and Dylan.

But times change. I found life, mine at least, had a way of getting more complicated. There were differences, conflicts, and eventually separation.

Over the years, I've thought back to those times in the mountains when all the strength I needed was in my legs, and all I wanted was to climb into the sky as high as I could. This mountain climbing, it's really much simpler than many things in life, but it's in this stark simplicity that I think we begin to get to the heart of things.

On McKinley in winter, we found more than adventure and an unearthly landscape. Our struggles also brought us closer to each other and to ourselves. I think of how Farine had no idea of what lay ahead, as he joked and strapped on his pack to head up the glacier. It so easily could have been me. Twenty years later, I can feel my despair at not being able to breathe life back into his still warm body. I remember John gasping at the bottom of another crevasse and fearing that it was happening again. I see Genet going out into the storm and coming back with enough cooking fuel to keep us alive. I can feel the blood beginning to freeze in my hands and feet. I hear Shiro's voice whispering in the back of my head, "check every possibility to the very end."

My mind drifts back to hours spent on the steep ice and sweet granite of the Cathedral Spires and Revelations, and to our grand adventure above the clouds on McKinley. In my mind the full moon is still rising over the Kahiltna and that silent world of glaciers, ice and rock. The stars are still burning in the black sky we looked up to from the summit. I can see the northern lights swirling out beyond the mountain and the sun breaking cold and golden over an icy ridge. Shimmering ice crystals are falling out of a clear sky. And there is the wind, ripping and pounding on the slopes, and in our heads. As my own life began to slip away, I was struck with an overwhelming sense of how wonderful it is to be alive, simply to breathe and walk about.

These experiences stay with you.

Appendix

Five Attempts on McKinley in Winter

WHEN WE CAME DOWN from the winter climb in '67 we wondered when someone would be crazy enough to go back to McKinley in winter. Knowing how climbers love to redefine the meaning of "impossible," we figured eventually someone would try a more difficult ascent. Without a major storm, they could have a great time up there. But we knew just the cold and darkness, day after day, could wear an expedition down—putting nerves on edge, threatening frostbite, and closing the margins of safety.

In the fifteen years following the first winter ascent there were a number of abortive attempts to make a second winter climb of McKinley. The parties were either inadequately prepared or were stopped by prolonged periods of bad weather. Then beginning in 1981 a number of strong, experienced climbers began coming to the mountain to try winter climbs more difficult and dangerous than we had dared imagine in 1967. Here is a brief account of how five expeditions succeeded or failed, and, more often than not, experienced both triumph and grief.

January 1981: John Waterman Solo

A bizarre journey to McKinley in winter began on the shores of Cook Inlet, near Anchorage. John M. Waterman, whose solo accomplishments had transformed him into a legendary figure of sorts, set out alone, on snowshoes, to travel up the Susitna River to Talkeetna, then up to McKinley more than 100 miles away.

The dimensions of this venture are hard to grasp. In part, it was a throwback to the days of a Jim Bridger or Lewis and Clark when a toughened scout or trapper might find his way across hundreds of miles of frozen wilderness. But what kind of person would cap off such a trek by trying to climb North America's highest mountain, alone and in winter?

For Waterman this trip was the culmination of a series of extreme undertakings that inclined some to view him as a brilliant adventurer, living out there on the edge of impossibility. Others dismissed him as simply crazy, courting his own destruction. He was in fact, an unusually strong and experienced climber. In the Alaska range he had already climbed a terrifying new route on Mt. Huntington, and had spent 148 days alone on Mt. Hunter, putting up an extremely difficult new line of ascent. Another party of climbers was astonished to find him sitting by himself on the summit plateau, eating peanut butter sandwiches.

On his solo attempt of Denali in winter, Waterman had reached the Sheldon Amphitheatre of the Ruth Glacier by early March. He radioed Cliff Hudson to bring extra food he had cached in his Talkeetna cabin. Hudson checked the cabin, found some boxes and flew them to Waterman. Unfortunately, the boxes contained not food, but climbing equipment and personal possessions.

Undaunted, Waterman left the mountain hut in the Sheldon Amphitheatre on April 1. He had 14 days of food, a bivouac sack and a snowmobile suit, but neither a tent nor a sleeping bag. He told Jay Kerr, another climber in the area, that he planned to gain the East Buttress at about 11,900 feet, climb this ridge to Thayer Basin and continue to the summit. His descent would take him down the other side of the mountain, via the Harper and Muldrow Glaciers, to Wonder Lake.

Kerr last saw Waterman heading up the northwest fork of the Ruth Glacier, making a beeline through a heavily crevassed area. He recalled that Waterman was acting "strange but not suicidal."

On April 22, a helicopter search for Waterman was initiated. An abandoned camp was found, along with a single set of snowshoe tracks. Several cabins on the other side of the mountain were searched. John Waterman had disappeared.

Later, Waterman's father pointed out that his son was far too experienced to have invited such an accident, implying that John Waterman had set out on an ascent from which he knew there would be no return. A hint of this possibility may have been in Waterman's last communication: a short enigmatic note attached to his possessions at the mountain house. It read: "3/13/81 My Last Kiss 1:42 pm."

February 1982: The Cassin

Three young men were drawn together by the idea of doing a climb that would push the limits of winter mountaineering.

They were Roger Mear, a strong British climber whose easygoing manner concealed a restless urge to reach the remote corners of Nepal, Antarctica, and Alaska; Mike Young, a cerebral, athletic former Rhodes Scholar with a penchant for running out to test himself on peaks in the Himalayas, and Alaska Range; and another Jonathan Waterman, this one a Denali National Park climbing ranger and author of *Surviving Denali: A Study of Accidents on Mt. McKinley.* Their accomplishments in high cold places were impressive. If they could combine their individual strengths and experience they would make a formidable team.

"That first winter ascent of Denali—what an inspiration," said Waterman. "We wanted to take the next step—do a technically difficult route in winter and do it alpine style."

They decided to climb the Cassin, a steep elegant ridge on the south side of the mountain, and descend the easier West Buttress route. A difficult climb in summer, the Cassin in winter would be extreme. Climbing alpine style, the three would move continuously upward, instead of relaying reserves of food and fuel up the mountain. They would forego fixed ropes and well stocked camps in order to gain extra speed. This meant they would come to a point of no return where, without fixed lines, it would be too risky to descend. They would have to gamble that neither illness nor a storm would strike during the seven or eight days they would be extended and vulnerable.

They flew to the Kahiltna February 16. It was $-30°$ and blowing on the glacier. They spent a few days ferrying gear to the base of the Cassin. This interlude before the hard climbing on the ridge was a good time to get adjusted to the cold, thin air, and to each other. The three hadn't climbed together before, and developing good camaraderie would make the climb more enjoyable and much safer. However, It was soon apparent that the chemistry of the group wasn't very good. "Our tempers were as short as the daylight hours and we spent little time talking," said Jon, of the first few days. "Our lack of compassion for each other and the anxiety about the weather voided communication...we couldn't mix...beneath it all we wanted the Cassin in winter more than we wanted our friendship."

Strong as they were individually, their personalities just didn't mesh. This fostered a sort of free floating tension that would flare up at one thing and then another. One convenient target was Jon's health. He was limping on a reinjured ankle and was recovering from a case of bronchitis. The cold also set them on edge for they were never warm enough to be truly comfortable. The route itself created its own mental strain. It would be unforgiving and extremely difficult to down-climb in an emergency. "This wasn't climbing," said Jon, "it was desperate hard work...the sense of commitment was overwhelming."

On the ninth day they started up the Japanese Couloir, a narrow slot of ice and snow slanting up to $55°$ for 1,200 vertical feet. It was an hour after dark and the temperature $-25°$ when they reached the top. Above them, the Cassin rose another 10,000 feet stretched out over 3 miles of steep ice and rock bands.

The following morning, the wind picked up, but they had to keep moving. Jon described "...bracing ourselves in big gusts of wind, hunched over our ice axes, hiding inside our hoods, the totality of our commitment tugged on us...there was no retreating now. We were going for broke."

They reached a narrow icy ledge at sunset. It took an hour and a half of chopping to widen it enough for their tent. It was $-35°$, a clear moonlit night. Because they had only a two man tent, someone always had to sleep outside. This night it was Jon's turn. He tied himself onto a tiny ledge he had chipped in the ice. Then a burst of northern lights suddenly broke open the dark sky. Jon called to the others, and, in a moment of respite from their dissension and the hard climbing that lay ahead, the three men watched eerie bands of green and yellow light shift overhead.

The following night, about a thousand feet higher, the wind was gusting; Roger, suffering from a splitting headache, took his turn outside. Jon wrote in his journal: "the last four days have seemed an eternity, time has no meaning up here. I've never seen the hours creep so slowly or torturously, ever. We have got to get out of here...This will be my last climb, no more. I've wised up. I'm not going to forget...This is too crazy."

On the climb to 18,000 feet they unroped and climbed at their own pace, "as though [they] wanted no connection with one another." That night the wind was blowing 30 miles an hour so they all crammed into the tent. Sleep was difficult. When someone rolled about in the night, blows were exchanged. The next day might have brought them to the summit, but they got a late start. Jon was sick: "Standing still, I just couldn't get enough air to breathe. Our progress became pitiful and we argued about how far we were from the top. The situation was critical. One big wind would pin us down, or blow us right off the mountain... My altitude sickness was slowing us down when speed was the essence of our safety."

They stopped for the night not knowing how close they were to the summit. It was $-40°$. Mike's toes had blackened from frostbite. In the morning Jon could barely breathe; there was heaviness in his lungs—the signs of pulmonary edema which can bring death in hours. The only cure is to descend, as quickly as possible. But first they had to climb up in order to get off the Cassin. Jon couldn't keep his balance when he tried to stand. It was $-45°$, no wind.

Mike and Roger began climbing. Jon tried to follow. The two stronger climbers disappeared above. Lurching on, a step at a time, Jon sighted the summit ridge two hours later. By the time the two came down from the summit, Jon was crawling on all fours; he still hadn't reached the top of the Cassin. Roger hurried down to help him. Without the weight of his pack, Jon staggered up off the ridge. The summit was only a hair's breadth away. If not sick, Jon could have reached it in ten minutes. Now he was fighting for his life. With no hesitation, he turned and started down. He had lost feeling in his feet and knew frostbite was setting in. Jon pointed out the route to Mike and Roger and they descended.

They made it to the 17,200 foot level that night. Two more days and they were back down on the Kahiltna. In a freak accident close to their base camp, Roger fell 30 feet down a crevasse, badly tearing the ligaments in one leg.

The three finally piled into their base camp snow cave, started to warm up and turned on some taped music. They felt both joy and relief at the enormity of what they had accomplished and suffered. "Our injuries were relatively minor, none of us got killed, and we did the route," said Waterman. "But in important stuff like trust and teamwork: we failed."

February 1983: The West Rib

Four highly experienced climbers flew to the southwest fork of the Kahiltna on an ambitious mission. They came to attempt a winter ascent of McKinley on a new and technically challenging route—the West Rib.

The climbers were Robert Frank (38), Charles Sassara (20), Steve Teller (29), and Chris Hraback (27). By February 28, they had established a camp at almost 10,000 feet, just below the base of the West Rib. To keep their bodies strong and help ward off frostbite they planned to each drink 6–8 quarts of liquids and eat 6,000 to 10,000 calories every day. After acclimatizing for several days, they started up with eight days of food and fuel to supply both the ascent and descent of the entire West Rib route. Their strategy was to move relatively quickly without relaying supplies to higher camps.

The first day, hard ice conditions in the couloir, poor visibility and 70 pound packs slowed them. Nightfall found them in the rocks near the top of the couloir. They cut ledges for their tents just before dark and got to sleep about 2 am. The next day they moved up to 12,000 feet where they rested two days. The temperature was $-40°$ to $-50°$. Everyone felt strong.

On March 9, as they climbed the rock rib toward their high camp, the wind started blowing, picking up to about 45 knots. With only three full days of food left and the possibility of a storm coming, they had to decide whether to continue or retreat. After some discussion, the team elected to go on: to increase their speed, they lightened their load by discarding extra ropes and ice screws. They would try to complete the climb unroped.

When the four climbers reached 17,000 feet, they hacked out tent platforms at the base of the couloir. Exhaustion set in and all began showing signs of altitude sickness. They rested the next day, watching the weather. With food supplies dwindling, they knew they should climb the next day—either to the summit or back down. They also knew that if the wind presaged a major storm, they would be in a precarious position.

They rose at 3 am the next morning. The winds were light, the skies clear. Hraback, followed by Sassara and Frank took off for the summit. Teller, still feeling ill stayed at the high camp.

At about 18,000 feet Hraback was too exhausted to continue; he turned back. Sassara and Frank reached the summit plateau by 10 am. They stopped briefly to eat and tried to warm their feet, then climbed on, arriving at the summit at 11 am.

They were cold and tired, but they had made a great climb. All that remained was getting down. The temperature was $-45°$. The two had been climbing hard for more than 10 hours by the time they reached the steep slope of the West Rib. The following events were reported by the American Alpine Club:

> They were both fatigued and lethargic by the time they made it to the top of the West Rib. They started down climbing the rib by 12:30, facing into the 40 to 50 degree slope. The conditions were extremely variable with hard ice, soft corn snow, wind crust and hard snow. . .
>
> They had both been unroped for the entire day. Suddenly, Sassara heard Frank yell, "Falling," Sassara looked up just as Frank slid into him and knocked him off the slope. Sassara immediately tried to self-arrest and stopped about 30 meters down the slope. After he regained his stance and composure he looked for Frank.
>
> About 400 meters down the couloir, Frank was falling head over heels, with pieces of his equipment being discarded. Sassara descended the route of Frank's fall finding blood, a camera bag, a glove, and about three or four pieces of bone with flesh attached.

"I watched, in a trance-like state, as my friend tumbled to his death," recalled Sassara. "My mind was in a void. Totally conscious, suspended between life and death, I felt the urge to follow Robert."

"Instead I turned back to the slope, slowly chopped a small ledge and clipped into my ax. It was strange how relaxed I was, unroped on the steep slope, standing there on one leg, refixing the crampon that had been torn off my left foot."

Sassara reached the high camp by 4:30 and told the others that Robert Frank was dead. The weather took a turn for the worse, and the three stunned climbers holed up at the high camp until March 13. Descending the route of Frank's fall as much as it allowed, they found scattered pieces of equipment and clothing and concluded that Frank's body had come to rest in a crevasse on the western side of the south face.

On the 15th, they rose early, to begin the difficult and exposed descent of the steep couloir. They made 17 rappels using ice screws, pitons and slings around exposed rocks. Three days later they reached their base camp on the southeast fork of the Kahiltna.

"The experience was very bittersweet," Sassara recalled later. "We made a difficult winter climb alpine style. We reached the summit. No one got frostbite. We accomplished everything we wanted—except for that one misplaced step. When we started out we accepted the risk, but nothing is worth what happened. For nearly a year, dreams of that day would trouble my sleep."

February 1984: Uemura Solo

On the first day of February 1984, Naomi Uemura strapped on his snowshoes, pulled on an enormous pack and, as he had so many times before, set out to accomplish something that had never been done before. His goal this time was the dream that had taken John M. Waterman's life—a solo winter ascent of Mt. McKinley.

At that moment, Uemura was as ready for this task as any man alive. In July, fourteen years earlier, he had made the first solo ascent of McKinley, reaching the summit by the same West Buttress route that now lay before him in February. He knew the mountain. Moreover, the path that brought him to the mountain in winter had taught him how to survive in extreme conditions.

Uemura, born in Southwest Japan in 1941, was a university student when he discovered mountains. He was drawn not so much to steep, technical climbs as to wandering alone among the peaks, finding peace and solitude. In 1964, he went to Chamonix by himself and climbed in the European Alps, escaping a crevasse fall on Mont Blanc. The next five years, he wandered from continent to continent, developing the skills and reputation of an adventurer. He climbed Mont Blanc in Europe, Kilimanjaro and Kenya in Africa, Mt. Sanford in Alaska and Aconcagua, the highest peak in South America. He built a raft and floated the full length of the Amazon. In 1969, Uemura became the first Japanese to reach the summit of Mt. Everest.

Soon thereafter, Uemura became interested in polar travel. One of his first trips was an incredible 7,500 mile, 3-year dogsled journey from Greenland to Alaska across Northern Canada. In 1978, Uemura set out from Ellesmere Island with 17 dogs for a solo trek to the North Pole. His struggle across the ice began with an attack by a polar bear that chased off his dogs, tore open his tent, pawed at his sleeping bag while he was in it, and then unaccountably went away. He tracked down his dogs and continued north, cutting a path through jumbled ice blocks that had stopped larger expeditions. It was winter, with only a few hours of daylight each day and temperatures going down to $-50°$. Uemura made it to the pole.

So it was in 1984 that Naomi Uemura came again to McKinley in the winter, uniquely experienced and toughened for this solo ascent. Already, he was one of the world's most accomplished explorer-adventurers. In Japan he was something more than a legend, some immortal, indomitable spirit. Certainly no one else could have started up McKinley, alone, in February, with such calm self-assurance. He planned a very fast climb—one week—and talked of doing a solo dog mushing trip across Antarctica when he returned.

The weather was cold, but clear and stable. Uemura started up with a 40 pound pack of caribou meat, seal oil, and three liters of fuel. With no one to hold him back, he climbed quickly. On February 12, his 43rd birthday, Uemura was spotted above 18,000 feet. He radioed pilot Lowell Thomas, Jr. that he expected to reach the summit by 4 pm.

The next day when Thomas flew by the mountain again, he and his passengers didn't sight Uemura, but they did receive a radio message. He said he had reached the summit about 7 the previous night. He had descended for three hours to a camp and was tired, but okay. He wanted to be picked up in two days, February 15, at his base camp on the Kahiltna.

On February 15, pilot Doug Geeting flew to the Kahiltna base camp. Uemura was not there, nor was there any indication that he had been there since the start of the climb.

Geeting, joined by Thomas in another plane, flew the mountain looking for the climber. They reported that the sky was clear, but winds near the mountain were very turbulent. A cloud cap was forming over the summit. They saw no sign of Uemura. The pilots speculated that he was probably holed up in a snow cave, with maybe two days of food, waiting for the wind to die down.

Confusing messages began filtering back from the mountain. One pilot thought he saw Uemura waving from a snow cave at about 16,000 feet. Another thought he heard a short radio transmission—"I'm lost." For the next three days, the weather closed in around McKinley. Each day, Thomas and Geeting went up to look for Uemura. Each day, they returned without spotting him. No one knew how much food he had. But as long as the wind blew, it was logical for him to stay in a snow cave.

The weather finally broke on February 20. Geeting and Thomas were up flying at first daylight. Uemura should be descending. For more than five hours, the pilots searched the entire West Buttress route from the Kahiltna base to the summit. They didn't see Uemura. They didn't find any tracks. Two rescue climbers started up the mountain.

The good weather lasted only one day. A new storm closed in for another five days. On the 26th, the wind slacked off enough to allow the rescue team to be picked up at 14,300 feet. It was impossible to search the upper portions of the mountain where the two rescue climbers had found the snow conditions to be "very difficult and dangerous, with crusty snow and ice over a hard ice." One of them speculated that Uemura must have fallen during a desperate attempt to descend in the storm. Later, empty snow caves used by Uemura would be found as high as 17,200 feet.

Naomi Uemura had vanished.

February 1986: Johnston Solo

At the time Uemura was reported missing in 1984, Dave Johnston had already packed food for his own solo winter ascent. Dave wrote in his journal:

> Naomi loved Denali too. He gambled and sadly lost. Unthinkable, one of the world's experts on high altitude and cold weather has disappeared.
>
> Some of my friends, saddened by Naomi's death worried excessively about me. I tried to explain my style would be totally different: 90 days of food and fuel...backed by two 300′ fixed ropes for really holey spots.
>
> But my friends were upset. I hate bending people out of shape with worry. The timing is just off.

Dave canceled his 1984 plans to solo Denali in winter, but he would return. In mid February 1986, 19 years after he, Genet and Davidson made the first winter ascent, Dave headed out from his cabin to pack into the mountain 60 miles away. His only companion on the trip would be "Bridgit." Now, Bridgit was not along to keep him warm at night, but to keep him out of crevasses. She was a very special girl, thin, strong, 20 feet tall and weighing only 18 pounds. Bridgit was a collapsible aluminum framework Dave had invented to protect him in case of a crevasse fall. If he fell through the snow covering a crevasse, Bridgit would, hopefully, span the crevasse and hold him from falling in.

Dave set out in perfect winter weather: a stable high pressure area kept the sky cloudless and temperatures between 0 and 20°. He had wanted to make the climb quietly with only a handful of people knowing he was up there. But by the time he reached Kahiltna Pass and turned toward Windy Corner, the newspapers discovered what was happening and began covering his progress.

The good weather held for Dave and he quickly ferried a good supply of food and fuel up to his high camps.

Dave could move as fast as anyone at altitude. But he wasn't trying to blitz his way up and down the mountain like Uemura. Nor was he throwing his fate to the elements as Waterman had. Dave was climbing cautiously, while having the time of his life—trucking along, a big grin on his face, taking his giant strides, and singing to himself.

By March 1, he had hauled supplies up to the 13,500 foot level, almost within striking distance of the summit. He rested, gathered himself, and watched the weather closely. When the moment felt right, he would set out for the top with his sleeping bag, a week's worth of food, and a snow shovel. If the weather held, he could reach the top and be back in one or two days. If a storm clamped down on the mountain, he'd simply dig a snow cave and burrow in. Dave was in his element.

Then the wind came up. Dave dug into the slope. After huddling in his snow cave for hours, he heard strange noises outside. "It went pitter-patter wheeekk, just like the sound of footsteps squeaking in the snow. It wasn't an hallucination. I heard it for sure."

He dismissed the kind of ghostly apparitions that some climbers on Everest and other high peaks have reported—appearances of mystery climbers or other mountaineers known to have died there. Perhaps the wind was blowing his gear around. He had to see what was going on.

Dave found snow had blown into the entrance to his cave. Both his shovels were outside, so he began digging with a cooking pot. He dug through four feet of snow, but the entrance was still sealed shut. Dave was being entombed in the mountain by the wind and driving snow.

"I was getting a little antsy," Dave said, "so I broke a hole out through the roof. I popped outside. I was really getting hammered—the wind was blowing 60, 70 miles an hour."

He set about rebuilding the cave, patching the roof, digging a new entrance. He got the job done, but his feet had suffered. "I went back in and brewed up some tea. Two toes were white. I rubbed them. Here came that old familiar feeling—like a dog nipping on your toes."

Dave had frostbite. "It's so ironic. It's the old frostbite injury from our winter climb in '67. It never completely recovered. It's a little numb in the best of times, that's why I didn't feel it getting cold." On March 1, exactly 19 years earlier Dave had first frozen his feet. It happened in that storm at Denali Pass with Art Davidson and Ray Genet; Dave got frostbite digging the snow cave that saved their lives.

Now, alone on McKinley, his freezing feet left him no choice. When the wind slacked off, Dave skied back to his cabin at Trapper Creek. "I know I could have made the summit," he said. "It's real disappointing. I got all that work done—doing 150-pound relays—only to get stopped by a little thing like my toe."

Dave had skied alone for 150 miles. As he said he would, he returned to share the joy of it—"It's so beautiful up there, the trip was worth it just to be on the mountain again."

OTHER TITLES YOU MIGHT ENJOY FROM THE MOUNTAINEERS BOOKS:

STRANGE AND DANGEROUS DREAMS:
The Fine Line Between Adventure and Madness
Geoff Powter
Adventurers are among the world's most celebrated heroes, but cross a line and potential glory can become derision, madness, and death.

THE AVALANCHE HANDBOOK,
3rd Edition
David McClung and Peter Shaerer
The unrivaled source for information on avalanches and snow safety—now completely updated!

HYPOTHERMIA FROSTBITE AND OTHER
COLD INJURIES: Prevention, Survival,
Rescue, and Treatment, 2nd Edition
Gordon Giesbrecht and James Wilkerson.

HIGH ALASKA: A Historical Guide to Denali,
Mount Foraker, & Mount Hunter
Jonathan Waterman
A blend of history and route guide to these great peaks.

SURVIVING DENALI: A Study of Accidents on
Mt. McKinley 1910-1990, 2nd Edition
Jonathan Waterman
An analysis of unfortunate victims on Denali. Provides compelling reading and invaluable advice.